PENGUIN

ARKANA

THE BOOK OF CHUANG TZU

Martin Palmer is Director of the International Consultancy on Religion, Education and Culture (ICOREC). A student of Chinese for over twenty years, he has translated many Chinese classics and folk religion texts, as well as having commented upon the major religious traditions of China in print and also on radio and television. As Director of ICOREC he works as religious adviser to the World Wide Fund for Nature (WWF) around the world, directing religion-based environmental programmes. Currently he is working with the China Taoist Association on a project to protect the main Taoist Sacred Mountains of China.

Elizabeth Breuilly is a member of ICOREC. She specializes in educational books and in assisting faith groups in articulating their fundamental teachings clearly to non-specialist audiences.

Chang Wai Ming, a practising lawyer, was Martin Palmer's first teacher of Chinese. Her interest in Chinese philosophy has been an abiding passion for many years.

Jay Ramsay has collaborated with Martin Palmer on a number of translations of Chinese texts, bringing his gifts as a poet to bear upon the translations. He is the founder of the Chrysalis poetry project.

清谿放棹

曾見雲溪外峰　神韻天然俗不到

The Book of
Chuang Tzu

Translated by Martin Palmer

*with Elizabeth Breuilly, Chang Wai Ming
and Jay Ramsay*

ARKANA
PENGUIN BOOKS

ARKANA

Published by the Penguin Group
Penguin Books Ltd, 80 Strand, London WC2R 0RL, England
Penguin Putnam Inc., 375 Hudson Street, New York, New York 10014, USA
Penguin Books Australia Ltd, Ringwood, Victoria, Australia
Penguin Books Canada Ltd, 10 Alcorn Avenue, Toronto, Ontario, Canada M4V 3B2
Penguin Books India (P) Ltd, 11 Community Centre, Panchsheel Park, New Delhi – 110 017, India
Penguin Books (NZ) Ltd, Cnr Rosedale and Airborne Roads, Albany, Auckland, New Zealand
Penguin Books (South Africa) (Pty) Ltd, 24 Sturdee Avenue, Rosebank 2196 South Africa

Penguin Books Ltd, Registered Offices: 80 Strand, London WC2R 0RL, England

www.penguin.com

Published by Arkana 1996
8

Copyright © ICOREC, 1996
Illustrations copyright © Circa Photo Library, 1996
All rights reserved

The moral right of the translators has been asserted

Set in 10/12.5 pt Bembo Monotype
Typeset by Datix International Limited, Bungay, Suffolk
Made and printed in Great Britain by Clays Ltd, St Ives plc

For Sandra

Contents

Preface

Translating an author as rich, diverse and as intense as Chuang Tzu is an immense undertaking. There are few full translations of Chuang Tzu, so I felt that there was space for another, especially one aimed at a more popular market. For this reason, there are one or two ways in which this translation differs from others.

Firstly, I have adopted a simplified form of romanization of Chinese names. There are two commonly used systems: Wade-Giles and Pinyin. The differences can be seen in the way they spell the capital of China: Peking (Wade-Giles) or Beijing (Pinyin). In many instances, Pinyin gives a more accurate phoneticization of the Chinese – as in 'Beijing'. But in Pinyin, 'Chuang Tzu' becomes 'Zhuang Zi' – which is not as close to the original as the Wade-Giles. In using Wade-Giles, I have opted for a more familiar system for the average reader. However, to help the flow of reading, I have dropped the diacritical marks, and capitalized all parts of the name. Thus, in chapter 5, I have changed the name of the man with the terrible appearance from Ai T'ai-t'o to Ai Tai To. In chapter 4, the minister, Ch'u Po-yu, becomes Chu Po Yu. I hope purists will forgive me this in the interests of greater ease for readers.

Secondly, I have dropped some of the more obscure names which are given and only make a great deal of sense if one is able to see the puns in Chinese. For example, the last paragraph of chapter 18 in the Chinese contains detailed names for every bug and insect. I have dropped all but the most necessary because they get very confusing!

Thirdly, in the first seven chapters, we have marked out the text to show that it does not flow sequentially. The first seven chapters in particular contain self-contained stories and discussions. Trying to read Chuang Tzu sequentially is a mistake. The text is a collection, not a developing argument. In the first seven chapters, we have indicated this with clear breaks.

Approaching a text as ancient and as fascinating as Chuang Tzu, any translator needs all the help possible! Having translated a number of ancient Chinese texts in the last few years (The *Tao Te Ching*, the *I Ching*) I feel relatively at home in the linguistic and cultural world of China between the sixth and third centuries BC. But I was delighted to have three guides who either in part or in whole had made the journey into the *Chuang Tzu* and lived to tell the tale. In confirming or debating my own translations, I turned to these three other translators for inspiration or for argument. The three translators are, first and foremost, the excellent translator of the first seven chapters, Fung Yu-Lan, professor of Chinese in the USA and China during most of this century. His excellent translation *A Taoist Classic Chuang-Tzu* is published by the Foreign Languages Press, Beijing, from an original edition first published in 1931. It is masterful.

The second translator, who has translated the whole text, is Burton Watson of the Columbia University translation program. His *The Complete Works of Chuang Tzu*, published by Columbia University Press in 1968 and still in print, is a joy to read. Clear and informative, it provides the most readable translation I have come across. I owe a great debt to Burton Watson, even if at times I differ from some of his usage and interpretations.

Finally, that master of translation – not necessarily for the ease of his translation but for the depth of his work – James Legge. Produced in the 1880s, his *The Writings of Kwang Tze* is a rich resource for any translator. It is to be found in volumes 39 and 40 of *Sacred Books of the East*, edited by Max Muller, Oxford University Press, 1891.

Apart from these books, I owe an immense debt of gratitude to colleagues. The Taoist scholars at the White Cloud Temple in Beijing, home of the China Taoist Association, taught me a great deal about how to read Chuang Tzu. To my old friend and first mentor in Chinese, Chang Wai Ming, I owe more than I can say. Over twenty years ago she taught me to love and enjoy the Chinese language and culture and I have never looked back. Her intensity of love for her own culture and language is truly infectious.

Jay Ramsay cannot read a word of Chinese – thank goodness! He thus makes a perfect sparring partner. As a poet he has a sense for English which challenges and thrills me as a writer. As someone who has entered into the Chinese world through the translations we have done together, he has a sense of Chinese symbolism and literature which is quite extraordinary. I owe him a great deal for making the most of my turns of phrase.

Elizabeth Breuilly is really the main other translator. Like Jay she knows no Chinese but she has a rigorous and vigorous understanding of English. She took sheets of barely legible scrawl sent back from all round the world – I translate as I travel – and turned it into readable English. She has given untold hours to this, as has Jo Edwards, who put most of it on disk. I cannot say how grateful I am to both of them for their work and for enjoying the old rogue Chuang Tzu as much as I have.

Martin Palmer
August 1995

Introduction

When the School of Taoism first began to look for its roots, sometime around 100 BC, it identified three great founder teachers. These were, and still are, Lao Tzu, Chuang Tzu and Lieh Tzu.

Taoism is the search for the Tao, the Way of Nature which, if you could become part of it, would take you to the edge of reality and beyond. One of the core teachings of Taoism is that:

> The Tao that can be talked about is not the true Tao.
> The name that can be named is not the eternal Name.[1]

In the light of this, perhaps it should not cause too much surprise to discover that, of these three founder-figures, only one can be definitely rooted in a given time and place! For Lao Tzu may well never have existed, and even if he did, he certainly didn't write the *Tao Te Ching*, the book usually ascribed to him as author. Lieh Tzu may also be a fictional figure. Again, even if he did exist, the book which bears his name contains few of his actual words and was probably composed some six hundred or more years after his supposed lifetime.

Which leaves us with Chuang Tzu. Of all the figures whom Taoism claims as its own from the extraordinary period of intellectual ferment of the sixth to third centuries BC, only Chuang Tzu emerges from the mists as a discernible figure. And the figure who does emerge is one of the most intriguing, humorous, enjoyable personalities in the whole of Chinese thought and philosophy.

---

1. *The Illustrated Tao Te Ching*, translated by Man Ho Kwok, Martin Palmer and Jay Ramsay, Element Books, 1993, p. 27.

The only 'historical details' we have of Chuang Tzu's life come from the first great historian of China, Ssu Ma Chien (died *c*. 85 BC). In his *Historical Records*, he tried to trace the histories of Lao Tzu and Chuang Tzu. He virtually gives up on Lao Tzu, lamenting that he found it almost impossible to discover any facts or details about him.

With Chuang Tzu he had more success. He says that Chuang Tzu was born in the town of Meng, which is thought to be somewhere in the present-day provinces of Anhui or Henan. His personal name was Chuang Chou, and it is as Chuang Chou that he is usually referred to in the book which we know as *Chuang Tzu*. The title 'Tzu' found in the names of the three founder-figures is an honorific title meaning 'Master'. In the text as translated here I have changed 'Chuang Chou' to 'Chuang Tzu' to avoid confusion.

Ssu Ma Chien goes on to say that Chuang Tzu worked as a minor official at Chi Yuan, which can be translated as 'The Lacquer Garden'. Quite what this means is unclear. Was this just a name of a place, in the same way that Salford means 'The Ford by the Willows', or was it actually an area of natural beauty? As with so much in the early histories of Taoism, we don't know.

The historian says that Chuang Tzu lived at the same time as Prince Hui of Liang (370–319 BC) and Prince Hsuan of Chi (319–301 BC). He also says that Prince Wei of Chu (338–327 BC) visited him. This puts him firmly into the last half of the fourth century and leads Needham to give his dates as 369–286 BC.[2] For once, we can be fairly sure about the approximate dates of such a figure.

Ssu Ma Chien continues his account by noting that Chuang Tzu was noted for his erudition, which was eclectic but rooted in the sayings of Lao Tzu, of which more later. He says that, because of this, Chuang Tzu's writings were largely imaginative or allegorical – a fact which is most definitely borne out by even a cursory glance at his book. It is also noted that his surviving writings in the first century BC were over 100,000 words in length.

Ssu Ma Chien then discusses three specific chapters of the book,

2. Joseph Needham, *Science and Civilisation in China*, Cambridge University Press, 1956, volume II, p. 35.

chapters 31, 29 and 10, in that order, and claims they were written explicitly to refute the arguments of the Confucians and to 'glorify the mysteries of Lao Tzu'. It is then noted that some of the characters in his writings are figments of his imagination but that such was his erudition and skill in public debate that not even the greatest scholars of his time could defend themselves against his pitiless attacks on both the Confucians and the followers of Mo Tzu. Ssu Ma Chien goes on to state that Chuang Tzu's writings and teachings were like a tidal wave which swamped everything and could not be stemmed, and his work so free-flowing that no ruler has ever been able to encapsulate it or harness it to specific statecraft – unlike the *Lao Tzu*, which has often been subtitled 'A Manual of Leadership'.

To illustrate this and to highlight Chuang Tzu's own sense of personal freedom from the niceties of power or the temptations of title – a theme which he often explores – Ssu Ma Chien relates a story which is actually recorded in the book itself:

Someone offered Chuang Tzu a court post. Chuang Tzu answered the messenger, 'Sir, have you ever seen a sacrificial ox? It is decked in fine garments and fed on fresh grass and beans. However, when it is led into the Great Temple, even though it most earnestly might wish to be a simple calf again, it's now impossible.' (Chapter 32, this translation)

In the version told by Ssu Ma Chien, Chuang Tzu goes on:

Go away! Don't mess with me! I would rather enjoy myself in the mud than be a slave to the ruler of some kingdom. I shall never accept such an office, and so I shall remain free to do as I will.

This exchange captures to perfection the spirit of Chuang Tzu which emerges from his writings. For unlike the *Tao Te Ching*, which tells no stories, contains no anecdote or personal details about anyone, the *Chuang Tzu* is full of stories, personalities, characters and incidents. It is a bag of tricks, knaves, sages, jokers, unbelievably named people and uptight Confucians! And through it strides the occasionally glimpsed figure of Chuang Tzu himself, leaving a trail of humour, bruised egos and damaged reputations.

xvi   The Book of Chuang Tzu

There are two particular insights which the book affords us of the personality and personal history of Chuang Tzu himself, which bring him vividly to life in a way unusual for philosophers. The first is his great friendship and rivalry with the philosopher Hui Tzu. The two represented different strands of philosophy but were close enough to enjoy the delights of sparring. In particular, Hui Tzu took exception to one of Chuang Tzu's key points, that meaning depends entirely upon the context and that there is no such thing as a 'fact' which stands apart from the context of the speaker. The most famous example of this comes at the end of chapter 17:

Chuang Tzu and Hui Tzu were walking beside the weir on the River Hao, when Chuang Tzu said, 'Do you see how the fish are coming to the surface and swimming around as they please? That's what fish really enjoy.'

'You're not a fish,' replied Hui Tzu, 'so how can you say you know what fish enjoy?'

Chuang Tzu said: 'You are not me, so how can you know I don't know what fish enjoy?'

Hui Tzu said: 'I am not you, so I definitely don't know what it is you know. However, you are most definitely not a fish and that proves that you don't know what fish really enjoy.'

Chuang Tzu said: 'Ah, but let's return to the original question you raised, if you don't mind. You asked me how I could know what it is that fish really enjoy. Therefore, you already knew I knew it when you asked the question. And I know it by being here on the edge of the River Hao.'

The intensity of this friendship of rivalry is poignantly captured in a story told in chapter 24:

Chuang Tzu was following a funeral when he passed by the grave of Hui Tzu. He looked round at those following him and said, 'The man of Ying had on the end of his nose a piece of mud as small as a fly's wing. He sent for the craftsman Shih to cut it off. Shih swirled his axe around and swept it down, creating such a wind as it rushed past that it removed all trace of the mud from the man of Ying, who stood firm, not at all worried. The ruler Yuan of Sung heard of this and called craftsman Shih to visit him.

'"Would you be so kind as to do this for me?" he said.

'Craftsman Shih replied, "Your servant was indeed once able to work like that, but the type of material I worked upon is long since dead."

'Since the Master has died, I have not had any suitable material to work upon. I have no one I can talk with any longer.'

This sad story brings me to the second detail which we can glean about Chuang Tzu from the book. Unlike perhaps our standard vision of the philosopher-sage of Taoism, whom we associate with remote mountains and an ascetic lifestyle, Chuang Tzu was married and brought up a family, though one does get the impression that, perhaps luckily for them, the bulk of the responsibility for rearing the children fell to his wife. These details come out in a story told in chapter 18:

Chuang Tzu's wife died and Hui Tzu came to console him, but Chuang Tzu was sitting, legs akimbo, bashing a battered tub and singing.

Hui Tzu said, 'You lived as man and wife, she reared your children. At her death surely the least you should be doing is to be on the verge of weeping, rather than banging the tub and singing: this is not right!'

Chuang Tzu said, 'Certainly not. When she first died, I certainly mourned just like everyone else! However, I then thought back to her birth and to the very roots of her being, before she was born. Indeed, not just before she was born but before the time when her body was created. Not just before her body was created but before the very origin of her life's breath. Out of all of this, through the wonderful mystery of change she was given her life's breath. Her life's breath wrought a transformation and she had a body. Her body wrought a transformation and she was born. Now there is yet another transformation and she is dead. She is like the four seasons in the way that spring, summer, autumn and winter follow each other. She is now at peace, lying in her chamber, but if I were to sob and cry it would certainly appear that I could not comprehend the ways of destiny. This is why I stopped.'

What is so wonderfully typical of these stories is the way Chuang Tzu uses incidents around him to deliver himself of a philosophical reflection or comment. Unlike the *Tao Te Ching*, which simply gives a saying or proverb and then comments upon it in a somewhat dry fashion, Chuang Tzu teaches through narrative, humour and detail. At times when translating this book, I was swept along by the desire to find out what happened next, or what point he was going to draw out of some incident. It must also be one of the few books written well over two thousand years ago that can make a translator burst out laughing aloud!

All of which brings me to the vexed question which has dominated the study of Chuang Tzu for centuries. Which parts of the book can be ascribed to Chuang Tzu himself and which come from different, later pens? The custom in many cultures of the past was to ascribe a book to a great figure from the past. By doing so you were not necessarily trying to claim that they had written every word. But neither were you too worried if people thought so, so long as they read it! Indeed Chuang Tzu himself comments upon the tendency to claim that one's own words are those of some great figure of the past as a way of gaining an audience. He saw nothing inherently wrong in this (see the opening of chapter 27).

So it was that around sayings or writings of a key figure, other writings which were felt to complement or expand those of the Master would be gathered. Eventually these would be edited and the entire collection known as the writings of, for example, Lao Tzu or Chuang Tzu. A similar process took place in Judaism at roughly the same time. Thus, for example, the five books of the *Torah* (Genesis to Deuteronomy) were ascribed to Moses, despite the fact that they record his death!

That this happened to the book we know as *Chuang Tzu* is without doubt. We even know who did the final editing job which produced the text as we have it with three sections. It was Kuo Hsiang, who died in 312 AD. He divided the text into three parts:

Chapters 1–7: The Inner Chapters. Traditionally believed to have been written by Chuang Tzu;

Chapters 8–22: The Outer Chapters. Traditionally seen as being the product of the Yangist school of philosophy.

Chapters 23–33: Miscellaneous Chapters. A catch-bag of odds and ends.

It is thought that Kuo Hsiang edited his text down from a

collection of fifty-three chapters, so what we have is a reduction from an even wider collection of material.

Almost from Kuo Hsiang's time onwards, the debate has raged about which bits Chuang Tzu wrote and which bits he did not. It has become customary to hold chapters 1–7 as being from Chuang Tzu. Yet some would maintain that when Kuo Hsiang spoke of 'Inner Chapters', he wasn't giving them any greater authority, but simply stating that their titles came from their content, whereas the next fifteen chapters take their titles from the first words of each chapter – from their outer skin as it were.

It is interesting that of the three chapters which Ssu Ma Chien specifically highlights in his life of Chuang Tzu, written some two hundred years after Chuang Tzu and some four hundred years before Kuo Hsiang, one appears in the miscellaneous section and two in the Outer Chapters. None appears in the Inner Chapters. This alone should caution us against making easy or simplistic judgements based upon the present order of the chapters. Personally speaking, having now worked my way through the whole text in Chinese, I would find it very hard to cut up the book into bits that are obviously from Chuang Tzu himself and bits that are obviously not. Rather, I believe that we have a great deal of material which comes from Chuang Tzu or which was directly inspired by Chuang Tzu's life and teachings. For example, the story of Chuang Tzu and the fish comes from chapter 17 and the tale of passing Hui Tzu's grave comes from chapter 24. Neither of these are allowed as authentic Chuang Tzu chapters by certain purists, yet they breathe the very spirit of Chuang Tzu just as much as, for example, the famous 'butterfly passage' of chapter 2.

There is a considerable industry in the remote and dustier shelves of Chinese studies, which engages itself in detailed and unending debate about which sections are genuine or not. But ironically, it seems that the author can speak more clearly to us if we do not concern ourselves with his existence or his authorship. For in the end, it really does not matter which bits come from the pen or life of Chuang Tzu and which are additions. The book simply should not be viewed as one consistent discourse. It is a catch-bag, an anthology of stories and incidents, thoughts and reflections which have gathered around the name and personality of Chuang Tzu. Trying to read the book through logically will only produce faint, ghostly laughter. And the one who will be laughing at you from afar will be the spirit of Chuang Tzu. For if there is one constant theme in the book, it is that logic is nonsense and that eclecticism is all, if you wish to open yourself to the Tao and the Te – the Way and the Virtue of all.

The *Book of Chuang Tzu* is like a travelogue. As such, it meanders between continents, pauses to discuss diet, gives exchange rates, breaks off to speculate, offers a bus timetable, tells an amusing incident, quotes from poetry, relates a story, cites scripture. To try and make it read like a novel or a philosophical handbook is simply to ask it, this travelogue of life, to do something it was never designed to do. And always listen out for the mocking laughter of Chuang Tzu. This can be heard most when you start to make grand schemes out of the bits, or wondrous philosophies out of the hints and jokes. For ultimately this is not one book but a variety of voices swapping stories and bouncing ideas off each other, with Chuang Tzu striding through the whole, joking, laughing, arguing and interrupting. This is why it is such an enjoyable book to enter, almost anywhere, as if dipping into a cool river in the midst of summer.

So you will find no great theories set out in this Introduction as to what Chuang Tzu means. Rather I want to try and set him, his terminology and some of his ideas into context and at times draw out certain comparisons with our own times.

To begin with, we must avoid calling Chuang Tzu a Taoist. He wasn't. There were no 'Taoists' in his day. There were thinkers who explored the notion of the Tao – the Way of Nature which, if you could become part of it, would carry you in its flow to the edge of reality and beyond, into the world of nature. Most of the great philosophers of the time struggled with the notion of the Tao, not least of them Kung Fu Tzu (better known in the West as Confucius). As is obvious from the number of times he crops up in the *Chuang Tzu*, Kung Fu Tzu was fascinated by the Tao. Indeed, he appears more often in the *Chuang Tzu* than either Lao Tzu or Chuang Tzu himself – albeit often in the role of a butt for Chuang

Tzu's humour. But the point remains that, in his own writings, Kung Fu Tzu talks more about the Tao than the *Tao Te Ching* does, page for page.

What marks out the three books of the *Tao Te Ching*, *Chuang Tzu* and *Lieh Tzu* from, for example, the writings of Kung Fu Tzu is their insistence on experiencing the Tao as a path to walk, rather than as a term to be explained. Experience is all.

For example, take the story which Chuang Tzu tells in the first half of chapter 17, concerning the Lord of the Yellow River and the god of the North Ocean, Jo. The Yellow River has flooded because of the autumn rains, and the god of the Yellow River believes he is the greatest, mightiest being in the world – until he flows into the North Ocean. Then he realizes that he is puny in comparison to the North Ocean.

Jo of the North Ocean replied, 'A frog in a well cannot discuss the ocean, because he is limited by the size of his well. A summer insect cannot discuss ice, because it knows only its own season. A narrow-minded scholar cannot discuss the Tao because he is constrained by his teachings. Now you have come out of your banks and seen the Great Ocean. You now know your own inferiority, so it is now possible to discuss great principles with you.'

In other words, the god Jo of the North Ocean can now begin to teach the Lord of the Yellow River because the Lord has experienced the limits of his own knowledge.

This approach – that the Tao which can be talked about is not the true Tao – marks out those writers whom later generations titled as Taoists. It is captured in the famous phrase '*wu-wei*', which I have usually translated here as 'actionless action'. This is beautifully captured in what seems to be a direct quote from Chuang Tzu found in chapter 13:

Chuang Tzu said,
'My Master Teacher! My Master Teacher!
He judges all life but does not feel he is being judgemental;
he is generous to multitudes of generations
but does not think this benevolent;
he is older than the oldest

but he does not think himself old;
he overarches Heaven and sustains Earth,
shaping and creating endless bodies
but he does not think himself skilful
This is what is known as Heavenly happiness.'

Further on in the same chapter he spells out *wu-wei* even more clearly:

'Heaven produces nothing,
yet all life is transformed;
Earth does not support,
yet all life is sustained;
the Emperor and the king take actionless action,
yet the whole world is served.'

Wu-wei also encompasses the approach of Chuang Tzu to official status and power. He rejects anything which elevates one aspect of life over another. To him, all are equal, and he brings this out in various ways, such as the stories of Robber Chih. For example, at the end of chapter 8 he tells of Po Yi, a former king, who abdicated in favour of his brother and later died of starvation rather than serve an unjust ruler. For this he was held up by Confucians and others as a model of righteousness. Robber Chih, an invented figure, is used by Chuang Tzu at various places through the book as an example of utter greed, cruelty and ruthlessness. Yet in this text Chuang Tzu puts the two men side by side:

Po Yi died for the sake of fame at the bottom of Shou Yang mountain, Robber Chih died for gain on top of the Eastern Heights. These two both died in different ways but the fact is, they both shortened their lives and destroyed their innate natures. Yet we are expected to approve of Po Yi and disapprove of Robber Chih – strange, isn't it?

The term 'innate nature' is a key one in Chuang Tzu. '*Hsing*', as it is pronounced phonetically, is used throughout the text to indicate that which is naturally the way a given species or part of creation either simply *is* in its givenness, or how it reacts to life. In contrast to this innate nature, this *hsing*, which I sometimes have put as true nature, Chuang Tzu presents the artifices and ways of 'civilization' as contrary and destructive to the innate nature. Thus at the start of chapter 9 we have:

Horses have hooves so that they can grip on frost and snow, and hair so that they can withstand the wind and cold. They eat grass and drink water, they buck and gallop, for this is the innate nature of horses. Even if they had great towers and magnificent halls, they would not be interested in them. However, when Po Lo [a famous trainer of horses] came on the scene, he said, 'I know how to train horses.' He branded them, cut their hair and their hooves, put halters on their heads, bridled them, hobbled them and shut them in stables. Out of ten horses at least two or three die . . .

The potter said, 'I know how to use clay, how to mould it into rounds like the compass and into squares as though I had used a T-square.' The carpenter said, 'I know how to use wood: to make it bend, I use the template; to make it straight, I use the plumb line.' However, is it really the innate nature of clay and wood to be moulded by compass and T-square, template and plumb line? It is true, nevertheless, that generation after generation has said, 'Po Lo is good at controlling horses, and indeed the potter and carpenter are good with clay and wood.' And the same nonsense is spouted by those who rule the world.

From that point on in chapter 9, Chuang Tzu launches into one of his characteristic attacks on the way in which the people's true innate nature has been lost and broken. He pictures a perfect world when all were equal and none had any sense of being greater or lesser. They just followed their innate nature. He then depicts the fall from this age of primal, innate, natural living:

Then the perfect sage comes, going on about benevolence, straining for self-righteousness, and suddenly everyone begins to have doubts . . . If the pure essence had not been so cut about, how could they have otherwise ended up with sacrificial bowls? If the raw jade was not broken apart, how could the symbols of power be made? If the Tao and Te – Way and Virtue – had not been ignored, how could benevolence and righteousness have been preferred? If innate nature had not been left behind, how could rituals and music have been invented? . . . The abuse of the true elements to make

artefacts was the crime of the craftsman. The abuse of the Tao and Te –
Way and Virtue – to make benevolence and righteousness, this was the
error of the sage.

Chuang Tzu sees all attempts to impose 'civilization' upon the
innate nature of the world, and especially on the people, as a terrible
mistake which has distorted and abused the natural world – the
world of the Tao, the flow of nature. And so he stands firmly
opposed to all that the Confucians stood for – order, control and
power hierarchies. This is why the *Book of Chuang Tzu* was always
ignored or despised by Confucians and why it, along with other
such 'Taoist' classics, was never formally counted as being amongst
the Classics of Academia in Imperial China. This man is a subversive,
and he knows it! The *Chuang Tzu* is a radical text of rejection and
mockery aimed at the pretensions of human knowledge and
powers.

This rejection of the constructions of meaning which we place
upon the world and which we then assume to be 'natural' is central
to Chuang Tzu as it was to Lieh Tzu as well. They are perhaps the
first deconstructionists. Let me give you an example from Lieh
Tzu. In chapter 8 of *Lieh Tzu* we are introduced to a gentleman by
the name of Mr Tien. He is about to set off on a long journey so
invites his friends and relatives to come for a farewell banquet. As
the dishes of fish and goose are brought in, Mr Tien looks benignly
on them and says, 'How kind Heaven is to humanity. It provides
the five grains and nourishes the fish and birds for us to enjoy and
use.'

In response to this quaint piece of anthropocentrism, everyone
nods in agreement, except for a twelve-year-old boy, the son of Mr
Pao. He steps forward and says,

'My Lord is wrong! All life is born in the same way that we are and we are
all of the same kind. One species is not nobler than another; it is simply that
the strongest and cleverest rule over the weaker and more stupid. Things
eat each other and are eaten, but they were not bred for this. To be sure,
we take the things which we can eat and consume them, but you cannot
claim that Heaven made them in the first place just for us to eat. After all,
mosquitoes and gnats bite our skin, tigers and wolves eat our flesh. Does

this mean Heaven originally created us for the sake of the mosquitoes, gnats, tigers and wolves?'

Here is the authentic voice of the Taoist. Here is the debunking of human pretensions and the re-assertion of the natural as the highest order. Here is the Tao of Chuang Tzu in the mouth of a twelve-year-old.

By stressing the abuses that have happened to our innate natures, Chuang Tzu constantly calls us to look with our heads on one side at what is 'normal'. He uses humour, shock tactics, silly names, the weirdest characters (such as Cripple Shu or Master Yu) and totally unbelievable scenarios (such as the 'willow tree' incident in chapter 18) to make us look again at what we hold to be true. He uses contradiction to explode convention. Take these exchanges from chapter 2:

There is the beginning; there is not as yet any beginning of the beginning; there is not as yet beginning not to be a beginning of the beginning . . . I have just made a statement, yet I do not know whether what I said has been real in what I said or not really said.

Under Heaven there is nothing greater than the tip of a hair, but Mount Tai [the greatest of the mighty sacred mountains] is smaller; there is no one older than a dead child, yet Peng Tsu [who, according to mythology, lived thousands of years] died young.

So where does all this leave Chuang Tzu in his understanding of life and his relationship to the rest of creation – the 'Ten Thousand Things', as it is put in Chinese? The next line in this quote from chapter 2 spells it out. If Chuang Tzu could conceivably be imagined uttering any kind of credal statement, perhaps this would be it:

Heaven and Earth and I were born at the same time, and all life and I are one.

This is the understanding that Chuang Tzu wishes us to return to.

The uselessness of language is the other key point of Chuang Tzu's discourses. He wants us to break beyond words and to realize how they imprison us. This is captured in a quote from chapter 2 which echoes the opening of the *Tao Te Ching*:

The great Way is not named,
the great disagreement is unspoken,
great benevolence is not benevolent,
great modesty is not humble,
great courage is not violent.
The Tao that is clear is not the Tao,
speech which enables argument is not worthy,
benevolence which is ever present does not achieve its goal,
modesty if flouted, fails,
courage that is violent is pointless.

I want to move on now from this glance at some of the key threads in Chuang Tzu's writings, to his place within 'Taoist' thought and belief. What was his relationship to the book we now know as the *Tao Te Ching*? Traditionally, the chronology of the three 'classics' of Taoism has been, first Lao Tzu with the *Tao Te Ching*, second *Chuang Tzu*, third *Lieh Tzu*.

Lao Tzu has been ascribed to the sixth to fifth centuries BC, while Chuang Tzu has always been known to be around the 330–290 BC era. It would thus seem that Chuang Tzu must have known of the book by Lao Tzu. However, as I have mentioned earlier, it is highly unlikely, even if such a person as Lao Tzu existed, that he wrote more than a few of the chapters of the *Tao Te Ching*. This book dates from around 300 BC at the earliest, though it uses much much older material.

When Jay Ramsay and I with our colleague Man Ho Kwok produced our translation and exploration of the *Tao Te Ching*, we discovered that each chapter consists of two very different strata, clearly discernible in the original Chinese. The first layer is a proverb, wisdom saying or oracle which has been passed down through generations and has become rounded and smooth as a result of re-telling. In quatrains which each have an identical number of characters, the saying is preserved in the midst or at the start of each chapter. Around it, written in a totally different style of Chinese, is a commentary, which indicates the fourth- to third-century BC world of China.

In *Chuang Tzu* we can see a similar process at work. At no point is there a direct quote from the *Tao Te Ching*. This is hardly surprising if the dates given above are accurate. The *Tao Te Ching* was not written down when Chuang Tzu was writing, or if it was, it was being compiled at roughly the same time. But it is clear that both books relied upon the same stock of folk wisdom, wisdom sayings and oracles. What is distinctive is the different ways each book handled the same common material. For example, compare how they each use a series of sayings about babies.

In chapter 55 of the *Tao Te Ching* we have:

'Those who have true *te*
Are like a newborn baby.'

– and if they seem like this, they will not be stung by wasps or snakes,
or pounced on by animals in the wild or birds of prey.

A baby is weak and supple, but his hand can grasp your finger.
He has no desire as yet, and yet he can be erect –
he can cry day and night without even getting hoarse
such is the depth of his harmony.

It's stupid to rush around.
When you fight against yourself, it shows in your face.
But if you draw your sap from your heart
then you will be truly strong.

You will be great.[3]

Chuang Tzu handles the same proverbial wisdom in a characteristi-cally different way in chapter 23. Lao Tzu has been asked by Nan Jung Chu how one can protect one's life. Lao Tzu replies:

'The basic way of protecting life – can you embrace the One?' said Lao Tzu. 'Can you hold it fast? . . . Can you be a little baby? The baby cries all day long but its throat never becomes hoarse: that indeed is perfect harmony. The baby clenches its fists all day long but never gets cramp, it holds fast to Virtue. The baby stares all day long but it is not affected by what is outside it. It moves without knowing where, it sits without

3. *The Illustrated Tao Te Ching*, p. 137.

knowing where it is sitting, it is quietly placid and rides the flow of events. This is how to protect life.'

. . . 'Just now I asked you, "Can you become a little baby?" The baby acts without knowing why and moves without knowing where. Its body is like a rotting branch and its heart is like cold ashes. Being like this, neither bad fortune will affect it nor good fortune draw near. Having neither bad nor good fortune, it is not affected by the misfortune that comes to most others!'

So a common source in this instance is even cited as having been used in discourse by Lao Tzu, but it is used in very different ways. This is no rigid adherence to a fixed text – for no such fixed *Tao Te Ching* text existed. It is the use of a common source which later solidified into sacred texts – both the *Tao Te Ching* and *Chuang Tzu*.

So what was the religious background out of which these two great texts arose? We have to rid ourselves of any notion that they arose from a Taoist world. As I have said, there was no Taoism until much later. Indeed the philosopher Hsun Tzu, who lived from *c.* 312 to 221 BC, thus overlapping in his earlier years with Chuang Tzu, puts Lao Tzu and Chuang Tzu into altogether different schools of philosophy in his list of such schools. By the time of Ssu Ma Chien, Chuang Tzu is being spoken of as a pupil of Lao Tzu's thought. It is obvious from Chuang Tzu himself that he holds Lao Tzu in very high esteem, even if he then goes off on his own path.

Perhaps it is more important in Chuang Tzu's case to see who he was *not* in favour of, for this gives us a clue to the religious thought from which he comes. He is an implacable enemy of the bureaucrats, the petty officials, the sages who teach benevolence and righteousness. He is opposed to all those who seek to tame or harness the innate nature of all aspects of creation, of nature – most especially that of the people. Ssu Ma Chien's inclusion of the story of Chuang Tzu rejecting outright any offer of a position of authority highlights this. But it is deeper than this. Chuang Tzu has a profound hatred of all that enslaves or controls the human spirit. In this he is against the state cult of Confucians, the cruel, almost fascist teachings of the

Legalists and Mohists, who felt that human nature was evil and therefore had to be brutally ruled, and yet he is also against the sentimentality of those who believe that everyone is really good.

Chuang Tzu is fed by shamanism, the earliest stream of Chinese spirituality, but is also in touch with the latest thinking in fourth-century BC cosmology. He draws his inspiration for the flow of nature from the shamanistic role of acting as an intermediary between the spiritual and physical worlds, where the Way of Heaven is the superior Way and the material world just a pale reflection of the true reality of the Heavenly world. This comes out time and time again when he compares the natural way of Heaven and Earth with the unnatural way of the rulers, sages and Emperors. But he is also a man who is teasing out the depths in new terms and models which were beginning to percolate into general Chinese thought. Most important amongst these is the role and significance of the individual as a being in his or her own right within the cosmos. There is no place here for the subsuming of the individual within the needs of the state. In contrast to the State Cult of China, where the ruler is the intermediary between the rest of humanity and Heaven, Chuang Tzu sees the rulers as the problem, and turns to the right of individuals to strike out for their own salvation, their own sense of place in a world which they are encouraged to deconstruct and then to re-assemble by turning to their innate nature.

This is quite the most radical aspect of his religio-social thought and lays the seeds for the later rise of Taoism as a specific religious expression where individual salvation, purpose and meaning became the central tenet of the new religion. For in elevating the free individual against the incorporation and subsuming of the individual within the corporate, he is moving in a much more radical direction than the *Tao Te Ching* does and is challenging the whole superstructure of conventional Chinese religious and social life.

So where does he get this idea from? Heaven knows! But I would conjecture that much of it is from pure speculation and from his own logical developments from the contextual nature of all knowledge, which lead him to see all previous attempts to impose order and meaning on the universe as just so much wordy wind in the air.

Because his critique of language and knowledge is so ruthless, he is left with nothing fixed, nothing 'given'. In such circumstances the human spirit can make great leaps forward. I believe that Chuang Tzu is one of the great innovators of human thought – a man whose time, maybe, has yet to come. Certainly the remarkable thing about him, to someone writing in the final days of the second millennium after Christ, is how modern he sounds, and yet how in his modern-ness he actually undermines that modern-ness's notion of its own modernity!

So I would claim that, while one can to some extent unravel the context of Chuang Tzu's arguments and the nature of his opponents, while one can see some antecedents of his thought in the shamanistic culture which these bureaucratic opponents were busy destroying, while one can see elements of what he was saying reflected in Lao Tzu, ultimately in Chuang Tzu we meet an original man. A thinker who broke through all the conventions of his time and entered new fields of thought. That he could do so with such humour, through such wonderful stories and with such amazing characters, puts him on a level with the most truly original and enjoyable thinkers the world has ever seen.

聽鸚畫
南田紵衣畫柳骨
一種瀟散出塵之
致真元易到

CHAPTER I

Wandering Where You Will

In the darkness of the north there is a fish, whose name is Vast. This fish is enormous, I don't know how many thousand miles long. It also changes into a bird, whose name is Roc, and the roc's back is I don't know how many thousand miles across. When it rises in the air, its wings are like the clouds of Heaven. When the seas move, this bird too travels to the south darkness, the darkness known as the Pool of Heaven.

The *Book of Wonders* records a variety of marvels. It tells how 'when the roc flies to the southern darkness, the waters are stirred up for three thousand miles, and he rises up in a whirlwind, soaring ninety thousand miles, not ceasing for six months'. It is like the swirling of the dust in the heat, blowing around below the deep blue of Heaven. Is this its true colour? Or is it because it is so far away that it appears like this? To one flying above looking down, the pattern is indeed the same.

If the waters are not great enough, they will not have the ability to carry a large boat. Spill a cupful of water into a small hollow and even a scrap will look like a boat. However, if you try and float the cup upon it, it will just sit there, for the water is not sufficient to carry such a boat. And if there is not enough wind, it will not have enough strength to bear up the great wings. The roc needs ninety thousand miles and the strength of the wind below him, so that he can rest upon the wind. Thus, with the light of Heaven on his back and with nothing to restrain him, the great bird can follow his course to the south.

A cicada taught a young dove, saying with a laugh, 'I try to fly, with considerable effort, into an elm or sandalwood tree, but I find that, before I can reach it, I am pulled back down to earth. So what chance does this creature have of rising to ninety thousand miles and heading south?'

Someone who goes into the countryside with his lunch, and returns in time for the evening meal will be as full as when he left. Someone travelling a hundred miles needs to take enough food to see him through. And someone who travels a thousand miles needs to carry food for three months. What do these two understand?

The understanding of the small cannot be compared to the understanding of the great. A few years cannot be compared to many years. How do we know this? The morning mushroom does not know of the waxing and waning of the moon. The cicada does not know of spring and autumn, for theirs are but short lives. To the south of Chu there is a vast creature for whom five hundred years is but a spring, and five hundred years is but an autumn. In ancient antiquity there was a giant tree called Chun, for whom spring was eight thousand years and for whom autumn was eight thousand years. Yet Peng Tsu[4] is the only man renowned for his great age, something envied by many people, which is rather pathetic!

When the Emperor Tang debated with Chi, a similar issue arose, for he said:

'In the barren north there is a dark sea called Heaven's Pool. Here there is a fish, several thousand miles wide and goodness knows how long. This creature is called Vast. There is also a bird, whose name is Roc, and whose back is like Mount Tai[5] and whose wings cover the heavens. He rises up on a whirlwind, ninety thousand

4. Mythological figure, reputed to have lived to a great age.
5. The greatest of the Sacred Mountains of China, believed to be the birthplace of creation and humanity.

miles high, soaring through the clouds and breaking through the clear blue sky, then turns to plot his course south, travelling to the southern darkness. A quail laughs at him, saying, "Where are you travelling to? I leap up high but come down again after just a few feet, falling to earth amongst the bushes. And frankly that is the best you can expect from flying! So where is that creature going?" This is what distinguishes the small from the great.'

Someone who can fulfil the duties of one office, or behaves well enough to please one district, or has enough virtue to please one leader and is used to rule one country, views himself in the same way as these creatures. However, Sung Jung Tzu[6] would laugh at such a person. The whole world might praise him but he would not do more as a result. The whole world might condemn him, but he would not be affected. He knew the difference between the inner and the outer and the boundaries between honour and disgrace, but he went no further. He did not care about the world's opinion, but there were boundaries he did not manage to overcome. The great Lieh Tzu[7] could ride the wind, going to the edges without concern, but returning after fifteen days. In the search for good fortune he knew no boundaries. Although he never had to bother with walking, nevertheless he needed some way of getting around. If instead he had risen through the naturalness of Heaven and Earth, travelled on the six elemental forces and voyaged into the unknown and unlimited, he would have had to depend upon nothing! As the saying goes

The perfect man has no self;
The spiritual man has no merit;
The holy man has no fame.

Yao,[8] giving up rule of the earth to Hsu Yu,[9] said, 'When the sun and moon have risen, there is no point in keeping the torches lit,

6. Philosopher who taught simple living and pacifism.
7. One of the three great 'Taoist' writers, along with Lao Tzu and Chuang Tzu.
8. One of the five original Emperors of Chinese mythology and pre-history. A model of Confucian wisdom.
9. A hermit who, according to legend, refused to take over the kingdom.

because it's a waste of light! When the rainy season comes, there is little point in continuing to water the ground! If you, great Master, were to take over the rule of everything under Heaven, then all would be well, whereas if I continue, all I am aware of is my failures. Please, take over ruling the earth.'

Hsu Yu said, 'Sir, you rule everything below Heaven, and everything below Heaven is well ruled. If I take over from you, Sir, won't people think I'm doing it just for the fame? But fame is nothing compared to reality. I would be like a guest, wouldn't I? The tailor bird makes its nest deep in the forest, but only uses one branch. The tapir drinks from the river Ho, but only takes what it needs. Return home, my noble Lord, for I have no interest in ruling the kingdom. The cook may not run his kitchen well, but the shaman does not jump up and take over.'

Chien Wu said to Lien Shu, 'I was listening to the words of Chieh Yu[10] – his words sounded fine, but there was no substance, going on and on but coming to no conclusion. I was considerably astonished by his words, for they seemed endless like the Milky Way; vast overstatements and not related to the world of humanity.'

Lien Shu said, 'What was he talking about?'

'He said, "Far away on a mountain called Ku She, there lives a holy man whose skin is like ice and pure snow, and his manner is like a shy virgin. He does not eat the five grains, but lives off the wind and dew. He climbs the clouds and rides the dragons, and travels beyond the boundaries of the known world. He has distilled holiness and uses this to heal all and to bring full harvests." Now I think this is nonsense and don't believe such words.'

Lien Shu said, 'Obviously. You wouldn't ask a blind man to appreciate a scene of beauty, nor a deaf man to enjoy the sounds of drums and bells. But it is possible to be blind and deaf in one's deep

10. A critic of Confucius, known as 'the Madman of Chu'.

understanding, as well as physically. Your very words show this, for you spoke like a young woman waiting for her appointed time!

'This man with such virtue can hold all existence and roll it into one. Reform is called for, so you, you fool, would just ask such a one to take over the empire! Such a man as this, nothing harms him, not even great floods pouring from the sky can drown him, nor the great drought which melts gold and stone and burns mountains and hills. One like him could make a Yao or Shun[11] just from his dust and debris, but he is not bothered by such things! A man from Sung who traded in official ceremonial hats travelled to Yueh, but the people of Yueh, who cut their hair and tattoo themselves, have no use for such things. Yao brought peace to the people of the earth and within the boundaries of the seas. But he went to visit the four masters of distant Ku She mountain, north of the river Fen, and he became aware that his rule was meaningless.'

Hui Tzu spoke to Chuang Tzu, saying, 'The King of Wei gave me the seeds of an enormous gourd, which I planted and it produced a fruit big enough to hold five bushels of anything, so I used it to hold water, but it was then too heavy to pick up. I cut it into two to make scoops, but they were too awkward to use. It was not that they weren't big, I just found I could not make use of them, so I destroyed them.'

Chuang Tzu said, 'Dear Sir, surely the problem is that you don't know how to use big things. There is a man in Sung who could make a cream which prevented the hands from getting chapped, and generation after generation of his family have made a living by bleaching silk. A pilgrim heard this and offered to buy the secret for a hundred pieces of gold. All the family came together to respond and said, "For generation after generation we have bleached silk, yet we have never made more than a few pieces of gold; now in

11. Shun took over the kingdom from Yao and is another model ruler.

just one morning we can earn a hundred pieces of gold! Let's do it.'' So the pilgrim got the secret and went to see the King of Wu. He was struggling with the state of Yueh. The King of Wu gave the pilgrim command of the army and in the depths of winter they fought the men of Yueh on the water, inflicting a crushing blow on the forces of Yueh, and the traveller was rewarded by the gift of a vast estate from the conquered territory. The cream had stopped the hands chapping in both cases: one gained an estate, but the others had never got further than bleaching silk, because they used this secret in such different ways. Now, Sir, you have a gourd big enough to hold five bushels, so why didn't you use it to make big bottles which could help you float down the rivers and lakes, instead of dismissing it as being useless? Because, dear Sir, your head is full of straw!'

Hui Tzu spoke to Chuang Tzu, saying, 'I have a big tree, which people call useless. Its trunk is so knotted, no carpenter could work on it, while its branches are too twisted to use a square or compass upon. So, although it is close to the road, no carpenter would look at it. Now, Sir, your words are like this, too big and no use, therefore everyone ignores them.'

   Chuang Tzu said, 'Sir, have you never seen a wild cat or weasel? It lies there, crouching and waiting; east and west it leaps out, not afraid of going high or low; until it is caught in a trap and dies in a net. Yet again, there is the yak, vast like a cloud in heaven. It is big, but cannot use this fact to catch rats. Now you, Sir, have a large tree, and you don't know how to use it, so why not plant it in the middle of nowhere, where you can go to wander or fall asleep under its shade? No axe under Heaven will attack it, nor shorten its days, for something which is useless will never be disturbed.'

納納溪梅逗曉
風水邨
山閣往
來通馬
歸程通
紅塵路
亞裡馳
逢迓偹
翁
梅元人
葉楚材
女婿陶敏

CHAPTER 2

Working Everything Out Evenly

Master Chi of the Southern District sat leaning forward on his chair, staring up at Heaven and breathing steadily, as if in a trance, forgetful of all around him. Master Yen Cheng Yu stood beside him and said, 'What is it? Is it true that you can make the body like a shrivelled tree, the heart like cold, dead ashes? Surely the man here now is not the same as the one who was here yesterday.'

Master Chi said, 'Yen, this is a good point to make, but do you really understand?

'I have lost myself, do you understand?
You hear the pipes of the people, but not the pipes of earth.
Even if you hear the pipes of earth, you don't hear the pipes of
　　Heaven!'

'Please explain this,' said Master Yu.
Master Chi replied,

'The vast breath of the universe, this is called Wind.
Sometimes it is unmoving;
when it moves it makes the ten thousand openings resound
　　dramatically.
Have you not heard it,
like a terrifying gale?
Mountains and forests are stormed by it,
great trees, a hundred spans round with dips and hollows,
are like noses, like mouths, like ears, like sockets,
like cups, like mortars, like pools, like gulleys;

sounding like a crashing wave, a whistling arrow, a screech;
　　sucking, shouting, barking, wailing, moaning,
the winds ahead howling *yeeh*,
those behind crying *yooh*,
light breezes making gentle sounds,
while the typhoon creates a great din.
When the typhoon has passed, all goes quiet again.
Have you not witnessed this disturbance settle down again?'

Master Yu said, 'What you've just described are the notes of the earth, while the notes of humanity come from wind instruments, but you have said nothing about the notes of Heaven.'

'The role of these forces on all forms of living things is not the same,' said Master Chi. 'For each is different, using what they need to be, not influenced by any other force!'

True depth of understanding is wide and steady,
Shallow understanding is lazy and wandering,
Words of wisdom are precise and clear,
Foolish words are petty and mean.

When we sleep, our spirits roam the earth,
when awake our bodies are alert,
whatever we encounter captures us,
day by day our hearts are struggling.

Often simple,
often deep,
often intimate.

Minor troubles make them unsettled, anxious,
Major troubles are plain and simple.

They fly off like an arrow,
convinced that they know right from wrong;
it is like one who makes a sacred promise,

standing sure and true and on their way to victory.
They give way, like autumn and winter,
decaying away with the ebb and flow of each day;
it is like a stream of water, it cannot be brought back;
they stagnate, because they are like old blocked drains,
brought on by old age,
which makes their minds closed as if near death,
and there is nothing which can draw their hearts into the power
    of the yang –
the life-giving light.

Joy and anger,
sadness and delight,
hope and disappointment;
faithlessness and certainty,
forcefulness and sloth,
eagerness and reticence,
like notes from an empty reed,
or mushrooms growing in dampness,
day and night follow each other before our very eyes and we
    have no idea why.
Enough, enough!
Morning and night exist,
we cannot know more about the Origin than this!

Without them, we don't exist,
Without us, they have no purpose.
This is close to our meaning,
but we cannot know what creates things to be thus.
It is as if they have a Supreme Guidance, but there is no way of
    grasping such a One.
He can certainly act, of that there is no doubt,
but I cannot see his body.
He has desires, but no body.
A hundred parts and nine orifices and six organs,
are parts that go to make up myself,
but is any part more noble than another?
You say I should treat all parts as equally noble:

But shouldn't I also treat some as better than others?

Don't they all serve me as well as each other?

If they are all servants, then aren't they all as bad as each other?

Or are there rulers amongst these servants?

There must be some Supreme Ruler who is over them all.

Though it is doubtful that you can find his true form,

and even if it were possible,

is it not meaningless to his true nature?

When someone is born in this body, doesn't life continue until
 death?

Either in conflict with others or in harmony with them,

we go through life like a runaway horse, unable to stop.

Working hard until the end of his life,

unable to appreciate any achievement,

worn out and incapable of resting,

isn't he a pathetic sight?

He may say, 'I'm still alive,' but so what?

When the body rots, so does the mind – is this not tragic?

Is this not ridiculous, or is it just me that is ridiculous and
 everyone else is sane?

If you allow your mind to guide you,

who then can be seen as being without a teacher?

Why is it thought that only the one who understands change and
 whose heart approves this can be the teacher?

Surely the fool is just the same.

But if you ignore your mind but insist you know right from
 wrong, you are like the saying,

'Today I set off for Yueh and arrived yesterday.'

This is to claim that what is not, is;

That what is not, does exist –

why, even the holy sage Yu cannot understand this,

let alone poor old me!

Our words are not just hot air. Words work because they say something, but the problem is that, if we cannot define a word's meaning, it doesn't really say anything. Is it possible that there really is something here? Or does it really mean nothing? Is it possible to make a proper case for it being any different from the chirruping of chicks? How is it that we have the Tao so obscured that we have to distinguish between true and false? What has clouded our words so that we can have both what is and what is not? How can it be that the Tao goes off and is no longer? How can it be that words are found but are not understood? When the Tao is obscured by pettiness and the words are obscured by elaboration, then we end up having the 'this is, this is not' of the Confucians and Mohists, with what one of them calls reality being denied by the other, and what the other calls real disputed by the first. If we want to confound what they call right and confirm what they call wrong, we need to shed light on both of them.

Nothing exists which is not 'that', nothing exists which is not 'this'. I cannot look at something through someone else's eyes, I can only truly know something which I know. Therefore 'that' comes out of 'this' and 'this' arises from 'that'. That is why we say that 'that' and 'this' are born from each other, most definitely.

Compare birth with death, compare death with life; compare what is possible with what is not possible and compare what is not possible with what is possible; because there is, there is not, and because there is not, there is.

Thus it is that the sage does not go down this way, but sheds the light of Heaven upon such issues. This is also that and that is also this. The 'that' is on the one hand also 'this', and 'this' is on the other hand also 'that'. Does this mean he still has a this and that? Does this mean he does not have a this and that?

When 'this' and 'that' do not stand against each other, this is called the pivot of the Tao. This pivot provides the centre of the circle, which is without end, for it can react equally to that which is and to that which is not. This is why it is best to shed light on such issues. To use a finger to show that a finger is not a finger, is not really as good as using something that is not a finger to show that a

finger is not a finger; to use a horse to show a horse is not a horse is
not as good as using something other than a horse to show that a
horse is not a horse. Heaven and Earth are as one as a finger is, and
all of creation is as one as a horse is.

What is, is, what is not, is not.
The Tao is made because we walk it,
things become what they are called.
Why is this so? Surely because this is so.
Why is this not so? Surely because this is not so.
Everything has what is innate,
everything has what is necessary.
Nothing is not something,
nothing is not so.
Therefore, take a stalk of wheat and a pillar,
a leper or a beauty like Hsi-shih,
the great and the insecure,
the cunning and the odd:
all these are alike to the Tao.
In their difference is their completeness;
in their completeness is their difference.

Through the Tao they are all seen as one, regardless of their
completeness or difference, by those who are capable of such
extended vision. Such a person has no need for distinctions but
follows the ordinary view. The ordinary view is firmly set on the
ground of usefulness. The usefulness of something defines its use;
the use is its flexibility; its flexibility is its essence and from this it
comes to a stop. We stop but do not know why we stop, and this is
called Tao.

To tax our spirits and our intellect in this way without realizing
that everything is the same is called 'Three in the Morning'. And
what is 'Three in the Morning'? A monkey trainer was giving
out acorns and he said, 'In the morning I will give you each three
acorns and in the evening you will get four.' The monkeys were
very upset at this and so he said, 'All right, in the morning you will
get four and in the evening, three.' This pleased the monkeys no
end. His two statements were essentially the same, but got different

reactions from the monkeys. He gained what he wanted by his skill. So it is with the sage, who manages to harmonize right and wrong and is content to abide by the Natural Equality of Heaven. This is called walking two roads.

The men of old understood a great deal. How much?

In the beginning they did not know that anything existed; this is virtually perfect knowledge, for nothing can be added. Later, they knew that some things existed but they did not distinguish between them. Next came those who distinguished between things, but did not judge things as 'being' or 'not being'. It was when judgements were made that the Tao was damaged, and because the Tao was damaged, love became complete. Is anything complete or damaged? Is anything not complete or damaged? There is completion and damage, just as Chao Wen[12] played the lute. There is nothing which is complete or damaged, just as Chao Wen did not play the lute.

> Chao Wen played the lute,
> Shih Kuang conducted,
> Hui Tzu debated.

The understanding of these three was almost perfect and they followed it to the end of their years. They cared about this because it was different, and they wanted to teach others about it. But it was not possible to make things clear, though they tried to make things simple. They ended up instead with the folly of the 'hard' and the 'white'.

Wen's son ended up continuing to play Wen's lute and achieved nothing for himself. If someone like this is called complete, then am I not also? And if someone like this is called incomplete, then surely

12. A famous musician.

neither I nor anyone else has ever been complete. Also, by the light shining out of chaos, the sage is guided; he does not make use of distinctions but is led on by the light.

Now, however, I have something to say. Do I know whether this is in the same sort of category as what is said by others? I don't know. At one level, what I say is not the same. At another level, it most definitely is, and there is no difference between what I say and what others say. Whatever the case, let me try and tell you what I mean.

There is the beginning; there is not as yet any beginning of the beginning; there is not as yet beginning not to be a beginning of the beginning. There is what is, and there is what is not, and it is not easy to say whether what is not, is not; or whether what is, is.

I have just made a statement, yet I do not know whether what I said has been real in what I said or not really said.

Under Heaven there is nothing greater than the tip of a hair, but Mount Tai is smaller; there is no one older than a dead child, yet Peng Tsu died young.

Heaven and Earth and I were born at the same time, and all life and I are one.

As all life is one, what need is there for words? Yet I have just said all life is one, so I have already spoken, haven't I? One plus one equals two, two plus one equals three. To go on from here would take us beyond the understanding of even a skilled accountant, let alone the ordinary people. If going from 'no-thing' to 'some-thing' we get to three, just think how much further we would have to go if we went from 'some-thing' to something![13]

Don't even start, let's just stay put.

The great Tao has no beginning, and words have changed their meaning from the beginning, but because of the idea of a 'this is'

13. This passage plays on the use of positive and negative signifiers in Chinese characters.

there came to be limitations. I want to say something about these limitations. There is right and left, relationships and their consequences, divisions and disagreements, emulations and contentions. These are known as the eight Virtues.

The sage will not speak of what is beyond the boundaries of the universe – though he will not deny it either. What is within the universe, he says something about but does not pronounce upon. Concerning the record of the past actions of the kings in the *Spring and Autumn Annals*, the sage discusses but does not judge. When something is divided, something is not divided; when there is disagreement there are things not disagreed about.

You ask, what does this mean? The sage encompasses everything, while ordinary people just argue about things. This is why I say that disagreement means you do not understand at all.

The great Way is not named,
the great disagreement is unspoken,
great benevolence is not benevolent,
great modesty is not humble,
great courage is not violent.
The Tao that is clear is not the Tao,
speech which enables argument is not worthy,
benevolence which is ever present does not achieve its goal,
modesty if flouted, fails,
courage that is violent is pointless.

These five are fine: they are, as it were, rounded. But if they lose this they can become awkward. This is why the one who knows how to stop at what he knows is best. Who knows the argument that needs no words, and the Tao that cannot be named? To those who do, this is called the Treasury of Heaven. Pour into it and it is never full; empty it and it is never empty. We do not know where it comes from originally, and this is called our Guiding Light.

In the olden days Yao said to Shun, 'I want to attack Tsung, Kuai and Hsu Ao. I have wanted to do this since I became king. What do you think?'

Shun replied, 'These three rulers are just primitives living in the backwoods – why can't you just forget them? In ancient times, ten suns rose and all life was illuminated. But how much more does Virtue illuminate life than even these suns!'

Yeh Chueh said to Wang Ni, 'Do you know, Master, what everything agrees upon?'

'How can I possibly know?' said Wang Ni.

'Do you know, Master, what you do not know?'

'How can I know?' he replied.

'Then does nothing know anything?'

'How could I know that?' said Wang Ni. 'Nevertheless, I want to try and say something. How can I know that what I say I know is not actually what I don't know? Likewise, how can I know that what I think I don't know is not really what I do know? I want to put some questions to you:

'If someone sleeps in a damp place, he will ache all over and he will be half paralysed, but is it the same for an eel? If someone climbs a tree, he will be frightened and shaking, but is it so for a monkey? Out of these three, which is wisest about where to live?

'Humans eat meat, deer consume grass, centipedes devour snakes and owls and crows enjoy mice. Of these four, which has the best taste?

'Monkeys mate with each other, deer go with deer. People said that Mao Chiang and Li Chi were the most beautiful women in the world, but fish seeing them dived away, birds took off into the air and deer ran off. Of these four, who really knows true beauty? As I see it, benevolence and righteousness, also the ways of right and wrong, are completely interwoven. I do not think I can know the difference between them!'

Yeh Chueh said: 'Master, if you do not know the difference

between that which is good and that which is harmful, does this mean the perfect man is also without such knowledge?'

'The perfect man is pure spirit,' replied Wang Ni. 'He does not feel the heat of the burning deserts nor the cold of the vast waters. He is not frightened by the lightning which can split open mountains, nor by the storms that can whip up the seas. Such a person rides the clouds and mounts upon the sun and moon, and wanders across and beyond the four seas. Neither death nor life concern him, nor is he interested in what is good or bad!'

Chu Chiao Tzu asked Chang Wu Tzu,

'I have heard from the Master
that the sage does not labour at anything,
does not look for advantage,
does not act benevolently,
does not harm,
does not pursue the Tao;
He speaks without speaking,
and does not speak when he speaks,
and looks beyond the confines of this dusty world.

'The Master sees all this as an endless stream of words, but to me they are like the words of the mysterious Tao. Master, what do you think?'

Chang Wu Tzu said, 'Such a saying as this would have confused even the Yellow Emperor,[14] so how could Confucius be able to understand them! However, you are getting ahead of yourself, counting your chickens before your eggs are hatched and looking at the bowl, imagining the roasted fowl. I will try to speak to you in a random way, so you listen to me likewise. How can the wise one sit beside the sun and moon and embrace the universe? Because he

14. The greatest of the five original Emperors of Chinese mythology, a symbol of wisdom and civilization.

brings all things together in harmony, he rejects difference and confusion and ignores status and power. While ordinary people rush busily around, the sage seems stupid and ignorant, but to him all life is one and united. All life is simply what it is and all appear to him to be doing what they rightly should.

'How do I know that the love of life is not a delusion? Or that the fear of death is not like a young person running away from home and unable to find his way back? The Lady Li Chi was the daughter of a border warden, Ai. When the state of Chin captured her, she wept until she had drenched her robes; then she came to the King's palace, shared the King's bed, ate his food, and repented of her tears. How do I know whether the dead now repent for their former clinging to life?

'Come the morning, those who dream of the drunken feast may weep and moan; when the morning comes, those who dream of weeping and moaning go hunting in the fields. When they dream, they don't know it is a dream. Indeed, in their dreams they may think they are interpreting dreams, only when they awake do they know it was a dream. Eventually there comes the day of reckoning and awakening, and then we shall know that it was all a great dream. Only fools think that they are now awake and that they really know what is going on, playing the prince and then playing the servant. What fools! The Master and you are both living in a dream. When I say a dream, I am also dreaming. This very saying is a deception. If after ten thousand years we could once meet a truly great sage, one who understands, it would seem as if it had only been a morning.

'Imagine that you and I have a disagreement, and you get the better of me, rather than me getting the better of you, does this mean that you are automatically right and I am automatically wrong? Suppose I get the better of you, does it follow that I am automatically right and you are therefore wrong? Is it really that one of us is right and the other wrong? Or are we both right and both wrong? Neither you nor I can really know and other people are even more in the dark. So who can we ask to give us the right answer? Should you ask someone who thinks you are right? But how then can that person give a fair answer? Should we ask someone who thinks I am right? But then if he agrees with me, how can he make a fair judgement? Then again, should we ask someone who agrees with both of us? But again, if he agrees with both of us, how can he make a true judgement? Should we ask someone who disagrees with both of us? But here again, if he disagrees with both of us, how can he make an honest judgement? It is clear that neither you, I nor anyone else can make decisions like this amongst ourselves. So should we wait for someone else to turn up?

'To wait for one voice to bring it all together is as pointless as waiting for no one. Bring all things together under the Equality of Heaven, allow their process of change to go on unimpeded, and learn to grow old. What do I mean by bringing everything together under the Equality of Heaven? With regard to what is right and wrong, I say not being is being and being is not being. But let us not get caught up in discussing this. Forget about life, forget about worrying about right and wrong. Plunge into the unknown and the endless and find your place there!'

The Outline said to the Shadow, 'First you are on the move, then you are standing still; you sit down and then you stand up. Why can't you make up your mind?'

Shadow replied, 'Do I have to look to something else to be what I am? Does this something else itself not have to rely upon yet another something? Do I have to depend upon the scales of a snake or the wings of a cicada? How can I tell how things are? How can I tell how things are not?'

Once upon a time, I, Chuang Tzu, dreamt that I was a butterfly, flitting around and enjoying myself. I had no idea I was Chuang Tzu. Then suddenly I woke up and was Chuang Tzu again. But I could not tell, had I been Chuang Tzu dreaming I was a butterfly, or a butterfly dreaming I was now Chuang Tzu? However, there must be some sort of difference between Chuang Tzu and a butterfly! We call this the transformation of things.

碧浪湖
遠夜放舟
斷篷帶
颯颯作
寒流
釣故雁
相思字
寫評雲
天尔許
愁事敎
剪鐙咏
浮湖天
清曉之
趣

CHAPTER 3

The Nurturing of Life

O̤ur life has a boundary but there is no boundary to
knowledge.
To use what has a boundary to pursue what is limitless is
dangerous;
with this knowledge, if we still go after knowledge, we will run
into trouble.
Do not do what is good in order to gain praise.
If you do what is bad be sure to avoid the punishment.
Follow the Middle Course, for this is the way to keep yourself
together,
to sustain your life, to care for your parents and to live for many
years.

Cook Ting was butchering an ox for Lord Wen Hui. Every movement of his hand, every shrug of his shoulder, every step of his feet,
every thrust of his knee, every sound of the sundering flesh and the
swoosh of the descending knife, were all in perfect accord, like the
Mulberry Grove Dance or the rhythm of the Ching-shou.[15]

'Ah, how excellent!' said Lord Wen Hui. 'How has your skill
become so superb?'

---

15. Two very ancient forms of music.

Cook Ting put down his knife and said, 'What your servant loves best is the Tao, which is better than any art. When I started to cut up oxen, what I saw was just a complete ox. After three years, I had learnt not to see the ox as whole. Now I practise with my mind, not with my eyes. I ignore my sense and follow my spirit. I see the natural lines and my knife slides through the great hollows, follows the great cavities, using that which is already there to my advantage. Thus, I miss the great sinews and even more so, the great bones. A good cook changes his knife annually, because he slices. An ordinary cook has to change his knife every month, because he hacks. Now this knife of mine I have been using for nineteen years, and it has cut thousands of oxen. However, its blade is as sharp as if it had just been sharpened. Between the joints there are spaces, and the blade of a knife has no real thickness. If you put what has no thickness into spaces such as these, there is plenty of room, certainly enough for the knife to work through. However, when I come to a difficult part and can see that it will be difficult, I take care and pay due regard. I look carefully and I move with caution. Then, very gently, I move the knife until there is a parting and the flesh falls apart like a lump of earth falling to the ground. I stand with the knife in my hand looking around and then, with an air of satisfaction, I wipe the knife and put it away.'

'Splendid!' said Lord Wen Hui. 'I have heard what cook Ting has to say and from his words I have learned how to live life fully.'

When Kung Wen Hsien saw the Commander of the Right he was surprised and said, 'Who is this man? Why has he only got one foot? Is this from Heaven or from man?'[16]

'From Heaven, not from man,' said the Commander. 'My life came from Heaven, which also gave me just one foot. The human appearance is a gift, which is why I know that this is from Heaven,

16. Amputation of one foot was a common form of punishment for criminals.

not from man. The marsh pheasant manages one peck every ten paces, and one drink every hundred steps, but it does not wish to be kept in a cage. Even if you treated it like a king, its spirit would not be happy.'

When Lao Tzu died, Chin Shih came to mourn for him. He uttered three shouts and then left.

A follower of the Master said, 'Wasn't the Master a friend of yours?'

'Certainly,' he replied.

'Then do you really think this way of mourning is best?'

'Certainly. To begin with I thought these were real men, but now I am not so sure. When I came in to mourn, there were old folk weeping as though they had lost a child; there were young people wailing as if for the loss of a mother. Such a gathering of everyone, all talking away though he didn't ask them to talk and weeping even though he didn't ask for tears! This is to turn from Heaven and to indulge in emotions, ignoring what is given. The ancient ones called this the result of violating the principles of Heaven. When the Master came, it was because he was due to be born. When he died, it was entirely natural. If you are prepared to accept this and flow with it, then sorrow and joy cannot touch you. The ancient ones considered this the work of the gods who free us from bondage.

'We can point to the wood that has been burned, but when the fire has passed on, we cannot know where it has gone.'

CHAPTER 4

Out and About in the World

Yen Hui[17] went to see Confucius and asked his permission to leave.

'Where are you going?' asked Confucius.

'To the state of Wei.'

'For what reason?'

He replied, 'Hui, Prince of Wei, is full of youthful vigour and determined in all he does. He treats his country with scant regard and is incapable of seeing his own faults. He has scant regard for the death of the people, and the dead lie across his country like scrub in the marshland. As for the people, they don't know where to turn. About Hui, I have heard you say, my Master, "Pay no heed to the state that is well run, but go to the state that is in real trouble. Around the door of the doctor gather many who are ill." Using these words of yours as a guide, I want to see if I can do anything for that state.'

'Alas!' said Confucius. 'You will certainly bring sorrow and even death upon yourself! The great Way doesn't get involved like this, mixing many things together. In such a mixture, the one true path gets lost in the many. With many paths comes confusion; with confusion comes problems; when problems arise, the situation cannot be resolved. The perfect man of old looked after himself first before looking to help others. If you look to yourself and find there are troubles, what use will you be if you try to sort out a dictator?

'Do you know how virtue is ruined, or where knowledge comes from? Virtue is ruined by fame and knowledge comes from argu-

17. The favourite follower of Confucius.

ment. Struggling for fame, people destroy each other, and knowledge is used for argument. Both of them are used for evil and you should have nothing to do with them. You may have great virtue and unquestionable sincerity. You may be kind-hearted and without interest in fame, but if you do not understand how people feel and think, you will do harm, not good. Such people try to force the people to be benevolent, to act properly and impose laws, and as a result they end up being hated precisely because they care about others. This is known as hurting others. Those who hurt will themselves be hurt and this is likely to be what will happen to you!

'Imagine, he could be the sort of king who values the good and hates the bad, so what point would there be in you trying to make him change his ways? Keep your advice for yourself. Kings and princes tend to assume they are right and will do all they can to win. You will find your eyes dazzled, your colour changing and your mouth trying to find words to apologize with, you will bend in contrition and your mind will agree with whatever he says. This is like trying to fight fire with fire, or water with water. This is to pile more on to more. Once you do this, you will be unable to argue with him again. Your words will be of no avail, for he will not believe them. As a result, you will be killed by a dictator like this.

'In earlier times, Chieh[18] murdered Kuan Lung Feng and Chou killed Prince Pi Kan.[19] Both these two were men who developed their characters best in order to pass the benefits down to their people. Those who ruled them were upset by the concern of these two, and as a result of their morality, they were destroyed by the rulers. Both the good and the bad struggle for fame. In ancient times, Yao attacked the states of Tsung Chih and Hsu Ao, Yu attacked the state of Yu Hu, and as a result these states were destroyed, their kings killed. Their desire for warfare had been insatiable and their wish for power inexhaustible. All of these sought fame and fortune – surely you know of them? The sages could not handle such people, how much less can you! However,

18. Chieh is the archetypal evil ruler who murdered his ministers when they tried to control him.

19. Pi Kan tried to restrain the last Shang Emperor's excesses.

you obviously have some plan in mind, so go on, tell me what it is!'

'If I am stern in intent and dispassionate, keen and single-minded, will this be enough?' asked Yen Hui.

Confucius said, 'Is that it? That will not do! This man acts as if he were supremely confident and puts himself about with style, yet you cannot judge what he really thinks from his demeanour. Ordinary people do not get in his way, so he has developed a taste for trampling upon other people's feelings. Given that normal virtues are wasted on him, how do you expect to present him with yet higher ones! He will dig his toes in and refuse to change. He may pretend to agree with you, but there will be no inner change. How can you imagine you will succeed?'

'I will retain my inner integrity, but outwardly be deceptive. I shall cite historical precedent. Inwardly genuine, I shall be guided by Heaven. Guided by Heaven, I shall know that both I and the Prince, the Son of Heaven, are both children of Heaven. Who then cares whether what he says is listened to or not? Surely someone like this is called a child by the people. This is what comes of being a child of Heaven. With this external guile, I can befriend people. Bowing and scraping, paying obeisance, this is what all ministers do. As this is what everyone does, no one will hold it against me. If I do just what others do, no one can criticize me. Citing historical precedent, I will be the dutiful student of antiquity. The words I shall use will condemn and reprove, but the point is they will be seen as the words of the old ones, not mine. This means I can tell the truth but be free from any blame. This is what I mean by citing historical precedent. If I do this, do you think it will work?'

Confucius said, 'Is that it? That will not do! There are too many schemes here, good ones but not well thought out. They may get you out of trouble, but they will not do what you want, as they are far from perfect. You are still being guided by your expectations.'

'I have nothing else to suggest,' said Yen Hui, 'so tell me what you would do.'

Confucius said, 'Go away and fast, then I will tell you what to do. While still plotting, do you think you can really be guided in what to do? The one who thinks he has it will not easily be guided by the Light of Heaven.'

'The Hui family is poor,' said Yen Hui, 'and we have not drunk wine or eaten meat for months. In this instance, will this count as having fasted?'

'This is fasting for the sacrifice, but not fasting of the heart.'

'Then what is fasting of the heart?'

'Your mind must become one, do not try to understand with your ears but with your heart. Indeed, not with your heart but with your soul. Listening blocks the ears, set your heart on what is right, but let your soul be open to receive in true sincerity. The Way is found in emptiness. Emptiness is the fasting of the heart.'

Yen Hui said, 'Previously, when I fasted, but not with the fast of the heart, I felt I was Hui; when I went on to the fast of the heart, I found I was not Hui. Is this what is called emptiness?'

The great Master said, 'Precisely! I'll tell you. Go and join this man in his cage, but don't set out to impress him. If he comes to like you, then you may sing for him. If he will not listen, keep quiet. Do not appear to be an open door, nor seek to be a balm. Be at one with all in his house and learn to bear what cannot be changed. Do this, and you might almost be successful. It's not difficult to stop walking, but to walk without touching the earth is more difficult. If you act like any other person, it is easy to be hypocritical, but if you act in the style of Heaven, the reverse is true. One hears of flying by means of wings, but never of flying without them; one hears of knowing as a result of knowledge, but never of knowing without knowledge. Take a look at the room that is shut off, the empty room where true light is born, and there is really contentment and stillness. But if you cannot remain still, then your mind goes racing off, even though physically you remain sitting. Use your ears and eyes to speak to what is within and use your heart and knowledge to speak to what is without. Then you will draw down the very gods themselves as well as other people. This is the mystery of all life: that which links Yu and Shun, that which Fu Hsi and Chi Chu[20] lived by. Just think how even more important it is for ordinary mortals!'

20. Two primordial founder figures. Fu Hsi is credited with discovering the eight Trigrams and with inventing writing.

Duke Tzu Kao of She, just before he left on a mission to the state of Chi, asked Confucius, 'The King has given me a most important mission to Chi. They will show me great courtesy, but they are unlikely to make much speed in the issue. Given how hard it is to push an ordinary person along, a nobleman is likely to be even more difficult. I really am worried. You used to tell me that "in whatever we set ourselves to do, no matter how great or small, following the Tao alone leads to success. To fail is to bring the judgement of others upon you. To succeed brings disturbance of the yin and yang. To escape any distress regardless of success or failure is only possible to a really virtuous man." I eat sensible food so that my kitchens are never overheated. However, this very morning I was given my commission and this evening I am drinking iced water. I wonder if I am getting sick. So already I have got into the bad state of disturbed yin and yang. If I fail, I shall have trouble from others. This means I am suffering on two fronts, and as a minister I doubt if I can carry out this commission. Perhaps you could give me some advice?'

'Under Heaven there are two great principles,' replied Confucius. 'The first is destiny, the other one is duty. The love of a child for its parents, this is destiny, it is there in his heart. A subject's service of his lord, this is duty, because he must have an overlord, this is how it is in the wide world. These are known as the two great principles. To be obedient to your parents and be prepared to follow them come what may, this is true filial piety. To serve your lord happily, regardless of what he asks you to do, this is real loyalty. To serve your own soul in such a way as to prevent either joy or sorrow within, but outwardly to handle what life throws at you as inevitable and not to be worried by this, this is the perfection of Virtue. Therefore, the person who finds himself in the position of a son or subject has at times to do what he has to do. Caught up in these affairs of state, he forgets his own life. He has no time to sit and contemplate the love of life or the fear of death! Therefore, my dear Sir, go on your mission!

'Let me tell you something else I have found out. In the ebb and flow of relationships between two states, if they live side by side and have regular links, they can show how mutual their interests are through their actions. If, however, they are separated by distance, then they have to rely upon the spoken word, and such messages have to be relayed by someone. But trying to convey the areas of joy and displeasure of both sides in such messages, is about the most thankless task under Heaven. When both sides are happy, the messages have to be laden down with excessive praise. When both sides are angry, the messages have to be laden with excessive aggression. Any exaggeration is false. Where there is falsehood, no one can trust a word and the messenger is in real trouble. This is why the *Fa Yen*[21] says, "Convey what each side wishes to say, but leave out the exaggerations." Do that and you may well be all right.

'When people gather to wrestle and sport, they always begin in a friendly mood, but always end with anger and aggression. As the pressure mounts, they resort to amazing tricks. When people gather to drink at special ceremonies, they begin in a proper and restrained manner, but soon degenerate into rowdiness. As this grows, their behaviour becomes more and more excessive. This is true of all things. People start off with sincerity but degenerate into rudeness. Things start simply enough, but soon become complex and confusing.

'Words are like the ebb and flow of the wind-blown seas: the purpose of them can become overwhelmed. The wind and seas are easily stirred, and what was attempted can be swamped and lost. Likewise, anger can be whipped up by cunning words and biased speeches. When anger comes, people bellow their rage like animals being driven to their death, their breath comes out in bursts of distress. Then the hearts of both sides are turned to rage. People are driven into a corner, having little idea how they got there but they respond with brutality. They do not know how this happens, so what hope is there of stopping all this? This is why the *Fa Yen* says, "Do not wander from the original charge you are given. Do not try to force the pace of negotiation. To go beyond what is asked is to be excessive." To go outside what your charge was, and to try to

21. A book of rules and proverbs.

solve everything yourself, is dangerous. It takes time to arrive at an appropriate settlement. A bad settlement, once made, cannot be changed! Therefore, take care, let your heart follow whatever happens. Accept what happens as it occurs in order to find your true place, follow the middle way. The best thing to do is leave it all to fate, even if this is not easy to do!'

Yen Ho was about to start as tutor to the eldest son of Duke Ling of the state of Wei, so he went to visit Chu Po Yu[22] and said, 'Here is a man whom Heaven has given a nature devoid of all virtue. If I simply allow him to go on in this way, the state is at risk; if I try to bring him back to a principled life, then my life is at risk. He can just about recognize the excesses of others, but not his own excesses. In a case like this, what can I do?'

'This is a good question!' said Chu Po Yu. 'Be on guard, be careful, make sure you yourself are right. Let your appearance be in agreement, let your heart be content and harmonious. However, both these strategies have their dangers. Do not let your outward stance affect your inner self, nor allow your inner self to be drawn out. If you allow yourself to be sucked into his way of things, you will be thrown down, ruined, demolished, and will fall. If your inner harmony becomes drawn out, then you will have fame and a name, you will be called an evil creature. If he acts like a child, then be a child with him; if he permits no restraints, do the same. If he goes beyond the pale, follow him! Understand him, and then guide him back subtly.

'Don't you know the story of the praying mantis? In its anger it waved its arms in front of a speeding carriage, having no understanding that it could not stop it, but having full confidence in its own powers! Be on guard, be careful! If you are over-confident in this way, you will be in the same danger.

'Don't you know what a tiger trainer does? He does not give them living animals for food, in case it over-excites them and breeds a love of killing. He does not even give them whole carcasses, for fear of exciting the rage of tearing the animals apart. He observes their appetite and appreciates their ferocity. Tigers are

22. Figures from the history of the fifth century BC.

a different creature from humans, but you can train them to obey their trainer if you understand how to adapt to them. People who go against the nature of the tiger don't last long.

'People who love horses collect their manure and urine in fine baskets and bottles. However, if a mosquito or gadfly lands on the horse, and the groom suddenly swipes it away, the horse breaks its bit, damages its harness and hurts its chest. The groom, out of affection, tried to do what was good, but the end result is the reverse of that. So should we exercise caution!'

Carpenter Shih was on his way to Chi, when he came to the place called Chu Yuan, where he saw an oak tree which was venerated as the home of the spirits of the land. The tree was so vast that a thousand oxen could hide behind it. It was a hundred spans round and it soared above the hill to eighty feet before it even began to put out branches. There were ten such branches, from any one of which an entire boat could be carved. Masses of people came to see it, giving the place a carnival atmosphere, but carpenter Shih didn't even look round, just went on his way. His assistant looked at it with great intensity, and then chased after his master and said, 'Since I first took up my axe and followed you, I have never seen wood such as this. Sir, why did you not even glance at it nor stop, but just kept going?'

He said, 'Silence, not another word! The tree is useless. Make a boat from it and it would sink; make a coffin and it would rot quickly; make some furniture and it would fall to pieces; make a door and it would be covered in seeping sap; make a pillar and it would be worm-eaten. This wood is useless and good for nothing. This is why it has lived so long.'

When Master Shih was returning, the tree appeared to him in a dream, saying, 'What exactly are you comparing me with? With ornamental fruit trees? Trees such as the hawthorn, pear trees, orange trees, citrus trees, gourds and other such fruit trees? Their fruits are knocked down when they are ripe and the trees suffer. The big branches are damaged and the small ones are broken off. Because they are useful, they suffer, and they are unable to live out the years Heaven has given them. They have only their usefulness to blame for this destruction wrought by the people. It is the same with all things. I have spent a long time studying to be useless, though on a couple of occasions I was nearly destroyed. However, now I have perfected the art of uselessness, and this is very useful, to me! If I had been of use, could I have grown so vast? Furthermore, you and I are both things. How can one thing make such statements about another? How can you, a useless man about to die, know anything about a useless tree?'

When carpenter Shih awoke, he told his apprentice what he had dreamt. The apprentice said, 'If it wants to be useless, why is it used as the shrine for the spirits of the land?'

'Hush! Don't say another word!' said Shih. 'The tree happens to be here so it is an altar. By this it protects itself from harm from those who do not realize it is useless, for were it not an altar, it would run the risk of being chopped down. Furthermore, this tree is no ordinary one, so to speak of it in normal terms is to miss the point.'

Nan Po Tzu Chi, wandering amongst the mountains of Shang, came upon a great and unusual tree, under which could shelter a thousand chariots, and they would all be covered. Tzu Chi said, 'What kind of a tree is this? It is surely a most wondrous piece of timber!' However, when he looked up, he could see that the smaller branches were so twisted and gnarled that they could not be made into rafters and beams; and looking down at the trunk he saw it was warped and distorted and would not make good coffins. He licked one of its leaves and his mouth felt scraped and sore. He sniffed it and it nearly drove him mad, as if he had been drunk for three days.

'This tree is certainly good for nothing,' said Tzu Chi. 'This is why it has grown so large. Ah-ha! This is the sort of uselessness that sages live by.

'In the state of Sung there is the district of Ching Shih, which is excellent for growing catalpas, cypresses and mulberry trees. However, those which are more than a handspan or so around are cut down by people who want to make posts for their monkeys; those which are three or four spans around are cut down to make beams for great houses; those of seven to eight spans are cut down by lords and the wealthy who want single planks to form the side of their coffins. As a result, the trees do not live out the years Heaven has allotted them, but instead are cut down by the axe in the prime of their life. This is all the result of being useful! At the sacrifice, oxen marked by the white forehead, pigs that have turned-up noses and men suffering from piles are useless as offerings to the River Ho. Shamans know this and as a result they consider such creatures as being inauspicious. However, the sage, for exactly this same reason, values them highly.

'Crippled Shu, now, is a man with his chin lost in his navel, his shoulders higher than the top of his head and his topknot pointing to Heaven, his five vital organs all crushed into the top of his body and his two thighs pressing into his ribs. By sharpening needles and washing clothes he earns enough to eat. By winnowing rice and cleaning it he was able to feed ten people. When the officials called up the militia, he walked about freely, with no need to hide; when they are trying to raise a large work gang, because of his deformities, no one bothers him. Yet when the officials were handing out grain to the infirm, he received three great portions and ten bundles of firewood. If a man like this, deformed in body, can make a living and live out the years Heaven sends him, how much more should a man who is only deformed in terms of his Virtue!'

Confucius went to Chu, and Chieh Yu, the madman of Chu, wandered to his gate and said, 'O Phoenix, O Phoenix! How your virtue has faded! The future cannot be awaited, nor the past reclaimed. When the whole world has the Tao, the sage can succeed. When the whole world has lost the Tao, the sage can only just survive. At a time like this, we are lucky if we can escape punishment. Happiness is as light as a feather, but who knows how to hold it? Misfortune is heavier than the very earth, but who knows how to escape it? Give up, give up trying to teach people Virtue! Watch out, watch out – rushing on into areas already marked out by you! Idiot, idiot, don't harm my path. I go on my way, walking crookedly, to preserve my feet from harm! The mountain trees are the cause of their own destruction. The fat throws itself into the fire. The cinnamon tree is edible, so it is cut down. The varnish tree is useful and it is cut about. Everyone knows the usefulness of the useful but no one knows the usefulness of the useless!'

CHAPTER 5

Signs of Real Virtue

In the state of Lu there lived a man called Wang Tai, who had lost a foot – yet the number of his followers was as great as those of Confucius. Chang Chi asked Confucius, 'Wang Tai has lost a foot, yet he manages to divide up the state of Lu equally with you, Master. He doesn't preach, he doesn't debate, but people come empty and leave full. Is it true that there is teaching without words, and that even if the body is not whole, the heart is complete? What kind of man is he?'

Confucius replied, 'This master is a sage, and the only reason I have not been his disciple is that I was slow in going to him. I will certainly now go to him as my teacher, and, therefore, how much more should those who are not equal to me! Why stop at just the state of Lu? I will bring all under Heaven to follow him.'

'He is a man who has lost a foot,' said Chang Chi, 'yet his authority is above yours! Sir, how very different he is from ordinary people. How exactly does his heart function?'

'Death and birth are matters of great significance,' said Confucius, 'but they have no effect on him. Even if Heaven and Earth were to collapse, he would not be disturbed. He truly understands the primary things in life and is not moved by mere things, he understands that some things are predestined and therefore holds true to the unchanging.'

'What do you mean?'

'If you look at things in terms of their difference,' replied Confucius, 'then the liver and gall are as different as the states of Chu and Yueh; however, study them from the perspective of their sameness, and all life is one. This is what this master does. Such a man is not guided by his eyes and ears, instead he lets his heart decide what is harmonious in its Virtue. He observes the unity and does not see that which is lost. He considers the loss of his foot as being like a lump of earth thrown away.'

Chang Chi said, 'In the way he has nurtured himself with knowledge, he has followed his heart, his true heart. Following his heart, he has cultivated an eternal heart, but why should it be that he becomes such a focal point?'

'People don't look at a flowing river for a mirror, they look at still waters, because only what is still stills things and holds them still. Of those things which are given life by the earth, only the pine and cypress are the best, for they remain green throughout winter and summer. Of those things given life by Heaven, only Shun was true, for he made his own life an example and so guided others' lives. Holding to the primal strength and eliminating fear, a lone brave knight can overcome nine armies. If this can be achieved by a brave man seeking renown, just imagine what can be achieved by one who is in control of Heaven and Earth and who encompasses all life, who simply uses his physical body as a place to dwell, whose ears and eyes he knows only convey fleeting images, who knows how to unite all knowledge, and whose heart never dies! Such a man as this, when he chooses a day to ascend on high, will be followed by many people. Yet why should he worry about such matters?'

Shen Tu Chia had lost a foot, and he was a student of Po Hun Wu Jen, along with Cheng Tzu Chan.[23] Tzu Chan said to Shen Tu Chia, 'If I go away from here first, please will you remain behind, and if you go away first, I shall remain behind.' The very next day they were both sitting together again on the same mat in the hall. Tzu Chan said to Shen Tu Chia, 'If I go away from here first, please will you remain behind, and if you go away first, I'll remain behind. Now I am just about to leave, and I really want to know, will you remain behind or not? When you see a top official, you don't even try to get out of his way. Do you think you are his equal?'

23. Prime Minister of Cheng, died 522 BC.

Shen Tu Chia replied, 'Within the house of our Master, does such a thing as a top official exist? You behave like a top official and are proud of your status. I recall the saying "If a mirror is bright, then no dust or dirt will collect upon it. And if they do, then the mirror is not bright. If you live for long around virtuous people, you are free from all excess." Now, you have chosen this master as a master to make you great, yet you can still utter these words. Are you not at fault?'

'Someone like you tries to be as great as Yao,' said Tzu Chan. 'Look at your Virtue, isn't that enough to make you stop and think about yourself?'

'There are many who have caused trouble but who think that they do not deserve punishment,' said Shen Tu Chia. 'However, those who do not cause trouble and who think they deserve nothing are few indeed. To know what is beyond your ability to change, and to live with this as your destiny, is the action of a virtuous one. Anyone who wanders into the middle of Archer Yi's[24] target will find that such a central place is exactly where you get hit! If they are not hit, then that is destiny. People with both feet often laugh at me for having only one and I used to get very angry. But when I come before our Master, I forget all about that. I don't know, maybe the Master has cleansed me of all that? I have followed the Master for nineteen years without worrying about the loss of my foot. Now you and I are trying to move beyond the physical body, yet you keep drawing attention to it. Isn't this rather excessive of you?'

Tzu Chan felt uncomfortable and wriggled about and said, 'Sir, please, say no more about this.'

24. The most famous archer of Chinese mythology.

In the state of Lu there was a mutilated man[25] called Shu Shan the Toeless. He came upon his stumps to see Confucius. Confucius said, 'You were not careful and therefore suffered this fate. It is too late to come and see me now.'

'Because of my lack of knowledge and through lack of care for my body, I lost my feet,' said Toeless. 'Now I have come to you because I still have that which is of greater value than my foot and I wish to save it. There is nothing that great Heaven does not cover, nor anything that the Earth does not sustain. I had hoped you, Sir, would be as Heaven and Earth to me, and I did not expect you to receive me like this!'

'I am being stupid!' said Confucius. 'Good Sir, please do not go away and I will try to share with you what I have learnt!'

However, Toeless left and Confucius said, 'Be watchful, my followers! Great Toeless has lost his feet but still he wants to learn in order to recompense for his evil deeds. How much more so should you who are able-bodied want to learn!'

Toeless told his story to Lao Tzu, saying, 'Confucius has definitely not become a perfect man yet, has he? So why does he try to study with you? He seems to be caught up with the search for honour and reputation, without appearing to understand that the perfect man sees these as chains and irons.'

Lao Tzu said, 'Why not help him to see that death and birth are one thing and that right and wrong are one thing, and so free him from the chains and irons?'

'Given that Heaven punishes him, how can he be set free?' asked Toeless.

Duke Ai of Lu said to Confucius, 'In Wei there was a man with a terrible appearance called Ai Tai To. But those around him thought the world of him and when women saw him they ran to their mothers and fathers saying, "I would rather be the concubine of this gentleman than anyone else's wife." This has happened more than ten times. He was never heard to take the lead in anything, but was always in accord with others. He was not powerful and thus able to save people from death, nor was he wealthy and able to feed

25. Mutilated as a punishment for crime.

people. Furthermore, he was so hideous he could scare the whole world. He never took the lead, just agreed with whatever was suggested, and he knew little about the world beyond his own four walls. But people came flocking to him. It is clear he is different from ordinary people, so I asked him to come and see me. He certainly was ugly enough to frighten the whole world. Yet he had only been with me for less than a month when I began to appreciate him. Within a year I had full trust in him. In my country there was no prime minister, so I offered him the post. His response to my request was to look most sorrowful and diffident as if he was going to turn it down. I was ashamed of myself but in the end simply handed over the country to him. Very soon after, he upped and left. I was distressed and felt this a great loss, for I had no one with whom to share the cares of the state. Now, what sort of man is this?'

Confucius said, 'I was once in the state of Chu on a commission, and I saw some piglets trying to suckle from their dead mother. After a while they started up and left her. She did not seem to notice them and so they no longer felt any affinity with her. What they loved about their mother was not her body but what gave life to the body. When a man is killed in battle, at his burial his battle honours are of little use to him. A man without feet has little love for shoes. In both cases they lack that which makes these of any significance. Indeed, the consorts of the Son of Heaven[26] do not cut their own nails or pierce their ears; a newly wed gentleman stays outside the court and is freed from onerous duties. With so much attention being paid to caring for the body, imagine what care should be given to preserving Virtue! Now Ai Tai To speaks not a word, yet he is believed. He does nothing and is loved. People offer him their kingdoms, and their only fear is that he will refuse. He must indeed be a man of perfect character, whose Virtue is without shape!'

'What do you mean by "perfect character"?' asked Duke Ai.

Confucius replied, 'Death, birth, existence and trouble, auspicious

26. A formal title for the Emperors, marking their special relationship with Heaven.

and inauspicious signs, wealth, poverty, value and worthlessness, glory and blame, hunger and thirst, cold and hot – all these are the way the world goes and the result of destiny. Day and night follow each other, but there is no way of knowing where they come from. Don't allow this to disrupt your innate balance, don't allow this to perturb your mind. If you can balance and enjoy them, have mastery over them and revel in this, if you can do this day in and day out without a break and bring all things together, then this brings forth a heart prepared for changes and this is perfect character.'

'But what do you mean when you say his Virtue is without shape?'

'Perfect balance is found in still waters. Such water should be an example to us all. Inner harmony is protected and nothing external affects it. Virtue is the result of true balance. Virtue has no shape or form yet nothing can be without it,' said Confucius.

A few days later, Duke Ai commented to Ming Tzu[27] on this discussion, saying, 'To begin with, I took up the position of authority and became a ruler of all under Heaven, caring for the people and concerned lest they die. I perceived this as being perfect. Now, hearing the thoughts of the perfect man, I fear that I really understood very little, for I cared more for my own self than for the country. Confucius and I are not in a relationship of subject and nobleman, for our friendship is founded upon Virtue.'

The Crooked Man with No Lips offered advice to Duke Ling of Wei, who greatly appreciated his words of advice, so much so that he thought ordinary people had backs too straight and lips too big. The Man with a Jug-sized Goitre offered advice to Duke Huan of Chi. Duke Huan appreciated his counsel, so much so that he thought ordinary people had necks which were too thin and short.

27. A disciple of Confucius.

If virtue is foremost, the physical body is ignored. When people do not ignore what they should ignore, but ignore what they should not ignore, this is known as true ignorance. The sage sees his role as that of a wanderer, sees knowledge as a curse, convention as a glue, virtue as just a means, and effort as common trade. The sage has no great plans, so what use has he for knowledge? He makes no divisions, so what use has he for glue? He has no problems, so what use has he for virtue? He has no career, so what need has he for common trade? These four, they are the nourishment of Heaven. Fed by Heaven, he is nourished by Heaven. As he loves being nourished by Heaven, he has no need of humanity! He has the form of a man, but not the emotions of a man. Because he has the form of a man, he can be amongst men, but not having the emotions of a man, he does not have to follow the ways of right and wrong. Inconsequential and small, he stays amongst men! Substantial and large, he is at one with Heaven!

Hui Tzu asked Chuang Tzu, 'Is it possible for someone to be without emotion?'

'Certainly,' said Chuang Tzu.

'A man without emotion – can you really call him a man?' asked Hui Tzu.

Chuang Tzu replied, 'The Way. gives him a face and Heaven provides a shape, so how can it follow he is not called a man?'

'But if he is already called a man, how can it follow that he has no emotion?'

'That's not what I mean by emotions,' said Chuang Tzu. 'When I say a man has no emotions, what I mean by this is someone who does not allow either the good or the bad to have any effect upon him. He lets all things be and allows life to continue in its own way.'

Hui Tzu said, 'If he doesn't interfere with life, then how does he take care of himself?'

'The Way gives him a face and Heaven provides a shape. He does not allow either the good or the bad to have any effect on him. But you now, you wear your soul on your sleeve, exhausting your energy, propping yourself up on a tree, mumbling, or bent over your desk, asleep. Heaven gives you a form and you wear it out by pointless argument!'

CHAPTER 6

The Great and Original Teacher

The one who understands Heaven and understands the ways of humanity has perfection. Understanding Heaven, he grows with Heaven. Understanding humanity, he takes the understanding of what he understands to help him understand what he doesn't understand, and so fulfils the years Heaven decrees without being cut off in his prime. This is known as perfection.

However, it is true that there are problems. Real understanding has to have something to which it is applied and this something is itself uncertain. So how can I know that what I term Heaven is not human? Or that what I call human is not Heaven?

Only the true man has understanding. So what is a true man? The true man of old did not fight against poverty, nor did he look for fulfilment through riches – for he had no grand plans. Therefore, he never regretted any failure, nor exulted in success. He could scale the heights without fear, plumb the depths without difficulties and go through fire without pain. This is the kind of person whose understanding has lifted him up towards the Tao.

The true man of old slept without dreaming and awoke without anxiety. He ate without tasting, breathing deeply, incredibly deeply. The true man breathes from his feet up, while ordinary people just breathe from the throat. The words of broken people come forth like vomit. Wallowing in lust and desire, they are but shallow in the ways of Heaven.

The true man of old did not hold on to life, nor did he fear death. He arrived without expectation and left without resistance. He went calmly, he came calmly and that was that. He did not set out to forget his origin, nor was he interested in what would become of him. He loved to receive anything but also forgot what he had received and gave it away. He did not give precedence to the heart but to the Tao, nor did he prefer the ways of humanity to those of Heaven. This is what is known as a true man.

Being like this, his heart forgets,
his appearance is calm,
his forehead is plain;
He is as chilly as autumn and as warming as spring.
His joy and anger arise like the four seasons.
He acts properly towards all things
and none know where this will lead.
So if the sage summons the army and conquers states,
he does not lose the affections of the people.
His magnanimous nature enriches ten thousand generations,
yet he has no affection for the people.
One who seeks to share his happiness with others is not a sage.
One who displays his feelings is not benevolent.
One who waits for Heaven is not a wise man.
The noble who cannot harmonize the good and the destructive is
   not a scholar.
One who seeks for fame and thereby loses his real self is no
   gentleman.
One who loses his true self and his path is unable to command
   others.
Men such as Hu Pu Chieh, Wu Kuang, Po Yi, Shu Chi, Chi
   Tzu, Hsu Yu, Chi To, Shen Tu Ti [28] –
all followed the example of others,
tried to get for them what they desired
but they did not seek for themselves what they desired.

The true man of old appeared aloof but was in no danger of
   falling.
He appears deficient, yet takes nothing.

28. Historical figures who were either reformers or upholders of the status quo, but who were all killed or committed suicide.

He does what he wills but is not judgemental.
His emptiness was clear, but there was no showing off.
Cheerfully smiling, he seemed to be content.
He responded immediately as if there was no choice.
If upset, he showed it.
If content, he was at ease with Virtue.
When calm, he appeared to be one with the world.
When superior, the world had no control over him.
His inner nature seemed unknowable.
Never being really aware, he forgot what to say.
He saw the law as the external form of government.
The rituals he saw as the wings,
knowledge as being the same as what is appropriate at the time.
Virtue he saw as what is proper.
Viewing law as the external form of government,
he was flexible in imposing the death sentence.
Viewing the rituals as the wings,
he got on well with society.
Viewing knowledge as being that which is appropriate,
he followed the natural course of events.
Viewing virtue as that which is proper,
he walked along with others who were capable of leading.
So he acted spontaneously,
but others thought it was at great cost.
Thus all that he sought was one.
What he disowned was also but one.
What is one is one, and what is not one is also one.
In the one, he was with Heaven.
In the not-one, he was one with humanity.
When heaven and humanity are not in dispute,
then we can say this is really the true man.

Death and birth are fixed. They are as certain as the dawn that comes after the night, established by the decree of Heaven. This is beyond the control of humanity, this is just how things are. Some view Heaven as their father and continue to love it. How much more should they show devotion for that which is even greater!

Some people consider their lord as being better than themselves and would willingly die for him. How much more should they do the same for one who is more true than their lord!

When the springs dry out, the fish are found stranded on the earth. They keep each other damp with their own moisture, and wet each other with their slime. But it would be better if they could just forget about each other in rivers and lakes. People sing the praises of Yao and condemn Chieh, but it would be better if they could forget both of them and just follow the Tao. The cosmos gives me the burden of a physical form, makes life a struggle, gives me rest in old age and peace in death. What makes life good, therefore, also makes death good.

A boat can be hidden in a gorge, and a fishing net in a pool, and you may think they are therefore safe. However, in the middle of the night a strong man comes and carries them off. Small-minded people just cannot see that hiding smaller things in larger things does not mean they will not be stolen. If you take everything under Heaven and try to store it under Heaven, there is no space left for it to be lost in! This is the real truth about things. To have a human form is a joyful thing. But in the universe of possible forms, there are others just as good. Isn't it a blessing to have these uncountable possibilities! The sage goes where nothing escapes him, and rests contented there with them. He takes pleasure in an early death, in old age, in the origin and in the end and sees them all as equally good – he should be an example to others. If this is so, then how much more should our example be that which holds together the whole of life and which is the origin of all that changes!

The great Tao has both reality and expression, but it does nothing and has no form.

> It can be passed on, but not received.
> It can be obtained, but not seen.
> It is rooted in its own self, existing before Heaven and Earth
>   were born, indeed for eternity.
> It gives divinity to the spirits and to the gods.
> It brought to life Heaven and Earth.

It was before the primal air, yet it cannot be called lofty;
it was below all space and direction, yet it cannot be called deep.
It comes before either Heaven or Earth, yet it cannot be called
  old.
It is far more ancient than antiquity, yet it is not old.
Hsi Wei[29] obtained it, and with it he framed Heaven and Earth.
Fu Hsi obtained it and through it he entered into the Mother of
  life's breath.
The Great Dipper constellation obtained it and from of old has
  never wavered.
The Sun and Moon obtained it and from of old have never
  ceased.
Kan Pi obtained it and was able to enter the Kun Lun
  mountains.
Feng Yi obtained it and was able to journey to the great river.
Chien Wu obtained it and was able to live on Mount Tai.
The Yellow Emperor obtained it and was able to ascend into the
  clouds of Heaven.
Chuan Hsu obtained it and was able to dwell in the Dark Palace.
The Queen Mother of the West[30] obtained it and was able to
  take her seat on Shao Kuang Mountain –
no one knew her origin, no one knows her end.
Peng Tsu obtained it and was able to live from the time of Shun
  to that of the Five Lords.
Fu Yueh obtained it and was able to become the Prime Minister
  of Wu Ting,
so he controlled all under Heaven.
Then, riding upon one constellation, he climbed upon another
  and soared to the Milky Way to dwell as a star.

Nan Po Tzu Kuei said to Nu Chu, 'Master, you are old, yet your
appearance is one of youthfulness. Why is this?'
  The reply came, 'I have studied the Tao.'

29. The following characters are all from the earliest myths of China.
30. Primal mother figure, an early Heavenly goddess, later adopted as a major
deity in Taoism.

'Can I study how to obtain the Tao?'

The reply was, 'Definitely not! Most definitely not! You are not the kind of man who could do this.

'Now there was Pu Liang Yi, who had the genius of a sage but not the Tao. I have the Tao, but not the genius. I wanted to teach him in order that he might become a sage. It seemed as if teaching the Tao to a man of genius would be easy. But no! I taught him for three days and he was able to ignore worldly matters. Having dispensed with worldly matters, I continued to teach him for seven days, so that he was able to ignore all external matters. Having disposed of all external matters, I continued to teach him for nine days, whereupon he could observe his own being as irrelevant. Having discerned his own self as irrelevant, he saw with true clarity. Having seen with true clarity, he could see by the One. Seeing by the One, he could ignore both past and present. Having ignored both past and present he was able to enter where there is neither death nor birth. The end of life is not death, and the coming to birth is not life. He could follow anything, he could receive anything. To him, all was being destroyed, all was being built. This is known as Tranquillity in Struggle. Tranquillity in Struggle means perfection.'

Na Po Tzu Kuei said, 'Master, where did you learn this?'

'I learned it through the medium of the spirit of writing; writing learned it from the offspring of continuous study; continuous study learned it from clarity of vision; clarity of vision heard it from quiet agreement; quiet agreement from being used; being used from great enjoyment; great enjoyment from deepest mystery; deepest mystery from absorption in mystery; absorption in mystery from the ultimate.'

The Masters, Ssu, Yu, Li and Lai, said one to another, 'Anyone who can conceive of nothingness as his head, life as his back and death as his tail and who knows that death and birth, being and no-being, are one and the same – one like this shall be our friend.' The four men smiled and agreed in their hearts and therefore became friends.

Shortly after, Master Yu fell ill. Master Ssu went to visit him and Yu said, 'How great is the Maker of All! He has made me deformed. My back is like a hunchback's, and all my organs are on top while my chin is lost in my navel and my shoulders rise up above my head and my topknot points to Heaven!' His yin and yang were in disarray. However, his heart was calm and he was not worried. He limped to a well and looked in at his reflection and said, 'Goodness me! The Maker of All has made me completely deformed!'

'Do you dislike it?' asked Master Ssu.

'Not really, why should I? For example, perhaps my left arm will become a cockerel and then I shall be able to tell the time at night. Maybe, eventually, my right arm will become a crossbow and then I can hunt a bird and eat it. Possibly my bottom will become wheels and my soul will be a horse which I shall climb upon and go for a ride. After all, I wouldn't then need any other vehicle again! I obtained life because the time was right. I will lose life because it is time. Those who go quietly with the flow of nature are not worried by either joy or sorrow. People like these were considered in the past as having achieved freedom from bondage. Those who cannot free themselves are constrained by things. However, nothing can overcome Heaven – it has always been so. So why should I dislike this?'

Later Master Lai fell ill. Gasping and heaving, he lay close to death. His wife and children were mourning around him. Master Li came to see him and Master Lai said, 'Hush, get out! Do you want to disrupt the processes of change?'

Leaning against the doorway Li commented,

'How great is the Maker of All!
What will you be made into next?
Where will you be sent?
Will you come back as a rat's liver?
Or will it be as a pest's arm?'

Master Lai said,

'When a mother and father tell a child to go somewhere,
be that east, west, south or north, the child obeys.
Yin and yang are the mother and father of humanity.
They have brought me close to death

and if I disobey this would be just perversity.
My death is not their problem!
The cosmos gives me form, brings me to birth,
guides me into old age and settles me in death.
If I think my life good, then I must think my death good.
A good craftsman, casting metal,
would not be too pleased with metal that jumped up and said,
"I must be made into a sword like Mo Yeh."[31]
Now, given that I have been bold enough
to take on human shape already, if I then said,
"I must be a human, I must be a human!",
the Maker of All would view me somewhat askance!
If Heaven and Earth are like a furnace and Nature is the
    craftsman,
then is it possible he could send me anywhere that was not
    appropriate?
Peacefully we die, calmly we awake.'

Masters Sang Hu, Meng Tzu Fan and Chin Chang, three good
friends, said to each other,

'Who can be together without any being together,
or collaborate with others without any collaboration?
Who can ascend to Heaven, ride the clouds, journey through the
infinite,
and forget about existence for ever and ever?'

The three men looked at each other and smiled, agreeing in their
hearts with one another and becoming firm friends.

Some time later Master Sang Hu died. Before he was buried,
Confucius heard of his death and sent Tzu Kung to participate in
the rituals. On arrival, Tzu Kung found one of the dead man's

31. A famous sword belonging to King Ho Lu (c. 500 BC) of Wu.

friends was making up songs while the other played a lute. Together they sang,

'Woe! Sang Hu! Woe! Sang Hu!
You have returned to the true form,
while we are still but men!'

Tzu Kung hurried forward and said, 'Is it really seemly and proper to sing before a dead body?'

The two men looked at him, laughed and said, 'What does a man like this know about proper ceremony?'

Tzu Kung went back to Confucius, told him what had happened, and asked, 'What kind of people are they? They are uncouth and pay no heed to their external appearance. They sing in the presence of a dead body without any change of face! There is no appropriate title for them. What kind of people are they?'

Confucius said, 'They go beyond the human world, while I travel within. That beyond and that within can never meet. It was a mistake to send you to join the mourning. They have truly become one with the Maker of All and now wander as the original breath of Heaven and Earth. They view life as a grotesque tumour, a swelling they inhabit. They view death as the removal of this growth. Since they see life like this, they simply do not consider whether death or birth comes first. They view their bodies as just so many collected different pieces. They forget their liver and gall and ignore their ears and eyes. They begin and cease without knowing what is beginning or ceasing. Unaware, they wander beyond the mundane world and stroll in the world of non-action. Why should they have to worry about proper conduct just to please ordinary people?'

'In that case, Master,' said Tzu Kung, 'why do you conform to convention?'

'I am one punished by Heaven,' said Confucius. 'Nevertheless, this is what I will share with you.'

'Can you tell me a little more?' said Tzu Kung.

'Fish enjoy water, humans enjoy the Tao. Enjoying water, the fish stick to the pond and find all they need to survive there. Enjoying the Tao, people do nothing and their lives are fulfilled.

The saying goes that fish forget about each other in the pond and people forget each other in the Tao.'

Tzu Kung said, 'May I ask about the man alone?'

'The man alone is only alone when compared to others, but he is alongside Heaven. It is said that the mean-minded man of Heaven is a nobleman amongst ordinary people and the nobleman is a mean-minded man of Heaven.'

Yen Hui asked Confucius, 'When Meng Sun Tsai's mother died, he cried without tears, there was no distress in his heart. When he mourned, there was no sorrow. Although he was deficient on these three points, nevertheless he is renowned throughout the state of Lu for his excellence as a mourner. Is it possible to obtain such a reputation, even when there is nothing to substantiate it? I find this very surprising.'

'Master Meng Sun Tsai did what was right,' said Confucius. 'He was far beyond mundane understanding. He could have restricted his actions even more but that was not really feasible. Nevertheless, he did cut out a great deal. Meng Sun Tsai does not know how he came to be born, nor how he will die. He just knows enough not to want one or the other. He doesn't know why he should continue, he just follows what happens without understanding! As we are all in a process of change, how can we know what unknown thing we will be changed into? As what we are changing into has not yet happened, how can we understand what change is? Perhaps you and I are in a dream from which we are yet to awake! In Meng Sun Tsai's case the body changes but this does not affect his heart. His body, housing his soul, may be affected, but his emotions are not harmed. Meng Sun Tsai alone has awoken. People cry, so he cries. He considers everything as his own being. How could he know that others call something their own particular self? You dream you are a bird and rise into the Heavens. You dream you are a fish and swim down deep into the lake. We cannot tell now if the speaker is awake or asleep. Contentment produces the smile; a genuine smile cannot be forced. Don't struggle, go with the flow and you will find yourself at one with the vastness of the void of Heaven.'

Yi Erh Tzu went to visit Hsu Yu, who asked him, 'In what way has Yao been helpful to you?'

Yi Erh Tzu said, 'Yao said to me, "Practise benevolence and justice. Speak up for what is right and against what is wrong."'

Hsu Yu said, 'So why have you troubled yourself to visit me? Master Yao has already branded on you the practice of benevolence and justice and mutilated you with the distinction between right and wrong. So how can you now expect me to help you meander alone in freedom and aimlessness, enjoying things as they happen through the process of change?'

'Maybe that is so,' said Yi Erh Tzu, 'but I'd like to find some small corner for myself.'

Hsu Yu said, 'No, it can't be done! If you have been blinded, it is impossible to appreciate beauty of face or form. Eyes with no pupils cannot see the beauty of fine, coloured silks.'

Yi Erh said, 'Wu Chuang paid no attention to her looks; Chu Liang ignored his strength; the Yellow Emperor disregarded his wisdom – all these were transformed by being worked upon. How can you know that the Maker of All will not remove the mark of my branding, heal my mutilation and, having thus restored me, enable me to follow you as my teacher?'

'Well!' said Hsu Yu. 'You never know. I will just tell you the basic outline of the teachings.

'Oh my Master, oh my Master!
He judges all life but doesn't believe himself to be a judge.
His blessings extend to all life, but he doesn't see himself as
    blessed.
Older than antiquity, yet not old.
Overarching Heaven, carrying Earth and forming all things, he
    is no craftsman.
It is through him that I wander.'

Yen Hui said, 'I'm getting better.'
Confucius said, 'What do you mean?'
'I have forgotten kindness and justice.'

'Fine, but that is not enough.'

On another occasion, they met again and Yen Hui said, 'I've improved.'

Confucius said, 'What do you mean?'

'I have forgotten rituals and music.'

'Good, but that is still not enough.'

On another occasion they met and Yen Hui said, 'I'm getting better.'

Confucius said, 'What do you mean?'

'I can sit right down and forget everything.'

Confucius was certainly disturbed by this and said, 'What do you mean by sit right down and forget?'

Yen Hui replied, 'My limbs are without feeling and my mind is without light. I have ignored my body and cast aside my wisdom. Thus I am united with the Tao. This is what sitting right down and forgetting is.'

Confucius said, 'If you are one with the great Way, then you no longer have preferences. If you are one with the cosmos, you are transformed. If this is what you have done, then I would like to follow you.'

Masters Yu and Sang were friends. It happened to rain for ten days, and Master Yu said, 'Master Sang may be in trouble!' So he packed some food to take to him. Arriving at Master Sang's door he heard strange noises and someone playing a lute, singing,

'Oh Father! Oh Mother! Oh Heaven! Oh humanity!'

It sounded as if the singer's voice was about to break and the singer was rushing to finish the verse. Master Yu entered and said, 'Master, why are you singing like this?'

He said, 'I was trying to work out what has reduced me to this. My father and mother wouldn't want me to be so poor, surely? Heaven treats all alike. Earth supports all alike. Heaven and Earth wouldn't wish me poor, would they? I seek to know who has done this, but I can't find an answer. When you come down to it, it must be simply fate.'

山寺鐘報
出暮煙
取意李咸之間
啟夏其視

CHAPTER 7

Dealing with Emperors and Kings

Yeh Chueh questioned Wang Ni. Four times he raised a question and four times he said he did not know. Yeh Chueh started jumping around in great excitement and went off to inform Master Pu Yi.

Master Pu Yi said, 'Have you only just discovered this? The noble ruler Shun[32] was not equal to the noble ruler Tai.[33] Noble ruler Shun tried to use benevolence to bind the people to him. This certainly worked, but he was unable to escape into being aware of no-man. Noble ruler Tai slept the sleep of innocence and awoke in calm collectedness. Sometimes he believed himself to be a horse, other times he might believe he was an ox. His wisdom was utterly true, his Virtue was profoundly real. He never came into awareness of no-man.'

Chien Wu went to visit the eccentric Chieh Yu, who asked him, 'What did Chung Shih say to you recently?'

Chien Wu replied, 'He said to me that the nobleman who has authority over people should set a personal example by proper regulations, law and practices. The corollary of this will be that no one will disobey him and everyone will be transformed as a result.'

32. One of the five original Emperors of mythology, a model of Confucian piety.
33. A mythological ruler of antiquity.

Eccentric Chieh Yu said, 'That would ruin Virtue. If someone tries to govern everything below Heaven in this way, it's like trying to stride through the seas or cut a tunnel through the river or make a mosquito carry a mountain. When a great sage is in command, he doesn't try to take control of externals. He first allows people to do what comes naturally and he ensures that all things follow the way their nature takes them. The bird flies high in the sky and thereby escapes from the risk of being shot with arrows. The mouse burrows down under the hill of the spirits and thus escapes being disturbed. Don't you even have as much understanding as these two creatures?'

Tien Ken was travelling to the south of Yin Mountain. He reached the river Liao, where he met the Man without a Name and said to him, 'I wish to ask you about governing everything under Heaven.'

The Man without a Name said, 'Get lost, you stupid lout! What an unpleasant question! I am travelling with the Maker of All. If that is too tiring, I shall ride the bird of ease and emptiness and go beyond the compass of the world and wander in the land of nowhere and the region of nothing. So why are you disturbing me and unsettling my heart with questions about how to rule all below Heaven?'

Tien Ken asked the same question again. The Man without a Name replied,

'Let your heart journey in simplicity.
Be one with that which is beyond definition.
Let things be what they are.
Have no personal views.
This is how everything under Heaven is ruled.'

Yan Tzu Chu went to visit Lao Tzu and he said, 'Here is a man who is keen and vigilant, who has clarity of vision and wisdom and who studies the Tao without ceasing. Such a person as this is surely a king of great wisdom?'

'In comparison to the sage,' said Lao Tzu, 'someone like this is just a humble servant, tied to his work, exhausting himself and distressing his heart. The tiger and the leopard, it is said, are hunted because of the beauty of their hides. The monkey and the dog end up in chains because of their skills. Can these be compared to a king of great wisdom?'

Yang Tzu Chu was startled and said, 'May I be so bold as to ask about the rule of a king who is great in wisdom?'

Lao Tzu said,

'The rule of a king who is great in wisdom!
His works affect all under Heaven, yet he seems to do nothing.
His authority reaches all life, yet no one relies upon him.
There is no fame nor glory for him but everything fulfils itself.
He stands upon mystery and wanders where there is nothing.'

In Chen there was a shaman of the spirits called Chi Hsien. He could foretell when people would die and be born; he knew about good fortune and failure as granted by Heaven; he knew about happiness and distress, life and its span, knowing the year, month, week and day, as if he were a god himself. As soon as the people of Cheng saw him coming, they would run away. Lieh Tzu went to see him and was fascinated by him. Coming back to Hu Tzu, he said, 'I used to believe, Master, that your Tao was perfection. Now I have found something even better.'

Hu Tzu said, 'What I have shown you is the outward text of my teaching, but not what is central. How can you think you have grasped my Tao? If you have hens but no cockerel, how can you have eggs? You flaunt your Tao before the world. This is why this man can read your fortune. Bring this shaman to me and let us meet.'

The next day Lieh Tzu brought the shaman to visit Hu Tzu. And as he left Hu Tzu's house with Lieh Tzu, the shaman said, 'Oh dear! Your Master is dying. There's virtually no life left – he has maybe a week at most. I saw a strange sight – it was like wet ashes!'

Lieh Tzu went in again, weeping so copiously that tears soaked his coat, and told Hu Tzu what had been said. Hu Tzu said, 'I made myself appear like the earth. I was as solid as the mountain, showing nothing to him. He probably perceived me to be a closed book, apparently without virtue. Bring him again if you can.'

The next day Lieh Tzu came again with the shaman to see Hu Tzu. As they went out, the shaman said to Lieh Tzu, 'How lucky for your Master that he has met me. He is getting better. Indeed he is truly alive. Life is flowing again.'

Lieh Tzu went back in and commented on this to Hu Tzu. Hu Tzu said, 'I made myself appear to him like Heaven, without fame or fortune on my mind. What I am wells up in me naturally. He saw in me the full and natural workings of life. Bring him again if you can.'

The next day they came again to see Hu Tzu. As they went out, the shaman said to Lieh Tzu, 'Your Master is never the same. I cannot grasp the fortune shown in his face. If he returns to some constancy then I will come and see him again.'

Lieh Tzu went back in and reported this to Hu Tzu. 'I showed him myself as the great Void where all is equal,' said Hu Tzu. 'He almost certainly saw in me the harmony of my innate forces. When water moves about, there is a whirlpool; where the waters are calm, there is a whirlpool; where the waters gather, there is a whirlpool. There are nine types of whirlpool and I have shown him just three. Bring him back again if you can.'

The next day they both came again to see him. However, before he had even sat down, the shaman panicked and ran off. Hu Tzu said, 'Follow him!'

Lieh Tzu ran after him. But he could not catch up with him. Coming back to Hu Tzu, he said, 'He has gone, I've lost him. I couldn't catch him.'

Hu Tzu said, 'I just appeared to him as hitherto unrevealed potential. I presented myself as not knowing who is who, nor what is what. I came flowing and changing as I willed. That's why he bolted.'

As a result of this, Lieh Tzu realized that he had so far learnt nothing real, so he returned home. For three years he did not go out. He cooked for his wife and tended the pigs as if they were humans. He showed no interest in his studies. He cast aside his desires and sought the truth. In his body he became like the ground itself. In the midst of everything he remained enclosed with the One and that is how he remained until the end.

Do not hanker for fame.
Do not make plans.
Do not try to do things.
Do not try to master knowledge.
Hold what is but do not hold it to be anything.
Work with all that comes from Heaven, but do not seek to hold it.
Just be empty.

The perfect man's heart is like a mirror.
It does not search after things.
It does not look for things.
It does not seek knowledge, just responds.
As a result he can handle everything and is not harmed by anything.

The Emperor of the South Sea is known as Change. The Emperor of the North Sea is called Dramatic. The Emperor of the Centre is called Chaos. Change and Dramatic met every so often in the region of Chaos. Chaos always treated them kindly and virtuously. Change and Dramatic said, 'Everyone has seven orifices so they can see, hear, eat and breathe. Chaos does not have these. Let us bore some holes into him.' Each day they bored a hole into Chaos . . . but on the seventh day Chaos died.

峡林簇々饒秋霽壞塔
亭々聳夕陽野水平橋人
獨立閒看鴉陣入溆花

CHAPTER 8

Webbed Toes

The big toe being webbed with the other toes, or an extra finger, may both be quite natural, but they do not spring from virtue. Swellings and tumours certainly arise from the body, but do not spring from what is natural. There are many acts of kindness and justice and they are often associated with the five vital organs.[34] But this is not the correct way according to the Tao (the Way) and Te (Virtue). In fact, webbed feet are simply useless extra pieces of skin; an additional finger is useless. So to associate these with the five vital organs is to confuse the use of kindness and justice. It places too much emphasis on hearing and sight. So heightened visual perception will cause confusion in distinguishing the five colours. One will be overwhelmed by interesting designs and dazzled by the bright and luminous shades of blue and yellow. As a result, it will be like Li Chu the keen-sighted. And doesn't an extraordinary faculty for hearing lead to confusion about the five notes, and excessive use of the six tones created by metal, stone, silk and bamboo together with the *huang chung* and *ta lu* pipes. As a result, it will be like the music master Kuang.

The result is that someone like this misuses the power of Virtue and destroys his inner self in a quest for fame and fortune, leading everything under Heaven to follow his music in pursuit of the unobtainable – is this not so? This results in Tseng and Shih.[35] A

34. The five vital organs of early Chinese medicine are the liver, lungs, heart, kidneys and spleen, and are linked to the five elements: water, wood, fire, earth and metal.

35. Models of benevolence and righteousness in Confucian teachings.

great skill in debate leads to the construction of arguments like a builder using bricks, or a netmaker working with string. He makes his arguments circular and his heart delights to go into pointless nitpicking debate about similarity and divergence. He goes slogging on uphill still spouting nonsense – is this not so? This results in Yang and Mo.[36] As a result, all of these types of people walk a complex road, with little to do with the correct Tao, the true path of all the world.

One on the true path does not lose his innate given nature.
To such a man that which is united presents no problem;
That which is divided is all right;
What is long is not too long;
That which is short is not too short.
The duck's legs for example are short, but trying to lengthen
    them would cause pain.
The legs of a crane are long, but trying to shorten them would
    produce grief.
What nature makes long we should not cut,
nor should we try to stretch what nature makes short.
That would not solve anything.

Perhaps then, benevolence and righteousness are not an inherent part of human nature? For look how much anxiety is suffered by those who wish to be kind.

If one toe is united to another by extra skin, trying to separate them will only cause tears. Likewise, if you try to bite off the extra finger, this will provoke screams: of these two, one has more, the other less, but the distress they cause is the same. The benevolent person of today looks at the evils of society with distressed eyes, while people who are not benevolent uproot their proper inborn nature and rush after wealth and honour. The conclusion, therefore, is that benevolence and righteousness are not part of the true nature of humanity! From the Three Dynasties[37] onwards they have created such trouble and nuisance for everyone.

36. Yang taught hedonism, while Mo Tzu taught love of all.
37. Hsia, Shang and Chou (2200–600 BC).

When a template or plumb line is used, or a compass and set-square, in order to get things right, this involves cutting away parts of what is naturally there. When cords or buckles, glue or varnish are used, this means we affect the original Virtue. Likewise, the bending and pauses in the rituals and music, or the smiles and happy face of benevolence and righteousness, are meant to hearten everyone, but they ignore the inbuilt principles of existence. Everything has its innate nature.

Given this, then, what is curved is not curved by the use of a template nor made straight by using a plumb line. It is not rounded by using a compass, nor made square by using a set-square; not made adhesive through glue and varnish, nor bound together by ropes and bands. Then everything under Heaven is made as it is by the ways of nature, without understanding why or how. Everything achieves what is intended, but does not understand why or how. Both today and in the ancient past it has always been so, and nothing can affect this. There is no point in holding to benevolence and righteousness, like a mixture of glue and varnish, ropes and bands, as a means of trying to journey in the Tao and Te – the Way and Virtue – for this merely confuses everything under Heaven.

A minor deception alters the sense of purpose. A major deception alters the very nature of a thing. How is it that I can be so certain this is so? Ever since the time of the ruler Shun,[38] who began to teach about benevolence and righteousness, everything under Heaven has been troubled and distorted by this and everything under Heaven has never ceased rushing about trying to live up to this. Is this not because benevolence and righteousness have changed our basic nature? I will try and explain what I mean by this. Ever since the Three Dynasties, and on down to today, everything under Heaven has had its innate nature affected by others. The mean or petty person has been willing to risk his very body for gain. The scholar risks his own self for fame. The senior officials risk their lives for their families. The sage risks his very self for everything under Heaven. All of these different types, with differing claims to

38. 2255 BC.

fame, have all damaged their innate nature and risked their lives in the same way.

For example, a slave boy and girl: the two of them were out, each looking after their sheep, but they lost the sheep. Ask the slave boy what happened – the fact is, he was holding his bamboo strips and reading; ask the slave girl what happened – the fact is, she was playing a game. These two were doing different things, but they both lost the sheep.

Po Yi[39] died for the sake of fame at the bottom of Shou Yang mountain, Robber Chih[40] died for gain on top of the Eastern Heights. These two both died in different ways but the fact is, they both shortened their lives and destroyed their innate natures. Yet we are expected to approve of Po Yi and disapprove of Robber Chih – strange, isn't it? In situations like this world-wide, if someone makes sacrifices for reasons of benevolence and righteousness, people call such a person a nobleman, a gentleman; if someone makes such sacrifices for wealth and power, then people call such a person a mean and petty man! The action of sacrifice is one and the same, yet we call one a gentleman and the other a petty man! In terms of sacrificing his life and harming his true nature, Robber Chih and Po Yi did the same. So why should we make a difference of one being a noble gentleman and the other a mean, petty person?

Those who apply themselves to benevolence and righteousness may travel the same path as Tseng and Shih, but I would not call them wise. Those who apply themselves to the five flavours may travel the same path as the chef Yu Erh, but I would not call them wise. Those who apply themselves to the five colours may travel the same path as Li Chu, but I would not call them very bright. My description of wisdom has nothing to do with benevolence and righteousness, it is to do with being wise in one's own virtue, nothing more. My description of being wise has nothing to do with benevolence and righteousness, it is that one should be led by one's innate nature, nothing more. When I talk about having good

39. Ruler who abdicated to his brother and then refused to serve an unjust ruler, so dying of starvation.
40. Famous for his wickedness.

hearing, I don't mean just listening, but listening to yourself. When I talk about good eyesight, I don't mean just looking, but looking at yourself. The fact is that those who do not see themselves but who see others, who fail to get a grasp of themselves but who grasp others, take possession of what others have but fail to possess themselves. They are attracted to what others enjoy but fail to find enjoyment in themselves. In such cases, whether he be Robber Chih or Po Yi, such a person is just as deceived and just as wrong. What I am ashamed of is of failing the Tao and Te – the Way and Virtue – so I don't try to elevate myself through acts of benevolence and righteousness, nor to sink down into useless and idiotic ways.

CHAPTER 9

Horses' Hooves

Horses have hooves so that their feet can grip on frost and snow, and hair so that they can withstand the wind and cold. They eat grass and drink water, they buck and gallop, for this is the innate nature of horses. Even if they had great towers and magnificent halls, they would not be interested in them. However, when Po Lo[41] came on the scene, he said, 'I know how to train horses.' He branded them, cut their hair and their hooves, put halters on their heads, bridled them, hobbled them and shut them up in stables. Out of ten horses at least two or three die. Then he makes them hungry and thirsty, gallops them, races them, parades them, runs them together. He keeps before them the fear of the bit and ropes, behind them the fear of the whip and crop. Now more than half the horses are dead.

The potter said, 'I know how to use clay, how to mould it into rounds like the compass and into squares as though I had used a T-square.' The carpenter said, 'I know how to use wood: to make it bend, I use the template; to make it straight, I use the plumb line.' However, is it really the innate nature of clay and wood to be moulded by compass and T-square, template and plumb line? It is true, nevertheless, that generation after generation has said, 'Po Lo is good at controlling horses, and indeed the potter and carpenter are good with clay and wood.' And the same nonsense is spouted by those who rule the world.

I think that someone who truly knows how to rule the world

41. A famous trainer of horses.

would not be like this. The people have a true nature, they weave their cloth, they farm to produce food. This is their basic Virtue. They are all one in this, not separated, and it is from Heaven. Thus, in an age of perfect Virtue the people walk slowly and solemnly. They see straight and true. In times such as these the mountains have neither paths nor tunnels, on the lakes there are neither boats nor bridges; all life lives with its own kind, living close together. The birds and beasts multiply in their flocks and herds, the grass and trees grow tall. It is true that at such a time the birds and beasts can be led around without ropes, and birds' nests can be seen with ease.

In this time of perfect Virtue, people live side by side with the birds and beasts, sharing the world in common with all life. No one knows of distinctions such as nobles and the peasantry! Totally without wisdom but with virtue which does not disappear; totally without desire they are known as truly simple. If people are truly simple, they can follow their true nature. Then the perfect sage comes, going on about benevolence, straining for self-righteousness, and suddenly everyone begins to have doubts. They start to fuss over the music, cutting and trimming the rituals, and thus the whole world is disturbed. If the pure essence had not been so cut about, how could they have otherwise ended up with sacrificial bowls? If the raw jade was not broken apart, how could the symbols of power be made? If the Tao and Te – Way and Virtue – had not been ignored, how could benevolence and righteousness have been preferred? If innate nature had not been left behind, how could rituals and music have been invented? If the five colours had not been confused, how could patterns and designs have occurred? If the five notes had not been confused, how could they have been supplanted by the six tones? The abuse of the true elements to make artefacts was the crime of the craftsman. The abuse of the Tao and Te – Way and Virtue – to make benevolence and righteousness, this was the error of the sage.

Horses, when they live wild, eat grass and drink water; when they are content, they entwine their necks and rub each other. When angry, they turn their backs on each other and kick out. This is what horses know. But if harnessed together and lined up under constraints, they know to look sideways and to arch their necks, to career around and try to spit out the bit and rid themselves of the reins. The knowledge thus gained by the horse, and its wicked behaviour, is in fact the fault of Po Lo.

At the time of Ho Hsu,[42] people stayed where they were, not knowing anything else; they walked but did not know where they were going; filled themselves with food and were happy slapping their bellies to show their contentment. This was what the people had. Then came the sage. He brought the cringing and grovelling of the rituals and music and infected all under Heaven with his offer of benevolence and righteousness, which he said would comfort the hearts of all.

As a result the people desired and longed for knowledge, and warred against each other to gain the advantage. Nothing could stop them. All this was the fault of the sage.

42. Mythological ruler of ancient China.

娑婆訶 八十四

此是觀世音菩薩解意根分別一切諸法

Broken Suitcases

To guard yourself against thieves who slash open suitcases, rifle through bags and smash open boxes, one should strap the bags and lock them. The world at large knows that this shows wisdom. However, when a master thief comes, he simply picks up the suitcase, lifts the bag, carries off the box and runs away with them, his only concern being whether the straps and locks will hold! In such an instance, what seemed like wisdom on the part of the owner surely turns out to have been of use only to the master thief!

I will try to explain what I am saying. What the world at large calls a wise man, is he not really just someone who stores things up for the master thief? Likewise, isn't the one they call a sage just a guardian of the master thief's interests?

How do I know all this?

Long ago in the state of Chi, all the little towns could see each other and the cockerels and dogs called to each other. Nets were cast and the land ploughed over an area of two thousand square miles. Within its four borders, ancestral temples were built and maintained and shrines to the land and the crops were built. Its villages and towns were well governed and everything was under the guidance of the sage. However, one morning Lord Tien Cheng killed the ruler and took his country. But was it just his country he took? He also took the wisdom of the laws of the state, created by the sages. So Lord Tien Cheng earned the title of thief and robber, but he was able to live out his days as secure as Yao or Shun had done. The smaller states dared not criticize him and the larger states did not dare attack. So for twelve generations his family ruled the state of Chi. Is this not an example of someone stealing the state of Chi and also taking the laws arising from the wisdom of the sages and using them to protect himself, although he was both robber and thief?

I will try to explain this. What the world at large calls someone of perfect knowledge, is this not in fact the person who stores up things for a great thief? Those commonly called sages, are they not responsible for securing things for the great thief?

How do I know all this?

Long ago Lung Feng was executed, Pi Kan was torn apart, Chang Hung was ripped open, and Tzu Hsu was smashed to pieces.[43] Good men though these four were, they could not escape their terrible ends. A member of Robber Chih's gang asked him, 'Is there a Tao for the thief?' Chih replied, 'What profession is there without its Tao? The robber works out what is worth stealing: this shows he is a sage; his courage is shown by being the first to break in; his righteousness is shown by being last to leave; his understanding is shown by deciding whether the raid is possible; his benevolence is shown by his dividing the spoils equally. Without these five attributes, no one in the world could become such a great thief.' Considering all this, it is clear that good men do not arise without following the Tao of the sages and therefore that Robber Chih had to also follow the sages' Tao, or he could not have succeeded. But in this world, the good men are few and far between, while the bad are numerous. So it is that the sage brings little to the world but inflicts much harm. It is said, 'When the lips have gone, the teeth get cold; the bad wine of Lu brought warfare to Han Tan.'[44] When the sage is born, the great thief arises. Beat the sages and let the thieves and robbers go, then the world will be all right. When the rivers dry up, the valley is empty. When the hill is levelled, the pool is filled.

43. Advisers who tried to reform their rulers and were executed for their pains.
44. At a great feast in Chu the Lord of Lu gave poor-quality wine, while the Lord of Chao (whose capital was Han Tan) gave good wine. The steward, having some desire for mischief, swapped them. The ruler of Chu took offence at the poor wine, attacked Chao and sacked Han Tan.

If the sage does not die, then great thieves will continue to arise. The more sages are brought forth to rule the world, the more this helps people like Robber Chih. Create weights and measures to judge by and people will steal by weight and measure; create balances and weights and people will steal by balances and weights; create contracts and legal agreements to inspire trust and people will steal by contracts and legal agreements; create benevolence and righteousness to ensure honesty and even in this instance benevolence and righteousness teach them to steal.

How do I know all this?

This one steals a buckle and he is executed, that one steals a country and he becomes its ruler. Yet it is at the gates of rulers that benevolence and righteousness are professed. Surely this is a case of the wisdom of the sages, benevolence and righteousness being stolen? So people rush to become great robbers, to seize estates, stealing benevolence and righteousness, and taking all the profits of the weights and measures, balances and weights, contracts and legal arguments. Try to prevent them with promises of the trappings of power, they don't care. Threaten them with execution, and this doesn't stop them. For by profiting those like Robber Chih, whom none can stop, the sage has made a great mistake.

It is said, 'Just as you do not take the fish away from the deep waters, so the means of controlling a country should not be shown.' The sage is the means of control, so the world should not see him clearly. Thus, if sages and wisdom were abandoned, great robbers would cease; destroy the jade and shatter the pearls, then petty thieves would not appear; burn the accounts and rip up the contracts, and the people will return to simplicity; break up the weights and the measures and the people will no longer argue; obliterate the laws of the world the sages have made, then the people can begin to be reasoned with. Throw away the six tones, destroy the pipes and lute, block the ears of Blind Kuang the musician, then every person in the world would for the first time be able to hear properly. If adornments were abolished, the five colours cast away and the eyes of Li Chu glued shut, then everyone in the world would be able to see clearly for the first time. Shatter the template and plumb line, discard the compass and T-square, break the fingers of a craftsman such as craftsman Chui, then for the first time everyone in the world will have and use real skills.

There is a saying: 'The greatest art in the world is like foolishness.'

Ignore the behaviour of Tseng and Shih, shut the mouth of Yang and Mo, purge benevolence and righteousness, and the true Virtue of all under Heaven will display its mystic power. When people have true clear vision, no one in the world will be duped; if everyone has true hearing, then no one in the world will be distracted; if everyone has true wisdom, then no one in the world will be fooled; if everyone has Virtue, then no one in the world will be debased. Those such as Tseng, Shih, Yang, Mo, the musician Kuang, craftsman Chui or Li Chu showed off their virtue on the outside. They made the world aflame with admiration and so confused the world: a way of proceeding which was pointless.

Sir, are you the only person who does not know about the age of perfect Virtue? In times past, in the era of Yung Cheng, Ta Ting, Po Huang, Chung Yang, Li Lu, Li Hsu, Hsien Yuan, Ho Hsu, Tsun Lu, Chu Jung, Fu Hsi and Shen Nung[45] the people followed their ways, knotting string and using the nets. They enjoyed their food; they took pleasure in their clothes; they were content with their lifestyles; they were at ease in their homes. Even though the states were so close to each other that they could hear their neighbours' dogs and chickens, nevertheless the people lived until a good age before dying and never travelled beyond their own borders. At that time, perfect harmony was the norm. Now the people are agitated, trying to see what is going on, saying, 'In such and such a place there is a wise man!' So they pack their bags and rush off, leaving their parents at home and failing to fulfil their duties to their ruler. You can see their footprints making a track from one state to another and the grooves made by their carriages, stretching for more than a thousand li. This is the fault of those in authority who search for good knowledge.

If those in authority search for knowledge, but without the Tao,

45. All mythological rulers or sages of antiquity.

everything under Heaven will be in terrible confusion. How do I know about all this? A great deal of knowledge is needed to make bows, crossbows, nets, arrows and so forth, but the result is that the birds fly higher in distress. A great deal of knowledge is needed to make fishing lines, traps, baits and hooks, but the result is that the fish disperse in distress in the water. A great deal of knowledge is needed to make traps, snares and nets, but the result is that the animals are disturbed and seek refuge in marshy lands. In the same way, the versatility needed to produce rhetoric, to plot and scheme, spread rumours and debate pointlessly, to dust off arguments and seek apparent agreement, is also considerable, but the result is that the people are confused. So everything under Heaven is in a state of distress, all because of the pursuit of knowledge. Everything in the world knows how to seek for knowledge that they do not have, but do not know how to find what they already know. Everything in the world knows how to condemn what they dislike, but do not know how to condemn what they have which is wrong. This is what causes such immense confusion. It is as if the brightness of the sun and moon had been eclipsed above, while down below the hills and streams have lost their power, as though the natural flow of the four seasons had been broken. There is no humble insect, not even any plant, that has not lost its innate nature. This is the consequence for the world of seeking after knowledge. From the Three Dynasties down to the present day it has been like this. The good and honest people are ignored, while spineless flatterers are advanced. The quiet and calm of actionless action is cast aside and pleasure is taken in argument. It is this nonsense which has caused such confusion for everything under Heaven.

CHAPTER 11

Leaving the World Open

I have heard of leaving the world open to its own way and not interfering, but I have never heard of trying to control the world.

We let the world be, fearful of spoiling its innate nature; we leave it alone, fearful of those who adversely affect the world's Virtue. If the nature of everything under Heaven is not distorted, if the world's Virtue is not despoiled, then what need is there to govern the world? In times gone by Yao controlled everything under Heaven, everyone was happy and the whole world was joyful, living in its true way. Nowhere was there stagnation. But when Chieh governed everything under Heaven, he made all life wearisome and distressed, and all people found their own nature turning bad and diseased. To be without peace, to be without fulfilment, is to turn against Virtue. No one can struggle against Virtue for long and still survive.

Are people too cheerful? If so, they harm the yang. Are people too vengeful? If so, they harm the yin. If both yin and yang are corrupted, then the four seasons will not follow each other, the balance of hot and cold will not be kept and this results in distress to the very bodies of the people! People will be unable to control a balance between joy and anger. It makes them restless, moving here, moving there, plotting to no purpose, travelling for no good reason or result. The consequence of this is that the world becomes concerned with mighty goals and plots, ambition and hatred, which brings in its wake the likes of Robber Chih, Tseng and Shih. As a result, the world may wish to reward the good, but there are not enough rewards available; nor can it adequately punish the bad, for there are not enough punishments.

The whole world is indeed vast, but it cannot provide enough rewards nor punishments. Given all this, how could people be expected to find enough time to rest quietly in the essential qualities of their innate nature?

Do people enjoy what they can see clearly?
In fact they are disturbed by colours.
Do they enjoy what they hear?
In fact they are spoiled by sounds.
Do they revel in benevolence?
In fact they confuse Virtue.
Do they take pride in righteousness?
In fact they reject reason.
Do they delight in ritual?
In fact they resort to pretence.
Do they take pleasure in music?
In fact they sink into dissolution.
Do they appreciate the sage?
In fact they take pride in falsehood.
Do they rejoice at knowledge?
In fact they celebrate quibblers.

While the world exists in its true nature, it is irrelevant whether these eight treasures exist or not. However, when the world exists in a way which distorts, twists, mixes up and confuses its true innate nature, these eight treasures cause immense confusion instead. It gets even worse if the world goes on to honour and value them! It is said, all this is passing! However, people go to great lengths, fasting, praying, teaching these treasures, beating drums and prancing around. I don't know what can be done about all this!

So it is that the noble master who finds he has to follow some course to govern the world will realize that actionless action is the best course. By non-action, he can rest in the real substance of his nature and destiny. If he appreciates his own body as he appreciates the world, then the world can be placed in his care. He who loves his body as he loves the world can be trusted to govern the world. If the noble master can prevent his five main organs from being destroyed, and his vision and hearing also; if he can become as lifeless as a corpse and develop his dragon powers; if he can thus still himself, his words will sound like thunder while his actions will be seen as the actions of a spirit from Heaven, who is guided by Heaven. If he is unconcerned and engaged in actionless action, his gentle spirit will draw all life to him like a dust cloud. How then would such a person have time for governing the world?

Tsui Chu questioned Lao Tzu, saying, 'If the world is not ruled, how can you improve people's hearts?'

Lao Tzu said, 'Take care how you play with people's hearts. People's hearts should not be shoved down nor pushed up, for this yo-yoing up and down makes the heart either a prisoner or an avenging fury. It can be gentle and giving, moulding even the hard and sharp, or it can be sharp and pointed, tough enough to cut, carve or chisel. It can be as hot as a searing fire; it can be as cold as ice. So swift that in the nodding of one's head it has twice roared over the four seas and beyond all boundaries. At rest, it is as deep as the abyss; when it is active, it is like a star in Heaven. It races beyond anything that seeks to bind it, for this is in truth the heart of humanity!

Long, long ago, the Yellow Emperor was the first to disturb the hearts of the people with all his cant about benevolence and righteousness. Yao and Shun came after him and wore themselves out trying to feed the material bodies of the people. They distressed their five vital organs with their benevolence and righteousness; they wore out their life's blood in drawing up codes of laws, and yet they failed. Yao had to send Huan Tou to Mount Chung, banish the three Miao tribes to the area of San Wei, and exile the Minister of Works to the Dark City. This is the measure of their failure to rule the world. This brings us to the Three Dynasties, when the world was in chaos. At the bottom we have people such as the dictator Chieh and Robber Chih; at the top we have people like Tseng and Shih. At this time the Literati and the Mohists also arose. As a result, contentment and fury squared up to each other, foolishness and wisdom rose against each other, good and bad insulted each other, the vainglorious and the sincere traded insults, and the whole of the world fell into decline. The great Virtue was no longer unified, and innate nature and destiny broke apart. The whole world sought knowledge and all the different peoples of the world were distracted. At this stage the axe and saw came into their own; the plumb line determined truth and brought execution; the hammer and gouge made their deep marks and the whole world fell into great disarray. The crime lies in playing around with people's hearts. The result was that leaders of worth hid below the mountains and princes in charge of vast armies hid shaking in their ancestor shrines.

In this generation, those condemned to death are piled up; those who wear the punishment yoke press upon each other; those sentenced to beatings are never out of sight of each other. Out of this lot now appear the Literati and Mohists, waving their arms. Oh dear! That this lot should be so audacious! They have no shame! Isn't it strange that we can see neither sageness nor wisdom, neither benevolence nor righteousness in the yoke and shackles of punishment! How can we tell whether or not Tseng and Shih are the arrows heralding the coming of Chieh and Chih? This is why I say, 'Destroy the sage, throw away wisdom and the whole world will have great order.'

The Yellow Emperor was the master of the world for nineteen years: the whole world followed his edicts. Then he heard of Master Kuang Cheng, who was dwelling on top of Kung Tung mountain, and he went to see him, saying, 'I understand that you, Master, have found the perfect Tao. I dare to ask you what is the essence of the perfect Tao? I would like to grasp the essence of Heaven and Earth and use them to assist the harvest of the five crops in order to help the people. I would like to be able to direct the yin and yang in order to bring all things to life. How can this be done?'

Master Kuang Cheng replied, 'What you ask about is the true element of all things; what you seek control over is in essence divided. Since you began governing all below Heaven, the very breath of the clouds has not yet formed, and yet it rains; the trees and bushes drop their leaves before they have turned yellow; the light of the sun and moon grows ever weaker. You are a man whose heart has become numbed by words, you are insubstantial and feeble. It would be unworthy to teach you the Tao.'

The Yellow Emperor withdrew and ceased ruling the world. He constructed a rude hut, filled only with a white grass mat, and he dwelt there for three months undisturbed. Then he went again to make his request.

Master Kuang Cheng was lying down facing south.[46] The Yellow Emperor, with an air of deference, came forward kneeling. He bowed low twice and said, 'I have heard it said, Master, that you are a master of the perfect Tao. I would like to ask, how should I govern my body in order to live a long life?'

Master Kuang Cheng sat up suddenly and said, 'This question of yours! Splendid! I will teach you about the perfect Tao. The essence of the perfect Tao is hidden in darkness, lost in silence. Nothing seen; nothing heard. Embrace the spirit in quietness, the body with its own rightness. Be still, be pure, do not make your body struggle, do not disturb your essence. All this will result in a long life. The eye does not see, the ear does not hear, the heart knows nothing, yet your spirit will guard your body and your body will have a long life. Guard what is within, block that which is outside, for much knowledge is dangerous.

'I will go with you up towards the great Light,[47] to the origins of the perfect other, the perfect yang. I will go with you through the gate of Deepest Mystery to the origin of the perfect other,[48] the perfect yin. Heaven and Earth have those who rule them, yin and yang have their places of concealment. Guard and take care of your body, then the rest takes good care of itself. I sustain the unity and dwell in harmony, thus have I remained alive for one thousand two hundred years and my body has not aged.'

The Yellow Emperor bowed his head to the ground twice and said, 'Master Kuang Cheng, to me you are Heaven itself.'

Master Kuang Cheng said, 'Splendid! I will teach you. This is inexhaustible, but people still think it has an end; this is incomprehensible, and yet people feel they can encompass it. The one who follows my Tao, if he is amongst the stars, will be elevated,

46. Traditionally, this position and direction was only taken by Emperors.
47. The sun.
48. The moon.

if down below, will be a king. The one who fails to follow my
Tao can see the brightness above but will still be just like the soil
below. Every creature born comes from the soil and returns to
soil. Therefore, I shall now leave you and enter the gate of that
which has no limit in the fields of the boundless. There I shall
combine with the sun and the moon. There I shall combine with
Heaven and Earth forever. I combine with whatever is with me!
What is apart from me, I ignore! All the people may die, but I alone
will survive!'

Yun Chiang was travelling east, carried along upon the wings of
a whirlwind. Suddenly he met Hung Mung, who was jumping
around, slapping his thighs and hopping like a bird. Yun Chiang
saw this and stopped dead, standing still in respect, and said, 'Elderly
man, who are you? What are you doing?'

Hung Mung continued to slap his thighs and hop like a bird, then
replied, 'Enjoying myself!'

Yun Chiang said, 'I would like to ask a question.'

Hung Mung looked at Yun Chiang and said, 'That's a shame!'

Yun Chiang said, 'The very breath[49] of Heaven is no longer in
harmony. Earth's very breath is ensnared, the six breaths do not
mix, the four seasons do not follow each other. Now I want to
combine the six breaths in order to bring life to all things. How do
I do this?'

Hung Mung slapped his thighs, hopped around and said, 'I don't
know, I don't know!'

Yun Chiang could go no further with this questioning. But three
years later, travelling east, he passed the wilderness of Sung and
came upon Hung Mung again. Yun Chiang, very pleased, rushed
towards him, stood before him and said, 'Heaven, have you forgotten me? Heaven, have you forgotten me?' Bowing his head twice,
he asked for teaching from Hung Mung.

Hung Mung said, 'Wandering everywhere, without a clue why.
Wildly impulsive, without a clue where. I wander around in this odd
fashion, I see that nothing comes without reason. What can I
know?'

49. *Chi* – the breath which animates all life and, when used up, causes death.

Yun Chiang replied, 'I am also wildly impulsive, but the people follow me wherever I am. I cannot stop them following me. Now, because they follow me, I want to have a word of teaching from you.'

'The disruption of the ways of Heaven distresses the true being of things, halting the fulfilment of Heaven's Mysteries,' said Hung Mung. 'This causes the animals to disperse, the birds to sing throughout the night, misfortune to hit the crops and the woods, and disaster to blight the very insects themselves. Alas, all this is caused by the people's error of thinking they know how to rule!'

'What should I do then?' said Yun Chiang.

'Oh, you distress them! Like a spirit, a spirit I will dance away,' said Hung Mung.

'I have had such trouble meeting you,' said Yun Chiang. 'Oh Heaven, just give me one other word.'

'Oh ho!' said Hung Mung. 'Strengthen your heart. Remain sure in actionless action, and all things will then transform themselves. Reject your body, throw out hearing and eyesight, forget that you are anyone, become one with the Vast and the Void. Loosen the heart, free the spirit, be calm as if without a soul. All living things return to their root, return to their root, not knowing why. Constantly in darkness, constantly in darkness, and throughout their physical existence they never depart from this. If they tried to understand this, they would depart from this. Ask not for its name, seek not for its shape. So all life comes to birth through itself.'

Yun Chiang replied, 'Heaven, you have honoured me with this Virtue, taught me through Mystery; my whole life I sought it, now I have it.' He bowed his head twice and got up. He said farewell and left.

Ordinary people are happy when someone agrees with them and distressed when others disagree with them. This happiness and distress comes from the desire to be marked apart from the common crowd, a desire set within their hearts. But if they have set their hearts upon distinguishing themselves from the rest, how does this draw them out beyond the rest? Better to go with everyone and be at peace rather than struggle, for, regardless of how clever you are, the others have more skills. However, when people want to rule a

country on someone's behalf, they do so by following the ways of
the kings of the Three Dynasties, but they do not see the evil which
comes with such methods. The country is at the mercy of their
fortune, but this usually ends in destruction! Only perhaps one in
ten thousand men can save the country by this; the chances are less
than one in ten thousand, so they ruin the country. It is very
distressing that those in power do not understand the risks of using
such people!

> The one who has a great country owns a great thing.
> Having such a great thing, he should not be treated as if he were
>   just anyone.
> Being himself something and yet not just a humble something,
> he should consider all others as just things.
> If he really, truly clearly comprehends
> that treating other things as just something,
> he is not himself just a humble something,
> he will not just be content with ruling all things under Heaven.
> He will go out and come in through the whole cosmos,
> ranging wide across all lands,
> solitary in going, solitary in returning.
> He is the sole possessor,
> and as sole possessor he is the most perfect of all.

The great man in what he teaches is like the shadow that follows
a body, the echo that follows a sound. Presented with a question, he
replies, confronting the questioner with such a depth of understanding, as if the whole of the cosmos was poured out. He lives in
silence; he acts no-where, guides those who are rushing hither and
thither in their search and journeys through that which has no
origin. His movements leave no trace as he goes in and out. He is as
the sun, beyond time. To describe him, you talk about his unity
with the great All. The great All has no self. Having no self, he does
not see himself having belongings! The one who wants possessions
is the nobleman of old, while the one who has nothing is the real
companion of Heaven and Earth.

> Most things are mundane but useful.
> The people are lowly but have to be relied upon.

Affairs are secretive but need to be fulfilled.
Laws are crude but necessary.
Righteousness is distant but is needed within.
Benevolence is intimate but needs to be made universal.
Rituals are restricted but need to be extended.
Virtue is central but needs to be raised higher.
The Tao is perpetually One but needs to be modified.
Heaven is spiritual but also practical.

So the sages contemplate Heaven but do not assist it.
They are concerned to perfect their Virtue but do not allow it to
    encumber them.
They set forth according to the Tao but do not make plans.
They work with benevolence but put no reliance upon it.
They draw extensively upon righteousness but do not try to
    build it up.
They observe the rituals but do not set great store by them.
They do what they have to and never shirk their responsibilities.
They try to make their laws applicable but do not believe them
    effective.
They value the people and do not take them for granted.
They make use of things and do not dismiss them lightly.
True, things are worthless but they must be used.
Those who do not see Heaven clearly will not be pure in Virtue.
Those who fail to follow the Tao cannot follow any other path.
What a disaster for those who cannot follow the Tao!

What is this Tao?
There is the Tao of Heaven;
there is the Tao of humanity.
Non-action brings respect: this is Heaven's Tao.
To be active is the Tao of humanity.
It is Heaven's Tao that is the ruler;
the Tao of humanity is the servant.
The Tao of Heaven and the Tao of humanity are poles apart.
Do not fail to reflect upon this.

清谿放棹

曾見雲谿外
峯尖神韻
天然不易到
真

CHAPTER 12

Heaven and Earth

Heaven and Earth are vast,
and their diversity comes from one source.
Although there are ten thousand forms of life,
they are one in their order.
Human beings are multitudinous,
but they are governed by one ruler.
The ruler is rooted in Virtue and perfected by Heaven.
It is said that long ago
the rulers of everything below Heaven
ruled through actionless action,
through Heavenly Virtue and nothing else.

If we look at words in the light of the Tao, then the title 'Ruler of the World' makes sense. If we look at the distinctions between rulers and others in the light of the Tao, then the separation of rulers and ministers is relevant and clear. If we look at their abilities in the same light of the Tao, then we see that the officials are in the right places. Look at anything in the light of the Tao and you will see that the response of all life is fulfilling. Pervading all Heaven and Earth there is Virtue; stirring all life is the Tao. The ruling classes govern those below them: this is hierarchy. Where ability is trained, this is called skill. Such skill is absorbed into administration and administration is righteousness. Righteousness is of Virtue; Virtue is of the Tao; the Tao is of Heaven. It is said that in olden times those who ruled everything under Heaven wanted nothing and the world was fulfilled; they practised non-action and the whole of life was transformed; they were immensely deep in their stillness and the many families of the world were calm. The *Records* say, 'Remain true to the One and all manner of tasks will be completed. Be without emotion and the very ghosts and spirits will submit.'

The great Master said, 'The Tao supports and sustains all life, so immense, so immense is its vastness! The nobleman should most definitely not have it on his heart.

'The action of non-action is called Heaven.
The words of non-action are called Virtue.
To love all humanity and to bring success to them is called
    benevolence.
To unite that which is not united is called greatness.
To go beyond barriers and boundaries is called open-handedness.
To have a vast multitude of diverse things is called wealth.
To have and to hold Virtue is called guidance.
To grow in maturity in Virtue is called stability
To be aligned with the Tao is called completion.
To refuse to allow anything external which distracts you is called
    perfection.

'The nobleman who clearly perceives these ten things will be also magnanimous in his ventures and his actions will benefit all life.

'Such a man will leave the gold in the mountain
and the pearls to lie in the deep.
He does not view money and goods as true profit,
nor is he attracted by fame and fortune,
nor by enjoyment of long life,
nor sadness at an early death;
he does not value wealth as a blessing,
nor is he ashamed by poverty.
He will not lust for the wealth of a generation to have as his
    own;
he has no wish to rule the whole world as his private domain.
His honour is clarity of understanding that all life are part of one
    treasury
and that death and birth are united.'

The Sage Master said,

'The Tao, how deep and quiet it lies;
how pure is its clarity!
Without it neither gold nor stone would resonate.
The gold and stones have sounds within them
but if they are not struck, then no sound comes forth.
All the multitudinous creatures have dimensions beyond
    calculation!

'The man of regal Virtue moves without complexity and is
ashamed to be found concerned with the affairs of state. His
knowledge is firmly rooted in the origin of self, and encompasses
even the spirits. His Virtue embraces widely. His heart goes out to
what is beyond him. Were there no Tao, then his body would have
no life, and without Virtue, his body has no brightness. One who
preserves his body and lives out his full life, who establishes Virtue
and clarifies the Tao, is he not imbued with regal Virtue? He
suddenly surges forth, wide and unlimited. He moves unexpectedly
and all life comes after him! This is what is meant by the man of
regal Virtue.

'He can see in darkest darkness,
hears where there is no sound.
In the midst of darkest darkness,
he alone sees clearly;
in the midst of no sound,
he alone hears the harmony.
Where depth plunges into depth,
he can discern things;
in world upon world of the spirits
he can discern the core of all.
So in his dealings with the multitude of beings
he can fulfil all their wants from perfect nothingness.
Always in pursuit
he returns for the night's rest.
Great and small, long and short, distant and near.'

The Yellow Emperor was travelling to the north of Red Water,
ascending to the summit of Kun Lun and looking out southwards.

Returning home he lost his dark pearl. He commissioned Know-ledge to look for it, but Knowledge was unable to trace it. He commissioned Li Chu to look for it, but he could not trace it. He commissioned Heated Debate to look for it, but he also could not trace it. Finally he commissioned Pointless to look for it and he traced it. The Yellow Emperor said, 'How strange! How is it that only Pointless could trace it?'

Yao's teacher was Hsu Yu; Hsu Yu's teacher was Yeh Chueh; Yeh Chueh's teacher was Wang Ni; Wang Ni's teacher was Pi I. Yao asked Hsu Yu, 'Could Yeh Chueh be counted the equal of Heaven? I could then ask Wang Ni to request that he take over from me.'

Hsu Yu said, 'Take care, for this could put everything under Heaven at risk! Yeh Chueh is sharp, clear-thinking, quick-witted and alert. By nature he is superior to others, but he can exploit what Heaven gives him. He would try to prevent flaws, but he does not understand where they spring from. Make him the equal of Heaven? Beware, for he would rely upon others rather than on Heaven, caring for his own self first and having little regard to the lives of others. He would pursue knowledge, and his actions would be like swift fire. He would be in bondage to his own ideas, in thrall to them, constantly looking all around to see how things are going. He would be at the mercy of demands, changing as they change and having no dependability at all. How could he be the equal of Heaven? There are small clans with common ancestors, and he could be the father of one such small branch, but not the father of the fathers of all the extended family. His rule would bring disaster, both to the ministers facing north and the ruler facing south.'

Yao was touring the sights of Hua. The guards of Hua said, 'Oh, a sage! Let me pray to the sage. Long life to the sage!'

Yao said, 'Never!'

'May the sage be wealthy!'

'Never!'

'May the sage have many sons!'

'Never!'

'Long life, wealth and many sons are what most people want,' said the guard. 'Why do you not want them?'

'Many sons bring many anxieties, wealth brings many troubles, long life brings many problems. These three things do not enhance Virtue. I dismiss them.'

The guard said, 'When I first saw you I thought you were a sage. Now I can see you are just a nobleman. Heaven gives life to all the multitudinous peoples and gives them their place. Many sons will have diverse assignments given to them, so there is nothing to fear! If you share your wealth with others, there is no trouble!

'The sage finds his place as a quail settles,
or as a fledgling is fed
and as a bird flying leaves no mark of its passage.
If the whole world has the Tao,
he is part of that well-being.
When the whole world has lost the Tao,
he develops Virtue and avoids involvement.
After a thousand years, wearied by the world,
he departs and rises to be with the immortals,
soaring up upon the white clouds,
arriving at the Supreme One's abode.
The three troubles you quote never affect him;
they do not touch his body;
Such a man suffers no shame!'

The guard then left. Yao pursued him, saying, 'I would just like to ask if . . .'

'Get lost!' said the guard.

When Yao ruled all under Heaven, Po Cheng Tzu Kao was made a governor. Yao passed the throne to Shun, then Shun passed it to Yu. At this point Po Cheng Tzu Kao resigned his commission and began farming. Yu went to see him and found him ploughing. Rushing up to him and bowing in deference, he halted and said, 'When Yao ruled the world, you, Sir, were made a governor. Yao gave way to Shun and Shun gave way to me and then you, Sir, resigned your commission and began farming. Dare I ask the reason why?'

Tzu Kao said, 'When Yao ruled the world, people worked, although he gave no rewards; the people were in awe of him, although he gave out no punishments. Now, you use both rewards and punishments but the people are without benevolence. Virtue will now decay and punishments will prevail. The chaos of the age to come has its origin here and now. So, Sir, why don't you leave? Do not disturb my work!'

He pushed on with his farming and did not look around.

At the great Origin there was nothing, nothing, no name.
The One arose from it; there was One without form.
In taking different forms, it brought life, and became known as
    Virtue.
Before any shape was given, their roles were assigned,
varied and diverse but all linked to one another.
This was their lot.
The forces worked on and things were created,
they grew and took distinct shapes, and these were called
    'bodies'.
The bodies contained spirits,
each distinct and mortal.
This is what we call the innate nature.
Train this innate nature and it will return to Virtue;
Virtue at its best is identical with the Origin.
Being of the One is to be ultimately formless, and this
    formlessness is vast.
This is like the opening and shutting of a bird's beak,
where the opening and shutting is like Heaven and Earth united.
This unity is chaotic and disorderly;
it looks stupid or foolish.
This is known as Mysterious Virtue,
being, without knowing it, part of the great Submission.

Confucius said to Lao Tzu, 'Some people try to grasp the Tao through argument. They try to make what is impossible seem possible. They try to make what is not seem as if it is. Like debaters, they make pointless distinctions and then claim they are actually significant – as real as this roof! Can such people as this be called sages?'

'Such people are the workers kept in bondage,' replied Lao Tzu, 'wearing out their bodies and bringing anxiety to their hearts. Like the dog who is tied to a leash because he catches vermin, or the monkey which is brought down from the mountains because it is skilful. Chiu,[50] I'm telling you, telling you something you have not heard of and cannot discuss. Those who have heads and feet but no heart and no ears are numerous. Those who have their bodies but who value that which is without body or form, are virtually unheard of! Life stops and starts, is born and dies, grows and declines, and there is nothing which can be done about this. People think the ruler of all this is humanity. Forget that, forget Heaven and be known as one of those who forget self. The person who forgets self can be known as the one who enters Heaven.'

Chiang Lu Mien travelled to visit Chi Che and said, 'The ruler of Lu asked me, saying, "Teach me." I refused, but he kept hold of me and I had to say something. I am not sure I chose the right path but I will tell you what I said. I said to the ruler of Lu, "You must be courteous and disciplined. Note and promote those who are public-spirited and loyal; note and oppose those who are selfish and subservient. If you do this, who could possibly wish to be against you?"'

Chi Che nearly choked with laughter and said, 'Your words, dear Sir, regarding the Virtue of Emperors and kings, are like the praying mantis waving his arms around in a fury, trying to stop a carriage – pretty pointless. If he followed your advice, he would end up building taller towers in which to store his increasing number of valuables, and the people would just follow his example.'

Chiang Lu Mien was taken aback and said in amazement, 'I am astonished at your words, Master, but I would dearly like to hear what you have to say on this issue.'

Chi Che said, 'If a great sage ruled the world, he would free the hearts of his people, make his teachings accessible and change people's behaviour. He would erase all falsehood and betrayal from their hearts and enable them to act as their own consciences dictate.

50. Confucius' own name.

It would arise from their very innate natures, yet they would not realize this. If he proceeded like this, why should such a person look up to Yao or Shun for guidance as to how to rule the people, or even bother to despise their methods? He simply wants all to be united in Virtue and in the tranquillity of the heart.'

Tzu Kung travelled south to Chu and as he returned through Chin, he was journeying along the side of the river Han. He saw a lone old man working on his land. The man had prepared the ground and had drawn water from the well and was carrying a jar of water to pour on the earth. Huffing and puffing, he was using up much of his strength and yet had little to show for it. Tzu Kung said, 'There are machines which can water a hundred fields in one day, for very little effort but with much to show for it. Wouldn't you like to have one, Master?'

The gardener looked up and said, 'How does this work?'

He said, 'It is made from wood, solid at the rear and lighter at the other end and it raises the water just as you would pour it out, or the way boiling water overflows. It is called a well dip.'

The gardener was furious, then laughed and said, 'I have heard from my teacher that where you have machines, then you get certain kinds of problems; where you get certain kinds of problems, then you find a heart warped by these problems. Where you get a heart warped, its purity and simplicity are disturbed. When purity and simplicity are disturbed, then the spirit is alarmed and an alarmed spirit is no place for the Tao to dwell. It isn't that I don't know of these machines, but I would be ashamed to use one.'

Tzu Kung was covered in confusion, hung his head and said nothing in reply. After a while, the gardener said, 'Sir, who are you?'

'A disciple of Confucius,' said Tzu Kung.

The gardener said, 'Sir, are you one of those types who expand their knowledge so as to try and appear to be a sage, seeking to impress everyone with your superiority, singing sad songs all alone in the hope of becoming famous in this world? It would be better for you to forget your breath and spirit and disregard the care of your body. Then you might make progress! As it is, you cannot care for yourself, so how do you expect to rule the world? Off you go, Sir, and do not disturb my work!'

Tzu Kung was disturbed and nonplussed by all this. He wandered off puzzled and disorientated, and he did not recover until he had travelled thirty li. His followers said, 'Who was that man? Master, why did you change colour when you saw him and change your bearing so that it took you all day to recover?'

He said, 'Previously I thought that there was only one true man in the world, because I did not know of this man. I have heard the Master say that in actions you aim for that which is true and in ventures you aim for success. Use little energy but have great results, this is the Tao of the sage. Now I don't believe this any more. Those who hold to the Tao are endowed with its Virtue. Being virtuous, they are complete in body. Being complete in their bodies, they are complete in spirit. Being complete in spirit, as a result they are in the Tao of the sages. They live in the world side by side with the people, travelling with them, but never knowing where they are going. Their simplicity is mind-boggling! They consider accomplishments, gain, machines, talents, to be inappropriate in the affections of the people. People like this do not go where they do not want to go nor do they do what their heart tells them not to do. Even if the whole world sings their praises and acclaims them, they will pay no attention at all; if the whole world blames them and accuses them of losing things, they are calm and unperturbed. Neither the praise nor the blame of the world gives them either gain nor loss. Such a one as this is called a man of complete Virtue! In contrast, I am just a wind-blown wave.'

When he returned to Lu, he reported the discussion to Confucius. Confucius said, 'That farmer is just a false man, a practitioner of the ways of Primal Chaos. He grasps the first thing, but does not know the second. He controls what is internal but cannot rule over that which is external. If you had met one who has the clarity of purity and simplicity, who through non-action can restore the original, give shape to his innate nature and enfold his spirit and thus wander at will throughout the world – had you met one such as this, then you would be alarmed! But this man of Primal Chaos, why do we need to worry about him?'

Chun Mang was travelling on his way east to the Great Gorge of the ocean and met Yuan Fung on the shore of the Eastern Ocean. Yuan Fung said, 'Master, where are you going?'

'I am going to the Great Gorge.'

'Why?'

'The Great Gorge is the sort of place that can never be filled by the waters entering it, nor emptied by the waters that flow out of it. I shall have a fine time, wandering beside it,' said Chun Mang.

Yuan Fung replied, 'Master, do you not care about the people? Can't you tell me about the way sages rule?'

'The way sages rule?' said Chun Mang. 'Only appoint those who are fit for the office; make appointments in accordance with the worthiness of those appointed; act only after studying the situation thoroughly. When deeds and words are in accord, the whole world is transformed. Consequently, a wave of the hand or a sharp look will bring the peoples of all the world rushing to you. This is the way sages rule.'

'Can I ask about the Virtuous ones?'

'The Virtuous one is still and without thought;
when he moves he is without design;
he keeps no tally of right and wrong, good or bad.
Virtuous ones share their gains with all within the four seas
and from this they derive pleasure.
They share what they have and are content.
Mournful, they are like a child who has lost his mother;
uncertain, they are like travellers who are lost.
Though blessed with great wealth and comforts,
they have no idea where it comes from;
they have more than enough to eat and drink,
but have no idea where it comes from.
This is the style of Virtuous ones.'

'What about the spiritual ones?'

Chun Mang said,

'Their spirits rise up to the brightest light
and their bodies disappear.

They are gloriously enraptured.
They live out their fate,
The spiritual one pursues to its end what is truly him
and dwells in the delight of Heaven and Earth
while his multitudinous cares fall away.
All things return to their true nature.
This is called Primal Mystery.'

Men Wu Kuei and Chih Chang Man Chi were observing the army of King Wu.[51] 'He is not of the stature of the noble Lord of Yu and that is why he has this problem,' said Chih Chang Man Chi.

Men Wu Kuei said, 'Was the world really well ruled under the noble Lord Yu? Or was it already in trouble and then Yu came and ruled it?'

'Everyone wants the world to be well governed,' said Chih Chang Man Chi. 'If it was already well governed, do you think anyone would have then commented upon the good rule of Yu?[52] He brought healing to wounds, a wig to cover baldness, medicines for the sick. He was like a dutiful son bringing medicines to a loving father, yet wearing a grim look. Any sage would be ashamed of this. In a time of perfect Virtue, the wise are not valued, the able are unemployed. The rulers are like the top branches of a tree, the people like deer: they do what is right but they do not understand righteousness. They love each other but they do not understand benevolence. They are dependable but they do not understand loyalty. They are trustworthy but do not understand good faith. In their movements amongst each other they care for each other but do not understand kindness. In this way they move without leaving any sign, act without leaving any recordable effect.'

The dutiful son who does not indulge his father and the loyal minister who does not flatter his ruler, these are the best of ministers and sons. The son who agrees with his parents in everything they

51. At the annual re-enactment of the Chou conquest of the Shang in the twelfth or eleventh century BC.
52. Name for the model Emperor Shun.

say and do is viewed by the ordinary people as an unworthy son. The minister who agrees with everything his ruler says and does is viewed by the ordinary people as an unworthy minister. Yet people don't seem to understand the truth of this. Those who agree with everything that the people say and think good whatever the people think is good, are never called just yes-men or sycophants. Does this mean popular opinion is of greater authority than parents or rulers? Someone is immediately angry if you tell him he is a yes-man or a sycophant. Nevertheless, throughout this life he will be a yes-man and all his life he will be a sycophant. His stories are designed to agree with people, his turns of phrase are intended to impress them. From start to finish, from beginning to end he never disagrees with them. He displays his robes, exhibiting the colours; his whole carriage is intended to impress and earn him favour with his peers and yet he cannot stand being called a sycophant! He just follows the fashion, liking this and disliking that as others do and yet he does not see himself as just one of the crowd. This is how far his stupidity has reached! The one who knows he is stupid is not that stupid; the one who knows he is confused is not that confused. The greatly deluded will never be rid of delusion; the monumentally foolish will never be very bright. If there are three men walking along together and one of them is confused, they will still reach their goal, because confusion is in the minority; but if two of them are confused, they will not arrive, because confusion is in the majority. So nowadays, with so much confusion in the world, I can indicate to the people where to go, but they do not follow me. Distressing, isn't it?

Classical music is wasted upon the simple peasant, but let them hear 'The Breaking of the Willows' or 'The Bright Flowers' and they will be very jolly. Similarly, wise words do not rest in the hearts of the people. Perfect words do not stay, because vulgar words are in the ascendant. Two basic drums can drown out the sound of the bell and deny the pleasure it could give. These days the whole world is confused. Even if I wanted to go in a particular direction, what good would it do? Since I understand this, if I were to try and force people to go my way, that would just be to fall into a delusion of my own. It is better just to let things be and not force them. If I don't get into such struggles, I shan't have anything to worry about. A leper has a son born at night-time and he rushes to find a light to look at him. His eagerness to see is based on his fear that the child will look like him.

A hundred-year-old tree is chopped up and from that is fashioned a sacrificial bowl, engraved and coloured green and yellow. The rest is thrown away into a ditch. Now, if we compare the sacrificial bowl and that which was cast away, there is certainly a difference between them in terms of beauty and ugliness, but they are one in that they have both lost their innate nature. Robber Chih, as distinct from Tseng and Shih, is very different from the others, but they are all one in having lost their innate nature. There are five ways in which the innate nature is lost. The first is when the five colours confuse the eye and deprive it of clarity of vision. The second is when the five notes confuse the ear and deprive it of the ability to hear. The third is when the five smells affect the nose and cause pains and distress to the forehead. The fourth is when the five flavours deaden the mouth and deprive the sense of taste of its ability to enjoy. The fifth is when pleasures and dislikes unsettle the heart and make the innate nature unstable. These five bring troubles to life. Now the followers of Yang and Mo start spreading out, thinking they have discovered something. But I would not describe this as news. What they have grasped only brings distress, so how can this be the right thing? If they have, then we could claim that the dove in the cage has found something worthwhile. Likes and dislikes, music and colours just confuse your inner self, while wearing caps of leather and feathered hats, carrying official decrees in hand and wearing ceremonial robes hinder appreciation of that which is external. Stuffed full of nonsense on the inside and bound by cords externally, people still look around, even when tied up like this, and claim they have grasped something. Why, they are no better off than criminals who are clamped in irons, their fingers in the screw, or tigers and leopards trapped in cages, yet they still think they have grasped something worth following.

CHAPTER 13

Heaven's Tao

It is Heaven's Tao to journey and to gather no moss,
thus all the forms of life are brought to perfection.
It is the Emperor's Tao to journey and to gather no moss,
which is why the whole world comes to his feet.
It is the sages' Tao to journey and to gather no moss,
thus all that lies within the oceans venerates them.
To understand Heaven clearly,
to comprehend the sages,
to journey through the entire cosmos
following the Virtue of the Emperors and the kings
but also to be spontaneous themselves:
this is the nature of those who comprehend,
seeming not to know
but being centred in stillness.

The sages are quiescent, not because of any value in being quiescent, they simply are still. Not even the multitude of beings can disturb them, so they are calm. Water, when it is still, reflects back even your eyebrows and beard. It is perfectly level and from this the carpenter takes his level. If water stilled offers such clarity, imagine what pure spirit offers! The sage's heart is stilled! Heaven and Earth are reflected in it, the mirror of all life. Empty, still, calm, plain, quiet, silent, non-active, this is the centredness of Heaven and Earth and of the Tao and of Virtue. The Emperor, king, and sages rest there. Resting, they are empty; empty, they can be full; fullness is fulfilment. From the empty comes stillness; in stillness they can travel; in travelling they achieve. In stillness they take actionless action. Through actionless action they expect results from those with responsibilities. Through actionless action they are happy, very happy; being so happy they are not afflicted by cares and worries, for these have no place, and their years of life are prolonged. Empty, still, calm, plain, quiet, silent, actionless action is the foundation of all life. If you are clear on this and facing south, it means you are a noble like Yao; if you are clear on this and facing north, you will become a minister like Shun.

Looking up to them, you observe the Virtue of Emperors, kings and the Sons of Heaven. Looking down on them, you observe the Tao of the dark sages and the uncrowned king. If you retire as they did, amongst the hermits of the rivers and oceans, mountains and forests, you will be considered like them as true scholars. Coming forward and offering help to this generation brings great fame and merit and the whole world becomes one. The sage is still; the king travels. Actionless action brings honour. The beauty radiated, since it arises from simplicity, outshines the rest of the world. Clarity is the Virtue of Heaven and Earth: this is the great Origin, the great Beginning. To have it is to be in harmony with Heaven, to bring equality with everything below Heaven and to be in harmony with all people. To be in harmony with all people is called human happiness; to be in harmony with Heaven, this is called Heavenly happiness.

Chuang Tzu said,

'My Master Teacher! My Master Teacher!
He judges all life but does not feel he is being judgemental;
he is generous to multitudes of generations
but does not think this benevolent;
he is older than the oldest
but he does not think himself old;
he overarches Heaven and sustains Earth,
shaping and creating endless bodies
but he does not think himself skilful.
This is what is known as Heavenly happiness.

'There is a saying: "If you know the happiness of Heaven, then you know that life is from Heaven and death is the transformation of things. In their stillness they are yin and in their journeying they are yang." To know Heavenly happiness means that you do not upset Heaven, nor go against others. You are not reliant on material things, you are not rebuked by the ghosts. There is a saying: "He moves with Heaven and rests with Earth, his heart is one, he is the king of the whole world; the ghosts do not worry him and his soul is not wearied, his heart is one with all living beings." This means his emptiness and stillness enter all beings in Heaven and Earth, travelling alongside all beings. This is known as the Heavenly happiness. Heavenly happiness is the heart of the sage; this is how he cares for all under Heaven.'

The Virtue of Emperors and kings considers Heaven and Earth as its parents, the Tao and Virtue as its master and actionless action as its core. Through actionless action they can make the whole world do as they will and yet not be wearied. Through action they cannot even begin to fulfil what the world requires. This is why the ancient ones valued actionless action. When both the leaders and those below them are in actionless action, then both the leaders and the underlings have the same Virtue. If those below and those above share the same Virtue, then none of them is in the position of a minister. If those below act and those above act also, then those above and those below share the same Tao. If those above and those below share the same Tao, then there is no one to be the lord. However, those above tend to care for the world by actionless action, while those below care for the world by action. This has always been the case. Thus the ancient kings of the world, who knew everything about Heaven and Earth, had no designs; even though they understood the whole of life, they did not speak out; though their skills were greater than any in the lands bounded by oceans, they did nothing.

Heaven produces nothing,
yet all life is transformed;
Earth does not support,
yet all life is sustained;
the Emperor and the king take actionless action,
yet the whole world is served.

There is a saying that there is
nothing as spiritual as Heaven,
nothing as rich as Earth,
nothing as great as Emperors and kings.

It is also said that the Virtue of Emperors and kings finds its match in that of Heaven and Earth. Thus can one ascend with Heaven and Earth, gallop with all life and harness all people to the Tao.

The beginning lies with those above, the outworking with those below; the important lies with the ruler, the details with the minister.

The three armies and five types of weapons[53] are the irrelevant aspects of Virtue.

Handing down rewards and punishments, advantage and loss and the inflicting of the five types of sentence,[54] these are the irrelevant aspects of teaching.

Rituals and laws, weights and measures and all the attention to self and name are the irrelevant aspects of governing.

The sound of bells and drums, the attention to feathers and hangings, these are the irrelevant aspects of music.

The attributes of official mourning are the irrelevant aspects of grief.

These five unimportant aspects await the movement of the spirit and the liveliness of the heart's skills before they can be of service.

The ancient ones were aware of all these aspects but did not give them any importance.

The ruler precedes and the minister follows;
the father precedes and the son follows;
the elder brother precedes and the younger brother follows;
the senior one precedes and the junior follows;
the man precedes and the woman follows;
the husband precedes and the wife follows.

53. The three armies are the standard subdivisions of a feudal state, and the five weapons are the spear, halberd, axe, shield and bow.
54. The five sentences are branding or tattooing, cutting off the nose, cutting off the feet, castration and execution.

This progression of the greater followed by the lesser mirrors that of Heaven and Earth. The sages take their example from this. Heaven is elevated, Earth lowly, and this reflects their spiritual illumination. Spring and summer precede and autumn and winter follow: this is the pattern of the four seasons. In the growth of all life, their roots and buds have their appointed place and distinct shape, and from this comes maturation and then decay, the constant stream of transformation and change. If Heaven and Earth, the most perfect in spirit, have their hierarchy of precedence and sequence, then how much more should this be so with the people!

In the ancestor shrine it is kinship which brings honour;
in the court it is nobility;
in the local areas it is age;
in the governing of things it is wisdom.

This is the pattern of the great Tao. To speak about the Tao but not about its pattern of sequence goes against the Tao itself. If we speak about the Tao that has no Tao, then there is no Tao to guide!

Thus it was that the ancient ones clearly grasped the great Tao, seeking first the meaning of Heaven and then the meaning of its Tao and Virtue.

When they clearly understood the Tao and Virtue,
they then understood benevolence and righteousness.
When they clearly grasped benevolence and righteousness,
they could see how to perform their duties.
When they grasped how to perform their duties,
they came to understand form and fame.
When they comprehended form and fame,
they were able to make appointments.
When they had made appointments,
they went on to examining people and their efforts.
When they had examined people's efforts,
they moved to judgements of good or bad.
When they had made judgements of good and bad,
they went on to punishments and rewards.

Following this, the foolish and the wise knew what they should do and the elevated and the lowly went to their appropriate places. The good and the worthy as well as those below them found in their own selves that all had assignments adapted to their skills, appropriate to their rank. Thus did they serve those above them and encourage those below; external matters were governed and their own selves developed. Knowledge and plotting were never used and they relied upon Heaven.

This is known as the great peace and perfect government.

The Book says, 'There is form and there is title.' Form and title were known to the ancient ones, but they gave it no importance. In the olden days, when they talked of the great Tao, they spoke of the five steps which brought them to 'form and fame', or they went to nine steps and debated 'rewards and punishments'. If they had just gone straight to discussing 'form and fame' they would have shown up their ignorance of the origin; or if they had plunged straight into 'rewards and punishments' they would have shown their ignorance of the correct beginning. Those who turn the Tao upside down before talking of it, who in fact oppose the Tao before speaking of it, will be governed by other people, for they could not rule others! Those who plunge straight in, gabbling on about 'form and fame' or 'rewards and punishments', may have some understanding of the means of governing but do not understand the Tao of governing. They may be of use to the world, but they cannot use the world. They are typical pompous scholars, just stuck in their little corner. Rituals, laws, weights and measures, all the point-scoring of correct forms and titles: the ancient ones had all this, but they were the tools of those below to serve those above. Those above did not use this to rule those below.

In days gone by Shun spoke to Yao, saying, 'Being Heaven's king, how do you use your heart?'

'I do not abuse those who are defenceless,' said Yao, 'nor do I ignore the poor. I mourn for those who die, caring for the orphaned child and for the widow. This is how I use my heart.'

'Righteous as far as righteousness goes, but not that great,' commented Shun.

'What ought I to do, then?' said Yao.

'When Heaven's Virtue is found, the hills rejoice, the sun and moon shine and the four seasons are in line. The regular pattern of each day and night follows properly and the rain clouds are moved accordingly.'

Yao said, 'So all I've really been doing is getting worked up and bothered! You seek compliance with Heaven, whereas I have sought compliance with humanity.'

Since earliest times Heaven and Earth have been known as great. The Yellow Emperor, Yao and Shun have all praised them. The ancient kings who ruled all under Heaven, did they need to act? Heaven and Earth were sufficient for them.

Confucius travelled west to place his books in the archives of Chou. Tzu Lu offered advice, saying, 'I have heard that the official in charge of the Royal Archives is Lao Tzu. But he has resigned and lives at home. Sir, if you want to place your books there, go and see him and ask his assistance.'

'Splendid,' said Confucius. So off he went to see Lao Tzu, but Lao Tzu refused to help. So Confucius took out his Twelve Classics,[55] and started to preach.

When he was halfway through, Lao Tzu said, 'This is too much. Put it briefly.'

Confucius said, 'In essence, it is benevolence and righteousness.'

'May I ask,' said Lao Tzu, 'are benevolence and righteousness of the very essence of humanity?'

'Certainly,' said Confucius. 'If the nobleman is without benevolence, he has no purpose; if without righteousness, he has no life. Benevolence and righteousness, these are truly of the innate nature of humanity. How else could it be?'

'May I ask, what are benevolence and righteousness?'

'To be at one, centred in one's heart, in love with all, without selfishness, this is what benevolence and righteousness are,' replied Confucius.

'Really! Your words reveal misunderstanding,' said Lao Tzu. '"Love of all", that's both vague and an exaggeration! "Without

55. It is unclear what the twelve were, but they certainly include the Six Classics of Confucianism.

selfishness", isn't that rather selfish? Sir, if you want people to remain simple, shouldn't you look to the ways of Heaven and Earth?

'Heaven and Earth have their boundaries which are constant;
the sun and moon hold their courses in their brightness;
the stars and planets proceed in the boundaries of their order;
the birds and creatures find their confines within their herds and flocks.
Think of the trees which stand within their own boundaries in order.

'So Sir, walk with Virtue and travel with the Tao, and you will reach the perfect end. Why bother with all this benevolence and righteousness, prancing along as if you were beating a drum and looking for a lost child? Sir, you will just confuse people's true nature!'

Shih Cheng Chi came to see Lao Tzu and asked him, 'I have heard tell that you, Sir, are a sage, so I came to see you, regardless of the length of the journey. Over the hundred nights of the journey my feet became blistered, but I did not stop nor rest. Now I find, Sir, that you are not a sage. Even though you were wealthy enough for even the rat holes of your house to be full of left-over rice, you nevertheless kicked your poor little sister out of the house. What an unkind action! When your food is placed before you, even if you cannot eat it all, you hoard it, whether it is raw or cooked.'

Lao Tzu showed no emotion and made no reply. The next day Shih Cheng Chi came to see him again and said, 'Yesterday I was rude to you, Sir. Today I have no heart for it. Why is this?'

Lao Tzu said, 'I think I have freed myself from knowledge, from the spiritual and from being a sage. If you had called me an ox yesterday, Sir, then I would have said I was an ox. If you had called me a horse, I would have said I was a horse. If people name a reality, but someone won't have it, then he just makes life more problematic. I am always like this, I don't just put it on for certain occasions.'

Shih Cheng Chi shrank back so as not to be even near Lao Tzu's shadow, then he came forward once more in a humble way and

asked how he could cultivate himself. Lao Tzu said, 'Your face is
unpleasant; your eyes glare; your forehead is broad; your mouth
hangs open; your style is pompous; you are like a tethered horse
waiting to bolt, ready to go like an arrow from a crossbow, you
examine everything in too much detail; you are cunning in your
use of knowledge, yet you lounge around. All this makes me
distrust you. Out on the frontier someone like you would be called
a bandit.'

The Master said,

'The Tao does not hesitate before that which is vast,
nor does it abandon the small.
Thus it is that all life is enlivened by it.
So immense, so immense there is nothing which is not held by
it;
so deep, so unfathomable beyond any reckoning.
The form of its Virtue is in benevolence and righteousness,
though this is a minor aspect of its spirit.
Who but the perfect man could comprehend all this?
The perfect man has charge of this age,
a somewhat daunting task!
However, this does not fool him or trap him.
He holds the reins of power over the whole world
but it is of little consequence to him.
His discernment unearths all falsehood
but he gives no thought to personal gain.
He gets to the heart of issues and knows how to protect the
foundation of truth.
Thus Heaven and Earth are outside him,
he ignores all life and his spirit is never wearied.
He travels with the Tao,
is in agreement with Virtue,
bids farewell to benevolence and righteousness
and ignores ritual and music,
because the perfect man has set his heart upon what is right.'

This generation believes that the value of the Tao is to be found
in books. But books are nothing more than words, and words have

value but only in terms of their meaning. Meaning is constantly seeking to express what cannot be said in words and thus passed on. This generation values words and puts them into books, yet what it values is perhaps mistaken, because what it values is not really all that valuable. So we look at things and see things, but it is only an outward form and colour, and what can be heard is just the name and sound. How sad that this generation imagines that the form, colour, name and sound are enough to capture the essence of something! The form, colour, name and sound are in no way sufficient to capture or convey the truth, which is why it is said that the knowledgeable do not speak and those who speak are not knowledgeable. But how can this generation understand this?

Duke Huan was sitting up in his hall reading a book. The wheelwright Pien was down below in the courtyard making a wheel. He put down his chisel and hammer, went up to the hall and asked Duke Huan, 'May I ask you, Sir, what words you are reading?'

Duke Huan replied, 'The words of the sages.'

'Are these sages still living?'

'They are long dead,' said Duke Huan.

'Then, Sir, what you are reading is nothing but rubbish left over from these ancient men!'

'How dare you, a wheelwright, comment on what I read! If you can explain this, fine, if not you shall die!' thundered Duke Huan.

The wheelwright Pien replied, 'Your Lordship's servant looks at it from the perspective of his own work. When I work on a wheel, if I hit too softly, pleasant as this is, it doesn't make for a good wheel. If I hit furiously, I get tired and the thing doesn't work! So, not too soft, not too vigorous, I grasp it in my hand and hold it in my heart. I cannot express this by word of mouth, I just know it. I cannot teach this to my son, nor can my son learn it from me. So for seventy years I have gone along this path and here I am still making wheels. The ancient ones, when they died, took their words with them. Which is why I can state that what Your Lordship is reading is nothing more than rubbish left over from these ancient ones!'

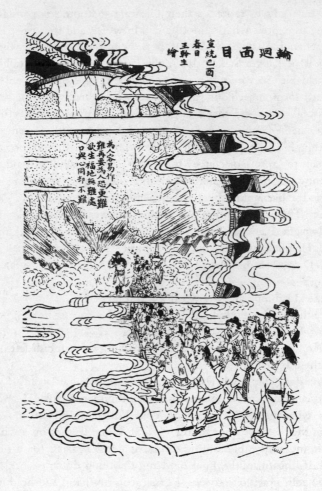

輪迴面目

宣統己酉
春日
王醉生
繪

為人容易作人難　再要為人恐更難
欲生福地無難處　口與心同卻不難

CHAPTER 14

Does Heaven Move?

Does Heaven move?
Does the Earth stand still?
Do the sun and moon argue about where to go?
Who is lord over all this?
Who binds and controls it?
Who, doing nothing, makes all of this be?
Is there some hidden cause that makes things as they are, whether
     they wish or not?
Or is it just that everything moves and turns because it has no
     choice?
Do the clouds come before the rain, or does the rain cause the
     clouds?
What causes them to be?
Who, doing nothing, brings all this joyful excess into being?
The winds come from the north,
going first to west then to east,
swirling up on high, to go who knows where?
Whose breath are they?
Who, doing nothing, creates all this activity?

Shaman Hsien said, 'Come, I will tell you. Heaven has six
directions and five cardinal elements.[56] Emperors and kings follow
them and there is good government. If they act against them, there
is bad government. Consider the Nine Lo, whereby harmony can
rule and Virtue can be established. The scholar will illuminate all
below and the whole world will be with him. This is what life is
like under the August Rulers.'

56. Fire, wood, earth, metal, water.

Tang, the Prime Minister of Shang, asked Chuang Tzu about benevolence. Chuang Tzu said, 'Tigers and wolves are benevolent.'

'What do you mean?'

'The father cares for his children,' said Chuang Tzu. 'Is this not benevolence?'

'But it is perfect benevolence that I am interested in.'

'Perfect benevolence has nothing to do with affection,' said Chuang Tzu.

But the Prime Minister replied, 'I have heard that where there is no affection, there is no love; where there is no love, there is no filial piety. Do you mean to say that perfect benevolence is without filial piety?'

'Certainly not. Perfect benevolence is of the highest order, and words such as "filial piety" cannot describe it. What you want to say is not that filial piety is surpassed, but that nothing even comes close to it. When a traveller goes south and then turns to face north when he has reached Ying, he cannot see Ming mountain. Why is this? Because it is far away. There is the saying: filial piety arising from respect is easy, filial piety arising from love is hard. If filial piety from love is easy, then to forget your parents is hard. It is easy to forget your parents, but it is hard to make my parents forget me. It is easy to make my parents forget me, but it is hard to make me forget the whole world. It is easy to forget the whole world, but it is hard for the whole world to forget me.

'Virtue ignores Yao and Shun and dwells in actionless action. Its benefits embrace every generation, though no one in the world understands this. Despite your protestations, how can you talk of benevolence and filial piety? Filial piety, mutual respect, benevolence, righteousness, loyalty, integrity, resoluteness and purity, all of these can be of service to Virtue. But they are not worthy in themselves. So it is said,

'"Perfect nobility disregards the honours of state;
Perfect richness ignores the wealth of the country;
Perfect fulfilment ignores fame and glory.
Alone of all, the Tao never alters."'

Cheng of the North Gate asked the Yellow Emperor, 'My Lord,

when you had the Hsien Chih music performed in the area around Lake Tung Ting, I listened and at first I was afraid; I listened again and I was weary; I listened to the end and I was bewildered. I became upset and incapable of coherent speech and finally I lost my self assurance.'

The Yellow Emperor said, 'That is what I would expect! I had it performed by the people, I attuned it to Heaven, I proceeded according to the principles of ritual and I rooted it in great purity. Perfect music must first of all find its response in the world of the people. It must conform to the principles of Heaven and walk with the five Virtues. It should merge with spontaneity; as a result of which it can order the sequence of the four seasons, bring great harmony to all life. This will be seen in the procession of the four seasons, bringing all life to birth. At one moment swelling, at one declining, constrained by both martial and civil boundaries. At one moment clear, at one obscure, the yin and yang are in harmony, the sounds pour forth. It is as if I were an insect awaking from hibernation or a crash of thunder; without end, without beginning, at one, death, at one, life, at one, finished, at one, surging forth. It is constant but there is no dependable pattern, this is what alarmed you.

'Next I played it with the harmony of yin and yang, and illuminated it by the light of the sun and moon. The notes changed from short to long, from gentle to harsh. They all hung upon a single harmony but were not determined by anything. The notes filled the valleys and the gorges, and it was useless for you to try to block them out or protect your spirit, for such notes move as they wish. The notes are measured and are clear and sharp. So the ghosts and the spirits hide in the dark, and the sun, moon and stars follow their own courses. I stopped when the music stopped but the sounds flowed on. This worried you; you could not understand it; you looked for them, but could not see them; you went after them, but could not find them. You were stunned and so you stood before the universal witness of the Tao or leaned against an old tree and groaned. Your eyes could not understand and so failed you; your strength collapsed beneath you. I could not catch it. Your body dissolved into emptiness and you lost control and so achieved release. It was this which wore you out.

'In the final section, I used notes that did not wear you out. I brought them together spontaneously. This seemed like chaos, like a thicket sprung from one root, like natural music produced from no one knows what, moving yet going nowhere, hidden in deep darkness. Some call this death, others life. Some call it fruit, others the flower. The notes moved, flowed, separated and changed, following no clear pattern. Understandably, the world is uncertain about them. The world sought advice from the sages, believing the sage to know true shape and true fate. When Heaven has not wound up the spring of life, but the five vital organs are all there ready, this is what is known as the music of Heaven, which delights the heart without words. So the Lord of Yen praised it saying, "Listening for it, you do not hear it; looking for it, you do not see its shape. It fills all Heaven and Earth, embracing the six directions." You desire to hear it, but it is beyond you, which is what confused you.

'I first performed the music which would induce awe, and because of this awe, fear arose like some spectre. Next I came up with weariness and this weariness brought on compliance in you. I ended with confusion and this made you feel stupid. But this stupidity reveals the Tao, the Tao that can be carried with you, wherever you are.'

Confucius was travelling in the west, in Wei State. Yen Yuan asked musician Chin, 'What do you think of the way my Master proceeds?'

Musician Chin replied, 'It's a shame! It seems likely to end in problems!'

'Why's that?' said Yen Yuan.

'The straw dogs,[57] before they are set out for the sacrifice, are kept in a basket which is covered by a beautifully designed embroidery. Meanwhile, the representatives of the dead and the official in charge of the rituals pray and prepare themselves to fetch the straw dogs. However, once they have been presented, they are just

57. Models used at sacrifices to distract evil spirits, which were thrown away afterwards.

trampled on, head and back, by those around. The left-over bits are swept up and burnt by the grass-cutters. That's all they're worth by then. If anyone takes them and puts them back in their baskets, covers them again with the embroidery and then hangs around or even lies down beside them to sleep, he will either have fearful dreams or, more likely, constant nightmares.

'Now your Master seems to have picked up some straw dogs originating from previous kings and has summoned his followers to lie down and sleep beneath them. The result was that the tree was chopped down in Sung; he was forced out of Wei; he got into considerable problems in Shang and Chou. Aren't these events like bad dreams? He was besieged in Chen and Tsai, and for seven days he had no cooked food, leaving him suspended between death and life. Aren't these events like nightmares?

'If you're travelling by water, using a boat is a good idea: if you're travelling by land, try using a carriage. The boat is fine for travelling by water, but if you try and drag it across the land, you can try for a whole lifetime but it is unlikely to go very far. Are not the past and the present like water and land? Are not the states of Chou and Lu like the boat and carriage? To try nowadays to behave in Lu as if you were in Chou is like trying to drag the boat across the land: a great deal of effort for no return, and harmful to one's self as well. Anyone who tries to do so does not understand that the efforts and the works of one age cannot, without great contortions, be made to fit another age.

'Have you never seen a well-pump in action? Pull it up, down it goes, let go and up it comes. So, people pull it, it is not the pump that is pulling the people. Thus, whether it rises or falls, the well-pump itself cannot be blamed by people. Therefore, it is the same with the rituals and prescriptions of the Three August Ones and the Five Emperors,[58] who gained their reputation not from being the same, but through their ability to govern. As a result we can compare the Three August Ones and the Five Emperors to haws,

58. The two main categories of mythological early rulers of China. The Three August Ones were Fu Hsi, Nu Kua and Shen Nung. The Five Emperors were the Yellow Emperor, Chuan Hsu, Kao Hsin, Yao and Shun.

pears, oranges and lemons. Their taste is quite distinct but all can enjoyably be eaten.

'So it is with rituals and prescriptions – they change according to the age. Now, take a monkey and dress it up to look like the Duke of Chou and the poor monkey will struggle and bite until he has got rid of the clothes. Look carefully and you will see that the past and present are like the monkey and the Duke of Chou. Take the case of Hsi Shih, the famous beauty, whose heart was troubled and so she often frowned on those around her. An ugly woman of the area saw the beauty of Hsi Shih, went home, lamented, and frowned on those around her. As soon as they saw her, the wealthy people in the area slammed their gates shut and refused to venture out! When the poor people saw her, they rushed to gather up their women and children and fled! This poor woman knew that a frown could be beautiful but she did not know why a frown could be beautiful. Poor soul!

'It's all up for your Master!'

Confucius had pottered along for fifty-one years and had never heard anyone speak of the Tao until he went south to Pei and went to see Lao Tzu.

Lao Tzu said, 'So you've come then, Sir? I have heard of you, that you are the wise man of the north. Have you, Sir, followed the Tao?'

'I have not yet followed it,' replied Confucius.

'Well, Sir, where have you looked?'

'I looked for it in what can be measured and regulated, but even after five years I still haven't been able to find it.'

'So, Sir, what did you do then?' asked Lao Tzu.

'I looked for it in yin and yang, but ten, twelve years went by and I still couldn't find it.'

'Obviously!' said Lao Tzu. 'If the Tao could be served up, everyone would serve it up to their lords. If the Tao could be offered, there is no one who would not offer it to their parents. If the Tao could be spoken of, there is no one who would not speak of it to their brothers and sisters. If the Tao could be passed on, there is no one who would not pass it on to their heirs. However, it obviously cannot be so and the reason is as follows.

'If there is no true centre within to receive it,
it cannot remain;
if there is no true direction outside to guide it,
it cannot be received.
If the true centre is not brought out
it cannot receive on the outside.
The sage cannot draw it forth.
If what comes in from the outside is not welcomed by the true
    centre,
then the sage cannot let it go.
Fame is something sought by all,
but don't go for too much of it.
Benevolence and righteousness are as the houses of the former
    kings,
useful for one night's shelter,
but don't stay there too long.
To stay long causes considerable adverse comment.

'The perfect man of old walked the Tao of benevolence, a path which he took on loan; he used righteousness as a place to lodge for a night. So it was that he ambled through the void and uncontrolled places; found food in the open fields and enjoyed the gardens which were not his. To be in such freedom, you must take actionless action. The open fields make living easy. He gives nothing and requires nothing. The ancient ones knew this as the wandering of the Truth Gatherer.

'Someone who believes wealth is the most important thing cannot give up their income; someone who seeks pre-eminence cannot give up the hunt for fame; those who love power cannot hand it over to others.

'Those who cling to things like these are usually fearful. Letting them go just once causes such agony that they will not consider even once doing so, although it would show them the folly of their ways. These are people bearing the punishment of Heaven. Hatred and kindness, taking and giving, correction and instruction, life and death, these eight things are tools of reform. However, only the one who abides by the great change and who does not stand in its way can use them. So it is said, to correct is to reform. If the heart cannot accept this, then the gate of Heaven is not opened.'

Confucius went to see Lao Tzu and talked with him about benevolence and righteousness. Lao Tzu said, 'If you get grit in your eye from winnowing chaff, then Heaven and Earth and the four directions get mixed up. A mosquito or gadfly which stings you can keep you awake all night. And benevolence and righteousness, when forced upon us, disturb your heart and produce great distress. You, Sir, if you want to stop everything below Heaven losing its original simplicity, you must travel with the wind and stand firm in Virtue. Why do you exert yourself so much, banging a big drum and hunting for a lost child? The snow goose doesn't need a daily bath to stay white, nor does the crow need to be stained every day to stay black. Black and white comes from natural simplicity, not from argument. Fame and fortune, though sought after, do not make people greater than they actually are. When the waters dry up and the fish are stranded on the dry land, they huddle together and try to keep each other moist by spitting and wetting each other. But wouldn't it be even better if they could just forget each other, safe in their lakes and rivers?'

After seeing Lao Tzu, Confucius went home and for three days he said nothing. His followers asked him, 'Master, now you have seen Lao Tzu, what do you make of him?'

'I have now seen a dragon!' said Confucius. 'A dragon coils up to show its form, it stretches out to display its power. It rides upon the breath of the clouds and is nourished by yin and yang. My mouth gaped open and I could not shut it. What can I say about Lao Tzu?'

Tzu Kung said, 'So it is really true that this man can be as still as the dead and see like a dragon, have a voice like thunder and be as still as deep waters? Can he travel through Heaven and Earth? Could I also set off to meet him?' So, with a note from Confucius, he set off to see Lao Tzu.

Lao Tzu sat himself down and spoke softly: 'I have seen many years roll by. What do you want, Sir?'

Tzu Kung replied, 'The Three August Ones and the Five Emperors ruled all under Heaven, but not in the same way, yet their fame is as the same. Sir, why do you not consider them as sages?'

'Come a little closer, my boy!' said Lao Tzu. 'Why do you say they were not the same?'

'Yao gave the throne to Shun and Shun gave it to Yu. Yu drew upon his strength and Tang resorted to war. King Wen was faithful to Chou and did not rebel. King Wu revolted against Chou and would not be loyal. This is why I say they were different.'[59]

'Come a little closer, my boy! I will tell you how the Three August Ones and the Five Emperors ruled the whole world. The Yellow Emperor ruled everything below Heaven in such a way as to make the hearts of all people one. If someone's parents died, but he did not cry, none of the people blamed him. Yao ruled the whole world in such as way as to make the hearts of the people truly affectionate. So, if someone wished to mourn for a longer or shorter period for other relatives than they did for their parents, none of the people blamed them.

'Shun ruled all under Heaven in such a way as to make the hearts of all the people divided. The wives gave birth to the children after ten months. By the time they were five months old, these children were talking; they were already calling people by their proper titles when they were still just babies. It was then that premature death first began.

'Yu ruled all under Heaven in such a way as to make the hearts of the people change. As a result, each person was felt to have their own heart and warfare was seen as legitimate. They killed thieves but not others. Everyone in the world seemed only concerned with his own self. This meant the whole world was full of anxiety, and from this came the Literati and the Mohists. For the first time ever they created the regulation of behaviour, but what would they say today about the customs of marrying wives and daughters?

'Let me tell you frankly about the Three August Ones and the

59. This paragraph describes the last rulers of the Three Dynasties and their successors or usurpers.

Five Emperors and their rule – for it can be called ruling, although it was nothing less than terrible chaos. The knowledge of the Three August Ones rose up like a cloud against the clarity of light of the sun and moon; bore down upon the tranquillity of the hills and rivers and levelled the distinctive aspects of the flow of the four seasons. Their knowledge was more deadly than the sting of the scorpion or the bite of a beast. Unable to be true to their innate natures and being, they still saw themselves as sages. Is this not shameful, that they were not ashamed?'

Tzu Kung was deeply shocked and knew not what to say.

Confucius said to Lao Tzu, 'I have mastered the *Poems*, the *Histories*, the *Rites*, the *Music*, the *I Ching* and the *Spring and Autumn* – all of the Six Classics. I know them inside out. However, I have discussed them with seventy-two rulers, telling them of the Tao of the first kinds and the illumination of the path trodden by Chou and Shao, but not one king has been interested. They've done nothing! It is so difficult to preach to such people! How can I make the Tao clear to them?'

Lao Tzu said, 'It is very lucky, Sir, that you did not discover a ruler who would try to govern this generation in such a way! The Six Classics are the tired footpaths of the first kings, not the actual feet that trod those paths! Now, Sir, what you are going on about is just these worn footpaths. But footpaths are created by the feet that first walked them. They are not the feet themselves! The white herons only have to look into each other's eyes without blinking for impregnation to happen. A male insect buzzes above and the female replies from below and impregnation takes place, borne upon the air. The creature called Lei contains both male and female and so impregnates itself. Innate nature does not change; fate is unalterable; time cannot be stopped and the Tao cannot be halted. Hold fast to the Tao and there is nothing it cannot do; lose it and there is nothing that can be done.'

Confucius did not go out for three months, then he went to see Lao Tzu and said, 'I've grasped it! The raven hatches its young; the fish spew forth their eggs; the slim-waisted wasp transforms, and when a younger brother comes along the elder brother weeps. For too long I have not been able to work in harmony with these changes. So, given that I did not play my part in harmony with others, how could I expect to change people?'

Lao Tzu replied, 'Well done. So now you've grasped it.'

CHAPTER 15

Rigid and Arrogant

To be rigid and arrogant;
to be above this generation and distant from its ways;
to talk of great principles;
to be critical and disparaging:
these are approved by scholars who dwell in the mountains, by
men who are not of this age, who are worn and weary or who cast
themselves into the deep.

To preach about benevolence, righteousness, loyalty and
    faithfulness;
to be humble, moderate, selfless and civil:
these are the marks of self-development and are the signs of the
scholars who wish to reform this generation. These are approved by
the one who wishes to preach and teach, whether at home or
abroad.

To talk of great achievements;
to make a great name;
to arrange the rituals between ruler and minister;
to sort out those above from those below;
to organize the ruling of the state:
this is what is approved by the scholar who values the court and
state, who loves his ruler and honours his country, who does what
he can and who seizes lands.

To live amongst the wilds and lakes;
to dwell in isolated places;

to fish alone;
actionless action:
this is what is approved by the scholar who retreats to the rivers
and seas, who leaves this generation alone, who is in no hurry.

Huffing, puffing;
grunting and groaning;
expelling the old breath and taking in the new;
undertaking physical exercises to preserve the body and soul;
long life his sole concern:
this is what is approved, this is the Tao of the scholar who infuses
his self with breath, feeding his body, hoping to live as long as Peng
Tsu.

To achieve loftiness without the burden of bias;
to follow the ways of improvement without benevolence or
    righteousness;
to rule successfully without achievement or fame;
who rest without rivers and oceans;
long life without organization;
to lose everything and yet to have all;
to drift calmly and endlessly, while all good things pay court to
    them:
this is the Tao of Heaven and Earth, the Virtue of the sages.

The saying goes, 'Calm, detachment, silence, quiet, emptiness and
actionless action, these are what maintain Heaven and Earth, the
Tao and Virtue.' The saying goes, 'The sage rests, truly rests and is
at ease.' This manifests itself in his calmness and detachment, so that
worries and distress cannot affect him, nothing unpleasant can
disturb him, his Virtue is complete and his spirit is not stirred up.

The saying goes, that the sage's life is the outworking of Heaven
and his death is the transformation of everything. When he is still,
his Virtue is like yin; when he is moving, his pervasiveness is like
yang. He brings neither good fortune nor bad. He acts and moves
in response to forces beyond. When he finds something, he rises up.
He ignores knowledge and nostalgia, following only the pattern of

Heaven. So he risks no disaster from Heaven, nor complications from things, no accusation from anyone, no charges from the spirits of the dead. In life he floats; at death he rests. He does not consider and plot, nor design for the future. He shines but is not seen; his good faith has no record; his sleep is dreamless and he wakes without fear. His spirit is pure and without blemish; his soul never tires. Empty, selfless, calm and detached, he is in harmony with Heaven's Virtue.

It is said that sadness and happiness are corruptions of Virtue; joy and anger are errors of the Tao; goodness and evil are contrary to Virtue. So, for the heart to be without sadness and happiness, is to have perfected Virtue. To be one and changeless, this is to have perfected stillness; to encounter no opposition is to have perfected emptiness; to have no dealings with anything is to have perfected indifference; to have no feelings of dissent is to have perfected purity. So it is said that, if the body is overworked and is allowed no rest, it will collapse, and if the spirit is employed without stopping, it becomes tired and eventually reaches exhaustion.

Water, if not mixed with other things, is by nature clear, and if it is not stirred up, it is level. However, if it is blocked and cannot flow, it cannot remain clear. This is like the Virtue of Heaven. It is said that to be innocent and pure, free from contamination, still and level, never changing, detached and acting without action, is to move with Heaven and to follow the Tao of sustaining the spirit. To have a sword like Kan Yueh, you must look after it in a special box and hardly dare use it, for this is the greatest of treasures. The spirit emanates in all four directions, without restriction, rising to Heaven and sinking down to enfold the Earth. It changes and nourishes all forms of life yet no one can find its shape. Its title is Harmony in the Supreme.

It is only the Tao of true simplicity which guards the spirit; if you are guarded and never lost, you become one with the spirit. In being one you are in communion with the Order of Heaven. Peasant wisdom says, 'The common people prize profit above all else; the worthy scholar, fame; the wise man, ambition and the sage his essential purity.' Simplicity means no mixing; purity means an unimpaired spirit. The one who manifests simplicity and purity can truly be called the true man.

CHAPTER 16

The Deceived and Ignorant Ones

These are the people who are called the deceived and ignorant ones: those who seek to improve their innate nature by means of vulgar learning in order to return to their origin, and those who wish to control their desires by following vulgar ways of thinking in the hope of achieving illumination.

The ancient ones ruled by the Tao:
they developed their understanding in calm;
knowledge was their life, yet they did nothing with knowledge.
When knowledge and calm nourish each other,
then harmony and order emerge as from innate nature.
Virtue is harmony; the Tao is order.
When Virtue enfolds everything, there is benevolence.
When the Tao is set out in order, there is righteousness.
When righteousness is clearly understood and all adhere to it,
    there is loyalty.
When the centre is pure and true and returns to its proper form,
    there is music.
When sincerity is articulated through the body and is expressed
    in style, there is ritual.

However, following ritual and music in an inappropriate way will lead the whole world into confusion. When someone tries to correct others, his own Virtue is clouded over, and his Virtue will no longer reach all others. Trying to do so will destroy everyone's innate nature.

Even in chaos, the ancient ones were centred, for they were one with their generation and followed the paths of simplicity and silence. In those times, yin and yang were in harmony, ghosts and spirits did nothing wicked, the four seasons followed each other, all forms of life were without injury and no living thing suffered early death. The people had knowledge but they did not use it; all this was perfect Oneness. In those times no one planned anything, for everyone maintained constant spontaneity.

This was the case until the time when Virtue deteriorated and then Sui Jen and Fu Hsi came to govern everything below Heaven, with the result that there was compliance but no unity. Virtue continued to deteriorate and then Shen Nung and the Yellow Emperor came to govern everything below Heaven, with the result that there was satisfaction but no compliance. Virtue continued to deteriorate and then Yao and Shun came to govern all below Heaven, with the result that, ruling by decrees and grand plans, they polluted the purity of nature and destroyed simplicity. The Tao was abandoned and Good substituted. Virtue was put at risk for the sake of opportunity. Then innate nature was abandoned and hearts allowed to determine their own way. Heart linked with heart through knowledge, but were unable to give the world peace. Pomp and ceremony were added to this knowledge. This displaced simplicity and the heart was swamped, resulting in the people being confused and disobedient, with no way back to true innate nature nor to their origin.

Perceiving this, we can see how the world has lost the Tao, and the Tao has lost this world. In this sort of world, how can the Tao lead the world, or a person of the Tao be seen by this world, or the world come to appreciate the Tao? The Tao cannot direct the world, nor the world direct the Tao. Even if the sage does not retreat to the centre of the forest and mountains, nevertheless his Virtue is still hidden, whether he likes it or not.

These hidden so-called scholars of old did not hide themselves and refuse to be seen. They did not close the doors on their words and refuse to let them out. They did not shut away their wisdom and refuse to share it. But those times were all haywire. If it had been possible for them to act, they could have done great things, bringing all to Oneness without any sign of doing so. However, the times were not favourable and it was not possible, so they put down deep roots, remained still and waited. This was the Tao by which they survived.

The ancient ones, wishing to keep themselves alive, did not use elaborate style to express their knowledge. They did not disturb everything in the whole world through their knowledge, nor use knowledge to try and disrupt Virtue. Alone and hermit-like they stayed where they were and looked to restore their innate nature. What more could they do than this? The Tao has no place for pettiness, and nor has Virtue. Pettiness is dangerous to Virtue; petty actions are dangerous to the Tao. It is said, rectify yourself and be done. Happiness which is complete is called the Timeliness of Purpose.

The ancient ones talked of the Timeliness of Purpose, but they did not mean having official carriages and badges of office. They simply meant that it was happiness so complete as to need nothing more. Today what is called Timeliness of Purpose means having official carriages and badges of office. Carriages and badges are of the body, they do not touch the innate nature. From time to time such benefits may come. When this happens, you cannot help it, no more than you can stop them going again. So having carriages and badges of office is no reason for becoming proud and arrogant in our purposes, nor are distress and poverty any reason for becoming vulgar. View both conditions as one and the same, so be free from anxiety and leave it at that. So if loss of what gives happiness causes you distress when it fades, you can now understand that such happiness is worthless. It is said, those who lose themselves in their desire for things also lose their innate nature by being vulgar. They are known as people who turn things upside down.

CHAPTER 17

Season of Autumn Floods

The season of the autumn floods had come and the hundred rivers were pouring into the Yellow River. The waters were churning and so wide that, looking across from one bank to the other, it was impossible to distinguish an ox from a horse. At this the Lord of the Yellow River was decidedly pleased, thinking that the most beautiful thing in the whole world belonged to him. Flowing with the river, he travelled east until he came at last to the North Ocean, where he looked east and could see no end to the waters. He shook his head, the Lord of the Yellow River, and looked out to confront Jo, god of the Ocean, sighing and saying,

'The folk proverb says, "The person who has heard of the Tao a hundred times thinks he is better than anyone else." This refers to me. I have heard people mock the scholarship of the Confucians and give scant regard to the righteousness of Po Yi, but I didn't believe them. Now I have seen your endless vastness. If I had not come to your gate, I would have been in danger, and been mocked by those of the Great Method.'

Jo of the North Ocean replied, 'A frog in a well cannot discuss the ocean, because he is limited by the size of his well. A summer insect cannot discuss ice, because it knows only its own season. A narrow-minded scholar cannot discuss the Tao, because he is constrained by his teachings. Now you have come out of your banks and seen the Great Ocean. You now know your own inferiority, so it is now possible to discuss great principles with you. Under Heaven there are no greater waters than the ocean. Ten thousand rivers flow into it, and it has never been known to stop, but it never fills. At Wei Lu the water disappears but the ocean never empties. Spring and autumn bring no changes. It pays no attention to floods or droughts. It is so much more than the waters of the Yangtze and the Yellow Rivers, it is impossible to estimate. However, I have never made much of this. I just compare myself with Heaven and Earth and my life-breath I receive from yin and yang. I am just a little stone or a little tree set on a great hill, in comparison to Heaven and Earth. As I perceive my own inferiority, how could I ever be proud?

'To compare all the space filled by the four oceans, is it not like a pile of stones beside a marsh in comparison with the vastness between Heaven and Earth? To compare China with all the space between the oceans, is it not like one single piece of grain in a granary? When talking of all life, we count them in tens of thousands, and humanity is just one of them. People inhabit the Nine Provinces, but humanity is just one portion of all the life that is sustained by grain, wherever carriages or boats can go. In comparison to all the multitudinous forms of life, isn't humanity like just a single hair on a horse?

'What the Five Emperors handed on, the Three Kings[60] argued over, the officials have struggled for, and benevolent people worry about, is nothing more than this. Po Yi was considered famous, because he gave up things, Confucius was known as scholarly, because he taught about it. Yet, in acting in such a way, making much of themselves, were they not like you who just now were so proud of yourself because of your flood?'

The Lord of the Yellow River said, 'Very well, so if I recognize Heaven and Earth as big and a tip of a hair as small, will that do?'

'No,' replied Jo of the North Ocean. 'You cannot define the capacity of things; time never stops; there is nothing constant in fate; beginning and end have no regulation.

'Great knowledge considers both that which is near and that which is far off, sees that which is small as not insignificant, sees that

---

60. The Three Kings were the founders of the Three Dynasties Hsia, Shang and Chou.

which is large as not necessarily significant, knowing that you cannot define the capacity of things.

'Great knowledge has a clear understanding of the past and present, which is why it can be unconcerned by the remoteness of the past and not worry about striving to grasp the present, for it knows that time never stops.

'Great knowledge understands the differences between fullness and emptiness, and is neither exalted by success nor disheartened by failure, for it knows of the inconsistency of fate.

'Great knowledge knows the straight and quiet road, so it does not get excited about life nor dejected by death, for it knows that neither beginning nor end is regulated.

'What people know is as nothing to what they don't know. The time since they were born is nothing in comparison to the time before they were born. When people take something minor and try to make it major, this is the path to mistake and confusion and they cannot achieve what they set out to do. Consider it thus: how can you know the tip of a hair can be used as a measure of smallness? How can we know that Heaven and Earth are equal to being the measure of the truly great?'

The Lord of the Yellow River said, 'The debaters of this generation say, "The tiniest thing has no body, the most enormous thing cannot be contained." Are these words true?'

Jo of the North Ocean replied, 'From the viewpoint of the tiniest, we look at what is so enormous and we cannot comprehend it. From the viewpoint of the most enormous, we look at what is tiniest and we cannot see it clearly. The tiniest is the smallest of the small, the biggest is the largest of the large; so we must distinguish between them, even though this is just a matter of circumstance. However, both the coarse and the refined have form. Without any form, there is no way to enumerate them. What can be said in words is the coarseness of things; what can be grasped through ideas is the subtlety of things. But words cannot describe nor ideas grasp, and this has nothing to do with coarseness or refinement.

'So it is that the great man through his actions will not set out to harm others, nor make much of benevolence and charity; he does not make any move for gain, nor consider the servant at the gate as lowly; he will not barter for property and riches, nor does he make much of his having turned them down; he asks for no one's help, nor does he make much of his own self-reliance, nor despise the greedy and mean, he does not follow the crowd, nor does he make much of being so different; he comes behind the crowd, but does not make much of those who get ahead through flattery. The titles and honours of this world are of no interest to him, nor is he concerned at the disgrace of punishments. He knows there is no distinction between right and wrong, nor between great and little. I have heard it said, "The Tao man earns no reputation, perfect Virtue is not followed, the great man is self-less." In perfection, this is the path he follows.'

The Lord of the Yellow River asked, 'Whether they are external or internal, how come we have these distinctions between noble and mean? Why do we distinguish between small and great?'

'Viewed from the perspective of the Tao,' said Jo of the North Ocean, 'things are neither elevated nor lowly. Viewed from the perspective of things, each one considers itself as elevated and the rest as lowly. Viewed from the perspective of the everyday opinion, neither elevation nor lowliness is to be understood from the perspective of individual things. Taking into account differing views, something which is seen as big because it is big means that, in all the multitudes of life, everything can be viewed as big. Likewise, if something is seen as small because it is small, then all forms of life can be viewed as small. If we know that Heaven and Earth are as tiny as a grain or the tip of a hair is as vast as a mountain range, then we will have grasped that our understanding of size is relative. In terms of what each does, we view something as useful because it is useful, which means that, in all the multitudes of life, everything can be viewed as useful. In the same way, if something is viewed as useless because it appears useless, then all forms of life can be viewed as useless. If we know that east and west are opposite each other, but also need each other, then we can understand how mutual exchange and interaction work. Viewed from the perspective of choice, if something is seen as good because it undoubtedly is good, then in all the multitudes of life there is nothing which is not good. Likewise, if something is viewed as wrong because it undoubtedly is wrong, then there is no form of life which cannot be viewed as wrong. If we understand that Yao and Chieh both considered themselves good, but saw the other as wrong, then we can understand how we perceive things differently.

'In the past Yao gave way to Shun and Shun ruled as Emperor. Ki Kuai[61] resigned and was disgraced. Chih ruled then and was finished off. Tang and Wu struggled and became kings. Duke Po[62] struggled and was executed. Looking at these models of struggle and defeat, acting like Yao or like Chieh, we can see that there is a time for noble behaviour and a time to be mean. There is nothing fixed about either. A battering ram can be used to storm a city wall but it is useless for filling a little hole: there is a difference here of function. The horses Chih Chi and Hua Liu could cover a thousand miles in a day, but were useless for catching rats, unlike a wild dog or weasel: there is a difference in skills. At night the horned owl can catch even a flea or spot the tip of a hair; in daylight, no matter how hard it tries, its eyes cannot see even a hill or mountain: there is a difference of nature. There is a saying, "Shouldn't we follow the right but not make wrong our ruler?" To do so shows that you have not been illuminated by Heaven and Earth and by the multitudinous differences of all life. This is like being a devout follower of Heaven and ignoring Earth, or like being a devout follower of yin and ignoring yang. It is quite clear this is not possible.

'Now, it is certainly the case that people talk like this endlessly, like fools or con-men. Emperors and kings have different ways of abdicating, and the Three Dynasties have different hereditary succession. Anyone who behaves differently from the customs of his time and contrary to its ways is called a rebel. Whoever complies and goes with the prevailing customs is called a friend of righteousness.

'Be quiet, be quiet, Lord of the Yellow River! How could you know anything about the gateway to nobility or meanness or the dwelling place of greatness or pettiness?'

61. King Ki Kuai of Yen was urged to imitate Yao and to abdicate. He did this in 316 BC and Tzu Chi, his minister, took over, but it was a disaster.
62. He launched an assault on his relatives, who ruled Chu, trying to emulate the Dynastic founders Tang (of the Shang) and Wu (of the Chou), but he failed.

'All right then,' said the Lord of the Yellow River. 'What am I to do and what may I not do? How can I decide what is worth keeping or rejecting and what is worth going for or leaving?'

Jo of the North Ocean said, 'Viewed from the perspective of the Tao, what is noble and what is mean are both just ceaseless changes. Don't cling to your own ideas, for this is contrary to the greatness of the Tao. What is little and what is much, these are terms of very limited use. Do not try to be just One, this just highlights how far away you are from the Tao. Be stern and strict like a ruler of a country who favours no one. Be gentle, be gentle like the local earth god to whom offerings are made and who does not grant fortune selfishly. Be open like air, like the four compass points shed light but do not permit boundaries. If you lovingly tend all forms of life, how could you favour one? This is known as being impartial. Consider all life as unified and then how could you talk in terms of long or short? The Tao has neither beginning nor end, but all living things have both death and birth, so you cannot be sure of them. One moment they are empty, the next moment full. They are unreliable. The years cannot be reversed nor time halted. Decay, maturity, fullness and emptiness, when they end, begin over again. So we can talk of great righteousness, and discuss the fundamental principle within all forms of life. The life force is a headlong gallop, speeding along, changing with every movement and altering every minute. As to what you should and should not do? Just go with this process of change.'

'If this is the case,' said the Lord of the Yellow River, 'then what is so important about the Tao?'

Jo of the North Ocean replied, 'To understand the Tao is to understand the principle. If you understand the principle, you know how to deal with things as they arise. Knowing this, you can ensure that nothing detrimental to yourself occurs. If someone has perfect Virtue, it is not possible for fire to harm, nor for water to drown, nor for either cold or heat to affect, nor birds and beasts to injure him. Not that I say that he dismisses all these things, but that he is able to discriminate between where he is safe and where he is in danger. He is at ease with both calamity and fortune, takes care as to what he approaches or avoids, and therefore nothing harms him.

There is a saying that Heaven is internal, humanity external and Virtue comes from the Heavenly. Know Heaven and humanity's actions, root yourself in Heaven and follow Virtue. Then you can bend, stretch, rush forward or hold back, because you will always return to the core and it will be said you have achieved the supreme.'

'But what do you call the Heavenly? What do you call the human?'

Jo of the North Ocean said, 'Oxen have four feet: this is what I call the Heavenly. When horses are harnessed and oxen have pierced noses, this I call the human way. There is the saying. "Don't allow the human to displace the Heavenly," don't allow your intentions to nullify what is ordained. Be careful, guard it and don't lose it, for this is what I call coming back to the True.'

The one-legged creature is envious of the millipede; the millipede is envious of the snake; the snake is envious of the wind; the wind is envious of the eye; the eye is envious of the heart.

The one-legged creature said to the millipede, 'I have one foot that I hop on and I can hardly go anywhere. But you, Sir, have a multitude of feet. How do you manage?'

The millipede said, 'Don't be so certain. Have you never seen someone spit? Out comes a big blob followed by a spray, which falls down like a shower of uncountable drops. Now I just set the Heavenly machinery in motion and as for the rest – I haven't a clue!'

The millipede said to the snake, 'I get about with all these feet, but I can't keep up with you, Sir, who have no feet. Why is this?'

The snake said, 'I am moved by the designs of Heaven, how can I control that? What could I use feet for!'

The snake said to the wind, 'By moving my backbone and ribs, I get along and at least I have some visible form. Now you, Sir, come hurtling along from the North Ocean and disappear off to the South Ocean but without any visible form. How is that?'

The wind said, 'True, I come hurtling along from the North Ocean and disappear off to the South Ocean. However, it is true that, if you point your finger at me, you are greater than me, or if you stamp on me, you also win. But it is also true that I can bring down great trees and bowl over great houses; only I can do this. Therefore, the one who can overcome all the small problems is in truth the great victor. To have a great victory, why, this is what a sage does.'

Confucius was travelling in Kuang and the men of Sung encompassed him with a number of rings of soldiers,[63] but he went on singing to his lute with no hesitation. Tzu Lu went in to see him and said, 'How is it, Master, that you are so contented?'

'Come!' said Confucius, 'I shall explain to you. For ages I've done my best to avoid difficulties. I have failed, but that's fate. For a long time I have tried to be given an appointment. I have not been given one, such are the times. In Yao and Shun's time, there was no one in the whole wide world who had difficulties, but it was not because of knowledge that this happened. In Chieh and Chou's time, no one in the whole wide world succeeded, but this was not as a result of lack of understanding. This was certainly a sign of the times. Those who travel the waters are not afraid of snakes or dragons: this is the courage of fishermen. To travel overland and not to tremble upon meeting rhinoceroses or tigers, this is the courage of hunters. To see swords clash and to regard death as a return, this is the courage of the bold soldier. To know that hardship is part of life, to know that success depends upon the times and to confront great disasters with fortitude, this is the courage of the sage. Be patient, and my fate will then become clear to you.'

Not long after, the leader of the troops came and humbly said, 'We thought you were Yang Huo and so we surrounded you. Now we know you are not, so we wish to apologize and retreat.'

Kung Sun Lung[64] asked Mou of Wei,[65] 'When I was younger, I learned the Tao of the earlier kings, and as I grew up, I saw clearly the significance of benevolence and righteousness. I brought together difference and similarity, discerned hardness and whiteness, what

63. Apparently they thought he was an enemy of theirs called Yang Huo.
64. A philosopher ridiculed by Chuang Tzu as one who argues about the difference between 'hard' and 'white'.
65. Author of a 'Taoist' text, now lost.

was certain and what was not, what was possible and what was not. I laboured at understanding the Hundred Schools of Philosophy[66] and spoke out against their teachings. I thought I had understanding of all things. Now, however, I have heard the words of Chuang Tzu, and to my surprise I am disturbed by them. Is it that my knowledge is not as good as his, or is it that his understanding is greater? I find I can't even open my mouth, so I ask you what I can do.'

Duke Tzu Mou leaned forward, sighed heavily, looked to Heaven, smiled and said, 'Dear Sir, have you not heard of the frog in the broken-down old well? He said to the turtle of the Eastern Ocean, "I have a great time! I leap on to the well wall, or I go down in the well, stepping along the broken bricks. When I enter the water, I float with it supporting my chin, feet up; on the mud, I dig my feet deep in. I look about me at the larvae, crabs and tadpoles and there is none that is as good as I. To have complete control of the waters of the gorge and not to wish to move but to enjoy the old well, this is great! Dear Sir, why don't you come down and see me sometime?"

'The turtle of the Eastern Ocean tried, but before he had put his left foot into the well, his right knee was stuck. At this he paused, shuffled out backwards and then began to speak about the ocean. "A distance such as a thousand miles doesn't come close to describing its length, nor a depth of a thousand leagues describe its deepness. In the time of Yu, nine years in every ten there were floods, but this did not raise the ocean an inch. In the time of Tang, seven years in every eight there were droughts, but this did not lower the ocean shore an inch. Nothing changes these waters, neither in the short term nor in the long term; they neither recede nor advance, grow larger nor smaller. This is the great happiness of the Eastern Ocean." When the frog in the broken-down old well heard this, he was utterly amazed and astonished; he was utterly astonished, dumbfounded and at a loss.

'For someone whose understanding can't handle such knowledge,

66. Traditional title for the remarkable flourishing of different schools of philosophy between the sixth and fourth centuries BC.

such debates about right and wrong, if they persist in trying to see through the words of Chuang Tzu, it is like a mosquito trying to carry a mountain on its back, or a scuttle bug rushing as fast as the Yellow River. This is plainly impossible. For someone whose understanding cannot handle such knowledge, such words of subtlety, all they are capable of is gaining some short-term reward. They are like the frog in the broken-down well, are they not? But Chuang Tzu is not planted firmly in the Yellow Springs of the Underworld, nor leaping, jumping into the stratosphere. There is neither south nor north: he scatters freely to the four points of the compass, and disappears into the depth. There is neither east nor west: starting in the darkest depth, he comes back to the great path. Then you, Sir, you in your astonishment try to sift his views to criticize them, or trawl through them in order to debate. Why, this is like trying to examine Heaven through a narrow tube or using an awl to explore the whole earth. Such tools are too small, aren't they? You, Sir, be on your way! Or possibly, Sir, you have not heard of the young students of Shou Ling and how things went for them in Han Tan? Having not yet learnt the lessons that the people of that country were trying to teach them, they forgot what they had learnt at home, so were reduced to crawling back home. So, Sir, if you don't get out now, you will forget, Sir, what you already knew and fail, Sir, in your career!'

Kung Sun Lung's mouth fell open and would not shut, his tongue stuck to the roof of his mouth and wouldn't drop down, and he shuffled off and ran away.

Chuang Tzu was one day fishing in the Pu river when the King of Chu despatched two senior officials to visit him with a message. The message said, 'I would like to trouble you to administer my lands.'

Chuang Tzu kept a firm grip on his fishing rod and said, 'I hear that in Chu there is a sacred tortoise[67] which died three thousand years ago. The King keeps this in his ancestral temple, wrapped and enclosed. Tell me, would this tortoise have wanted to die and leave

---

67. Used for divination and oracles.

his shell to be venerated? Or would he rather have lived and continued to crawl about in the mud?'

The two senior officials said, 'It would rather have lived and continued to crawl about in the mud.'

Chuang Tzu said, 'Shove off, then! I will continue to crawl about in the mud!'

Hui Tzu was made Minister of State in Liang and Chuang Tzu went to see him. Someone told Hui Tzu, 'Chuang Tzu is coming, because he wants to oust you from your office.' This alarmed Hui Tzu and he scoured the kingdom for three days and nights trying to find this stranger.

Chuang Tzu went to see him and said, 'In the south there is a bird known as the Young Phoenix, do you know about this, Sir? This bird, it arises in the Southern Ocean and flies to the Northern Ocean and it never rests on anything except the begonia tree, never eats except the fruit of the melia azederach and never drinks except from springs of sweet water. There was once an owl who had clutched in his talons a rotting rat corpse. As the Young Phoenix flew overhead the owl looked up and said, "Shoo!" Now you, Sir, you have the state of Liang and you feel you have to shoo me away?'

Chuang Tzu and Hui Tzu were walking beside the weir on the River Hao, when Chuang Tzu said, 'Do you see how the fish are coming to the surface and swimming around as they please? That's what fish really enjoy.'

'You're not a fish,' replied Hui Tzu, 'so how can you say you know what fish enjoy?'

Chuang Tzu said: 'You are not me, so how can you know I don't know what fish enjoy?'

Hui Tzu said: 'I am not you, so I definitely don't know what it is you know. However, you are most definitely not a fish and that proves that you don't know what fish really enjoy.'

Chuang Tzu said: 'Ah, but let's return to the original question you raised, if you don't mind. You asked me how I could know what it is that fish really enjoy. Therefore, you already knew I knew it when you asked the question. And I know it by being here on the edge of the River Hao.'

CHAPTER 18

Perfect Happiness

Is it possible anywhere in this whole wide world to have perfect happiness or not? Is there a way to keep yourself alive or not? Now, what can be done and what is to be trusted? What should be avoided and what adhered to? What should be pursued and what abandoned? Where is happiness and where is evil?

What the whole wide world values is riches, position, long life and fame.

What brings happiness is good times for oneself, fine foods, beautiful clothes, lovely sights and sweet music.

What is despised is poverty, meanness, untimely death and a bad reputation.

What is considered sour is a lifestyle which gives the self no rest, a mouth which never has fine foods, a body without good clothes, eyes that never rest upon lovely views, an ear that never hears sweet music.

Those who cannot get these things become greatly agitated and fearful. This is a foolish way to treat the body!

Those who are wealthy weary themselves dashing around working, getting more and more riches, beyond what they need. The body is treated therefore as just an external thing.

Those in positions of power spend day and night plotting and pondering about what to do. The body is treated in a very careless way. People live their lives, constantly surrounded by anxiety. If they live long before dying, they end up in senility, worn out by concerns: a terrible fate! The body is treated in a very harsh fashion. Courageous men are seen by everyone under Heaven as worthy, but this doesn't preserve them from death. I am not sure I know whether this is sensible or not. Possibly it is, but it does nothing towards saving them. Possibly it is not, but it does save other people. It is said, 'If a friend doesn't listen to the advice you offer him, then bow out and don't argue.' After all, Tzu Hsu argued and lost his life.[68] If he had not argued, he would not be famous. Is it possible that there really is goodness, or not?

Now, when ordinary people attempt to find happiness, I'm not sure whether the happiness found is really happiness or not. I study what ordinary people do to find happiness, what they struggle for, rushing about apparently unable to stop. They say they are happy, but I am not happy and I am not unhappy either. Ultimately, do they have happiness or not? I regard actionless action as worthy of being called happiness, though the ordinary people regard it as a great burden. It is said: 'Perfect happiness is not happiness, perfect glory is not glory.'

The whole world is incapable of judging either right or wrong. But it is certain that actionless action can judge both right and wrong. Perfect happiness is keeping yourself alive, and only actionless action can have this effect. This is why I want to say:

Heaven does without doing through its purity,
Earth does without doing through its calmness.

Thus the two combine their actionless action and all forms of life are changed and thus come out again to live! Wonder of wonders, they have not come from anywhere! All life is mysterious and emerges from actionless action. There is a saying that Heaven and Earth take actionless action, but yet nothing remains undone. Amongst the people, who can follow such actionless action?

Chuang Tzu's wife died and Hui Tzu came to console him, but Chuang Tzu was sitting, legs akimbo, bashing a battered tub and singing.

Hui Tzu said, 'You lived as man and wife, she reared your children. At her death surely the least you should be doing is to be

68. Wu Tzu Hsu tried to alert his master the King of Wu that a neighbouring kingdom would invade. In the end the King grew to distrust Tzu Hsu and made him commit suicide in 484 BC.

on the verge of weeping, rather than banging the tub and singing: this is not right!'

Chuang Tzu said, 'Certainly not. When she first died, I certainly mourned just like everyone else! However, I then thought back to her birth and to the very roots of her being, before she was born. Indeed, not just before she was born but before the time when her body was created. Not just before her body was created but before the very origin of her life's breath. Out of all this, through the wonderful mystery of change she was given her life's breath. Her life's breath wrought a transformation and she had a body. Her body wrought a transformation and she was born. Now there is yet another transformation and she is dead. She is like the four seasons in the way that spring, summer, autumn and winter follow each other. She is now at peace, lying in her chamber, but if I were to sob and cry it would certainly appear that I could not comprehend the ways of destiny. This is why I stopped.'

Uncle Legless and Uncle Cripple were touring the area of the Hill of the Dark Prince and the zone of Kun Lun where the Yellow Emperor stayed.[69] Without warning a willow tree suddenly shot up out of Uncle Cripple's left elbow. He was certainly most surprised and somewhat put out.

'Sir, do you dislike this?' said Uncle Legless.

'No,' said Uncle Cripple. 'What should I dislike? Life exists through scrounging; if life comes through scrounging, then life is like a dump. Death and birth are like the morning and the night. You and I, Sir, observe the ways of transformation and now I am being transformed. So how could I dislike this?'

Chuang Tzu went to Chu to see an ancient desiccated skull, which he prodded with his riding crop, saying, 'Sir, did you follow some unfortunate course which meant you brought dishonour upon your father and mother and family and so end up like this? Sir, was it perhaps the cold and hunger that reduced you to this? Sir, perhaps it was just the steady succession of springs and autumns that brought you to this?'

69. All symbols or places of immortality.

So saying, he pulled the skull towards him and lay down to sleep, using the skull as a head-rest. At midnight he saw the skull in a dream and it said, 'Sir, you gabble on like a public speaker. Every word you say, Sir, shows that you are a man caught up with life. We dead have nothing to do with this. Would you like to hear a discourse upon death, Sir?'

'Certainly,' said Chuang Tzu.

The skull told him, 'The dead have no lord over them, no servants below them. There is none of the work associated with the four seasons, so we live as if our springs and autumns were like Heaven and Earth, unending. Make no mistake, a king facing south could not be happier.'

Chuang Tzu could not believe this and said, 'If I got the Harmonizer of Destinies to bring you back to life, Sir, with a body, flesh and blood, and companions, wouldn't you like that?'

The skull frowned, looked aggrieved and said, 'Why should I want to cast away happiness greater than that of kings and become a burdened human being again?'

Yen Yuan went east to Chi and Confucius looked very anxious. Tzu Kung stood up and asked him, 'May I ask, as a junior master, why you have looked so anxious, Sir, since Hui has gone east to Chi?'

Confucius said, 'That is a very good question! Kuan Tzu[70] had a saying that I think is very apposite. He said, "A small bag cannot hold anything big and a bucket on a short rope cannot reach the water in the depths." Likewise it is also true that destiny has its particular structure and the body its proper uses, which you can neither add to nor subtract from. I am worried that when Hui arrives he will talk to the Duke of Chi about the Tao of Yao, Shun and the Yellow Emperor, and thereafter he will continue by talking about Sui Jen and Shen Nung.[71] The ruler will then try to see if he measures up to all this and will find he does not. As he is unable to measure up he will be distressed and when such a person is distressed – death!

70. Minister of Chi c. 650 BC, admired by Confucius.
71. Sometimes counted as two of the Three August Ones, but more often as mythological progenitors of the Chinese and their civilization.

'Have you never heard this story before? Once upon a time, a seabird alighted in the capital city of Lu. The Earl of Lu carried it in procession to the ancestral shrine, where he played the Nine Shao music and offered the offerings of the sacrifice to it. However, the poor bird just looked confused and lost and did not eat a single piece of meat, nor did it drink even one cup of wine, and within three days it died. The problem was trying to feed a bird on what you eat rather than what a bird needs.

'To feed a bird so it survives, let it live in the midst of the forest, gambol on the shores and inlets, float on the rivers and lakes, devour mudfish and tiddlers, go with the flock, either flying or resting, and be as it wishes. Birds dislike hearing human voices, never mind all the other noises and trouble! If you try to make them happy by playing the Nine Shao music in the area around their lakes, when the birds hear it they will fly away. If the animals hear it, they will run away and hide and if the fish hear it they will dive down to escape. Only the people, if they hear it, will come together to listen.

'Fish can live in water quite contentedly, but if people try it, they die, for different beings need different contexts which are right and proper for them. This is why the ancient sages never expected just one response from the rest of the creatures nor tried to make them conform. Titles should not be over-stretched in trying to capture reality and ideas should be only applied when appropriate, for this is not only sensible, it will bring good fortune.'

Lieh Tzu was following the Tao and one day he was eating by the roadside and saw a one-hundred-year-old skull, which he pulled clear of the weeds and addressed, saying, 'Just you and I know that you never died nor were you ever born. Does this distress you? Do I really enjoy myself?'

Where does everything come from?[72] From the water come creeping plants, from the water's edge comes Frog's Robe, this gives birth to Hill Slippers, and these in turn produce Crow's Feet,

---

72. This entire paragraph assumes traditional Chinese notions of how different species emerge as transmutations of other species.

and Crow's Feet become maggots, and the leaves become butterflies. The butterflies change and become insects to be found below the stove, which are similar to snakes and are called Chu To. A thousand days later they become birds called Dried Old Bones. From the spit of the Dried Old Bones comes a type of bug and these bugs turn into Vinegar Drinkers. Other bugs are born from the Vinegar Drinkers and Huang Shuang insects are born from Chiu Yu insects, which themselves are born from Mou Jui maggots, and Mou Jui maggots are born from Rotting maggots, which themselves are born from Sheep's Groom. Sheep's Groom comes together in intercourse with bamboo that has not put forth any shoots for years and they give birth to Green Peace plants. These give birth to leopards, leopards give birth to horses, horses give birth to humans, humans eventually sink back to what was in the beginning. All the multitudes of life arise from the mystery of beginning and return there.

蘇嚧蘇嚧
四十五

此是諸佛樹葉落聲

CHAPTER 19

Grasping the Purpose of Life

If you have grasped the purpose of life there is no point in trying to make life into something it is not or cannot be.

If you have grasped the purpose of destiny, there is no point in trying to change it through knowledge.

If you wish to care for your body, first of all take care of material things, though even when you have all the things you want, the body can still be uncared for.

Since you have life, you must first of all take care that this does not abandon the body. However, it is possible for the body to retain its life, but still not be sustained. Birth cannot be avoided, nor death be prevented. How ridiculous! To see the people of this generation who believe that simply caring for the body will preserve life. But if caring for the body is not sufficient to sustain life, why does the world continue to do this? It may be worthless, but nevertheless it cannot be neglected, we are unable to avoid it.

If someone wishes to stop doing anything to sustain the body, they are advised to leave this world, for by leaving they can be free from any commitments, and, being free from commitments, they can be virtuous and peaceful. Being virtuous and peaceful, they can be born again like others and, being born again, they approach close to the Tao. But why is it such a good idea to leave the troubles of this existence and to forget the purpose of life? If you leave the troubles of existence, your body will not be wearied; if you forget life, your energy will not be damaged. Thus, with your body and energy harmonized, you can become one with Heaven. Heaven and Earth are the father and mother of all life. Together they create a form, apart they create a beginning. If body and energy are without fault, this is known as being able to adapt. Strengthened and again strengthened, you come back again to assist Heaven.

Master Lieh Tzu asked gatekeeper Yin, 'Only the perfect man can walk underwater and not drown, can walk on fire without burning, and can pass over the multitude of forms of life without fear. I would like to ask, how does the perfect one do this?'

Gatekeeper Yin replied, 'It is because he preserves his original breath and this has nothing to do with knowledge, work, persistence or bravery. Sit down, and I will tell you all about it.

'Everything has a face, forms, sounds and colour: these are just appearances. How is it possible that this thing and that thing are separated from each other? Indeed, why should any of them be viewed as truly the first of all beings? They are just forms and colours, and nothing more. However, everything arises from what is formless and descends into that which is changeless.

'If you grasp and follow this, using it to the full, nothing can stand in your way! It means being able to reside within limits which have no limit, be secluded within boundaries which have no beginning, ramble to where both the beginning and the end of all life is; combine the essential nature, nourish the original breath, harmonize Virtue and, by following this path, commune with the origin of all life. Someone like this guards his unity with Heaven, his spirit is without fault, and thus nothing can get inside and attack him!

'If a drunk falls out of his carriage, even if the carriage is going very fast, he will not die. He is just the same as others, bone and joints, but he is not injured, for his spirit is united. Since he does not realize he was travelling, he has no idea that he has fallen out, so neither life nor death, alarm nor fear can affect him, and he just bumps into things without any anxiety or injury.

'If it is possible to stay united through being drunk on wine, just imagine how much more together one could be if united with Heaven! The sage retreats to the serenity of Heaven, as a result nothing causes him harm. Even someone who is out for revenge does not break his opponent's sword. Nor does someone get cross with a tile that just fell on him, no matter how upset he is. Instead, we should recognize that everything under Heaven is united. Thus it is possible to get rid of chaos, violence and warfare and of the rigours of punishment and execution, for this is the Tao.

'Do not hearken to the Heavenly in humanity, but listen to the Heavenly in Heaven, for paying attention to Heaven's Virtue is life-giving, while attending to humanity damages life. Do not cast aside the Heavenly, and do not ignore the human aspect: then the people will draw closer to the realization of Truth!'

Confucius was travelling to Chu and he went through the heart of a forest, where he saw a hunchback trapping cicadas, using a sticky pole with such ease that it seemed as if he used his hands. 'Sir, what skill!' said Confucius. 'Do you have the Tao?'

'Indeed, I have the Tao. The first five to six months I learned how to balance two balls on top of each other on a pole, and when they did not fall, I knew I could catch a few cicadas. Next I practised with three balls, and when they did not fall, I knew I could catch one cicada in ten. Next I practised with five balls, and when they did not fall, I knew I could catch cicadas very easily. I brace my body as if it were a straight tree trunk and stick out my arms like a pole. Never mind how vast Heaven or Earth are, or the vast numbers of the multitudes of living beings, I concentrate my knowledge on catching cicadas. Never tiring, never leaning, never being aware of any of the vast number of living beings, except cicadas. Following this method, how could I fail?'

Confucius turned and said to his followers, 'His will undivided and his spirit energized, that is how I would describe this hunch-backed gentleman!'

Yen Yuan commented on Confucius, saying, 'I was crossing the gorge at Chang Shan and the boatman guided the boat with real verve. I said to him, "Can one study how to guide a boat?" He said, "Indeed. Someone who can swim well will have no trouble. If someone can dive under water, he may not have seen a boat before but he will know what to do." I asked him what this meant, but he could not say, so I am asking you: what do his words mean?'

'A good swimmer learns quickly,' said Confucius, 'because he knows how to ignore the water. Someone who can swim under the water may indeed have never seen a boat, but he regards the waters as though they were dry land, and the overturning of a boat as nothing more serious than a waggon turning over. So he too learns quickly. All forms of life can be overturning or sliding downwards right in front of his eyes, but he is not affected, nor does it disturb his inner calm, so there is nothing bad that can disturb him! In an archery competition, you shoot as skilfully as possible, hoping to win. If you compete to win decorated buckles, you are concerned with your aim. If you compete for gold, it can make you very nervous. Your skills are the same in all these cases, but because one of these is more significant than the others, this puts external pressure on you. To pay too much attention to such external things makes you thoughtless about the internal things.'

Tien Kai Chih went to see Duke Wei of Chou, and the Duke asked him, 'I hear Chu Hsien is studying life. As Chu Hsien's companion, what have you heard of this, Sir?'

Tien Kai Chih replied, 'I just sweep the courtyard and guard the gate, so how could I have heard anything about it?'

'Master Tien, don't be so modest,' said Duke Wei. 'I want to hear more.'

'Well,' said Kai Chih, 'I have heard the Master say, "Someone who sustains life is definitely like a shepherd who watches for the stragglers and brings them into line."'

'What does this mean?' said Duke Wei.

'In Lu they had Shan Po, who dwelt in the caves, drank nothing but water and was not interested in profit like the rest of the people,' said Tien Kai Chih, 'and for seventy years he lived like this and had the complexion of a girl. Then, sadly, he encountered a fierce tiger which killed and ate him. You have Chang Yi, who knocked on all the doors of the wealthy and powerful, never missing an opportunity to visit. He continued like this for forty years, then caught a fever, became sick and soon died. Po took care of what was internal and a tiger devoured his externals, while Yu took care of his external image and the illness destroyed him from the inside. These two masters did not manage to keep their herd together.'

Confucius said, 'Don't hide inside, don't come out and shine like yang, but hold steadfastly to the middle ground. Follow these three rules and you will be known as one of the truest. When people are about to set out on a dangerous journey, if they hear that one person in ten has been killed, then fathers, sons, elder and younger brothers will all warn them to be careful and they will not set off until they have an armed escort. That is wise, isn't it? People should really worry about what truly worries them, the thoughts that come when they are lying awake in bed or at table eating and drinking. But they don't understand these warnings – what an error!'

The priest of the ancestors looked into the pigsty and said, 'What's so bad about dying? I fatten you up for three months, then I undergo spiritual discipline for ten days, fast for three days, lay out the white reeds, carve up your shoulders and rump and lay them on the place of sacrifice. Surely you're OK with that, aren't you?'

It is, however, true to say that from the perspective of the pig it would be better to eat oats and bran and stay there in the pigsty. It is also true that, looking at this from my perspective, I'd like to be honoured as an important official while alive and, when I die, be buried with a horse-drawn hearse, lying upon a bed of feathers. I could live with that! From the pig's point of view, I wouldn't give a penny for such a life, but from my point of view, I'd be very content, though I wonder why I perceive things so differently from a pig?

Duke Huan[73] was out hunting in the fields, accompanied by Kuan Chung[74] as his driver, when they saw a ghost. The Duke grabbed Kuan Chung's hand and said, 'Kuan Chung, what do you see?' He replied, 'I don't see anything.'

The Duke returned home, fell ill, got worse, and for a number of days did not venture out. A scholar of Chi called Huang Tzu Kao Ao said, 'Sire, you are harming yourself, for the ghost does not have the evil to harm you! When the original breath within is scattered and will not reunite, then weakness follows. If it goes up but will not come down, it makes a man bad-tempered. If it goes down but will not come up, it makes a man very forgetful. If it

73. Despotic ruler of Chi 684–643 BC.
74. Chief Minister of Duke Huan, who held him in very high esteem.

goes neither up nor down, but centres upon the body, at the heart, then illness comes.'

'Is it certain that ghosts exist?' asked Duke Huan.

'There are such things,' he replied. 'The hearth has one,[75] the store has one. The pile of rubbish outside the walls has one. The north-east under the eaves has two; the north-west under the eaves has one. In the water there is one; in the hills there is another. The mountains have their own, as do the meadows and the swamps.'

'Can I ask you what a swamp ghost looks like?' said the Duke.

'The swamp ghost is as big as a wheel rim, as high as a carriage axle, wears a purple gown, a fur hat and is hideous, as such things usually are. Hearing the sound of a waggon or thunder, it holds its head and rises. To see this creature means you will become a dictator.'

Duke Huan was absolutely delighted and laughed, and he said, 'So that is the man I saw!' Then he sat up, tidied himself and even before the day ended, though he did not realize it, he was better.

Chi Hsing Tzu was raising game birds for the King.

Ten days later he asked, 'Are the game birds ready?' 'Not yet,' said Chi Hsing Tzu, 'I need to work on their arrogance and control their spirit.'

Ten days later the King asked again, and he said, 'Not yet, they are easily alarmed.'

Ten days later the King asked again, and he said, 'Not yet, they glare about them and I need to control their spirit.'

Ten days later the King asked again and Chi Hsing Tzu told him, 'Good enough. A cock nearby can crow and they are not disturbed: if you saw them from afar, you'd think they look like wood. They have harmonized their Virtue, and other cocks will not challenge them, but run away.'

Confucius was sightseeing in Lu Liang, where the waterfall is thirty fathoms high and the river races along for forty miles, so fast that neither fish nor any other creature can swim in it. He saw one

75. In the Chinese, all the ghosts have specific names, which I have omitted to make the paragraph easier to read!

person dive in and he assumed that this person wanted to embrace death, perhaps because of some anxiety, so he placed his followers along the bank and they prepared to pull him out. However, the swimmer, having gone a hundred yards, came out, and walked nonchalantly along the bank, singing a song with water dripping off him.

Confucius pursued him and said, 'I thought you were a ghost, but now I see, Sir, that you are a man. I wish to enquire, do you have a Tao for swimming under the water?'

He said, 'No, I have no Tao. I started with what I knew, matured my innate nature and allow destiny to do the rest. I go in with the currents and come out with the flow, just going with the Tao of the water and never being concerned. That is how I survive.'

Confucius said, 'What do you mean when you say you started with what you knew, matured your innate nature and allow destiny to do the rest?'

He said, 'I was born on the dry land and feel content on the land, where I know what I know. I was nurtured by the water, and felt safe there: that reflects my innate nature. I am not sure why I do this, but I am certain that this is destiny.'

Woodcarver Ching[76] carved a piece of wood to form a bell support, and those who saw it were astonished because it looked as if ghosts or spirits had done it. The Marquis of Lu saw it, and asked, 'Where does your art come from?'

'I am just a woodcarver,' Ching replied. 'How could I have "art"? One thing is certain, though, that when I carve a bell support, I do not allow it to exhaust my original breath, so I take care to calm my heart. After I have fasted for three days, I give no thought to praise, reward, titles or income. After I have fasted for five days, I give no thought to glory or blame, to skill or stupidity. After I have fasted for seven days, I am so still that I forget whether I have four limbs and a body. By then the Duke and his court have ceased to exist as far as I am concerned. All my energy is focused and external concerns have gone. After that I depart and enter the

76. Historical figure, c. 569 BC.

mountain forest, and explore the Heavenly innate nature of the trees; once I find one with a perfect shape, I can see for certain the possibility of a bell support and I set my hand to the task; if I cannot see the possibility, I leave it be. By so doing, I harmonize the Heavenly with Heaven, and perhaps this is why it is thought that my carvings are done by spirits!'

Tung Yeh Chi was showing his driving skills to Duke Chuang. He drove up and down holding a straight central line like a plumb line, and turned to left and right with the grace of a curve drawn with a compass. Duke Chuang was impressed, and felt that no one could do better, so he commanded him to do a further hundred circuits.

Yen Ho came by and went in to see the Duke, saying, 'Chi's horses are almost worn out.' But the Duke said nothing. Shortly after, the chariot broke down and the Duke said, 'Sir, how did you know this would happen?' Ho replied, 'The strength of the horses was spent but he urged them on. That's why I said they would collapse.'

Workman Chui could draw as straight as a T-square or as curved as a compass, because his fingers could follow the changes and his heart did not obstruct. Thus his mind was one and never blocked. The feet can be forgotten when you walk in comfortable shoes. The waist can be forgotten when your belt fits comfortably. Knowledge can forget yes and no, if the heart journeys contentedly. Nothing changes inside, nothing proceeds from outside, if you respond to what occurs in a contented way. By starting with what is contented, not undergoing that which is disturbing, it is possible to know the contentment of forgetting what contentment is.

There was a man called Sun Hsiu who came to the gate of Master Pien Ching Tzu to call upon him, and said, 'I used to live in the countryside and no one I ever met said that I didn't behave properly, nor did anyone I met say that, when confronted with problems, I didn't display fortitude. However, when I worked in the fields, the crops were never good, and when I worked for the ruler, things didn't go well in the world. Therefore, I have been expelled from the countryside and exiled from the court, yet what is the nature of my offence against Heaven? How did this misfortune become my destiny?'

Ching Tzu replied, 'Sir, have you not heard of how the perfect man behaves? He forgets his liver and intestines and disregards his ears and eyes. With no defined goal he meanders through the rubbish. What he is good at is doing nothing. Indeed, it is called being but not expecting any reward, bringing up but not controlling. Now you display your knowledge in order to impress the foolish; you strive for fame to highlight your distance from others, polishing yourself so as to be as bright as the very sun and moon. Thus far you have harmonized with your body, having the usual nine apertures, and you have not been struck midway through life by blindness or deafness, lameness nor any deformity, so in comparison to many, you are fortunate. So why do you wander around grumbling about Heaven? Be gone, Sir!'

Master Sun left. Master Pien came in, sat down and rested, then turned his face to Heaven and moaned. His followers said, 'Teacher, why are you groaning?'

Master Pien said, 'I have just been visited by Hsiu and I told him about the Virtue of the perfect man. I fear he was disturbed and has ended up completely confused.'

His followers said, 'Not necessarily. Were the words of Master Sun correct? Were our teacher's words wrong? If wrong, then nothing can make it right. But what if Master Sun's words were wrong? And our teacher's words were right? This means he was already confused, so nothing has changed!'

Master Pien said, 'Not necessarily. Once upon a time a bird landed on the outskirts of the capital city of Lu. The ruler of Lu was very pleased and prepared a special sacrifice for it to enjoy and the Nine Shao[77] music was performed for its entertainment. The bird was distressed and bewildered and did not eat or drink. This is known as trying to sustain a bird with that which sustains us. If you want to feed a bird, then let him go in the midst of a forest, or float on a river and lake and devour snakes. This is what a bird wants.

77. Formal ritual music.

'Now Hsiu, he is foolish and has heard little, so when I try to tell him about the perfect man's virtue, it is as if I was trying to take a mouse for a ride in a horse-drawn waggon, or trying to make a quail happy by providing the sounds of bells and drums. It is not surprising that he was startled!'

佘王具平此下飛此山間布 歇汧噴薄
頃覺清凉之氣蒲滌肺腑眞不知人
間有煩熱也寫此示藻 神住念慈

CHAPTER 20

The Huge Tree

Chuang Tzu was walking through the heart of the mountains when he saw a huge verdant tree. A woodcutter stopped beside the tree, but did not cut it. When asked why he didn't he said, 'It's no good.' Chuang Tzu said, 'Because this tree is not considered useful, it can follow all the years Heaven has given it.'

The Master came out of the mountains and stayed a night at a friend's house. This man was delighted and told his son to kill a goose and cook it. The son answered, saying, 'One goose can cackle, the other one can't. Tell me which one to prepare?' The father replied, 'Prepare the one that does not cackle.'

On the next day Chuang Tzu's followers asked him, 'Yesterday there was a tree in the heart of the mountains which was able to live all the years Heaven gives because it is no use. Now, at your friend's house, there is a goose who dies because it is no use. Teacher, what do you think of this?'

Chuang Tzu laughed and said, 'Personally, I'd find a position between useful and useless. This position between useful and useless might seem a good position, but I tell you it is not, for trouble will pursue you. It would certainly not be so, however, if you were to mount upon the Virtue of the Tao;

'never certain, never directed,
never praised, never condemned,
on the one hand a dragon, on the other a snake,
going as it seems appropriate.
Now up, now down,
using harmony as your guide,
floating on the source of all life.

'Let things be, but don't allow things to treat you as just an object, then you cannot be led into difficulties! This is the path taken by Shen Nung and the Yellow Emperor. Now, however, because of the multitudinous varieties of species and the ethical codes of humanity, things certainly aren't what they were!

'There is unity only in order to divide;
fulfilment only in order to collapse;
a cutting edge is blunted;
those who are elevated are overthrown;
ambition is thwarted;
the wise are conspired against;
the fools are conned.

'So what can be trusted? My followers, just the Tao and its Virtue!'

I Liao[78] from the Southern Market came to see the Marquis of Lu.[79] The Marquis had a very troubled expression.

'Why does the ruler look so anxious?' said the Master of the Southern Market.

'I have studied the Tao of the first kings and the methods of the first rulers,' replied the Marquis of Lu. 'I honour the ghosts and worthy people, try to follow them and never depart from them. But nevertheless I cannot avoid failure, so yes, I am anxious.'

The Master from the Southern Market said, 'Marquis, your method for avoiding troubles is pretty feeble! The elegant, fur-dressed fox and the graceful snow leopard live in the mountain forests: this is where they are at peace. At night they set off but during daylight they stay at home, being cautious. It is hunger and thirst that drives them out one by one, after careful planning, to find food beside the rivers and lakes. Nevertheless, they do not avoid the misfortune of falling into traps and nets. Who is to blame? Their own fur is to blame. Now, the country of Lu, is this not the fur of the ruler? Cast away this body, get rid of the fur, cleanse your heart, scorn the passions and go where there is no one.

78. Hsiung I Liao of Chu lived c. 480 BC.
79. Ai of Lu.

In Nan Yueh there is a place called Virtuously Founded. In that country the people are fools, caring little for themselves, wanting little. They know how to produce, but not how to preserve; they give away, but expect nothing back; they don't know righteousness or what ritual requires. They are ill-mannered, careless and take no care how they proceed, and as a result they don't walk the way of the great skill. At birth they are happy, at death they celebrate. So I say to you, O ruler, cast aside your country, break with tradition and, helped by the Tao, travel on.'

'To follow the road there is both long and arduous,' said the Marquis, 'with some rivers and mountains to cross. I have neither a boat nor a carriage, so what should I do?'

The Master of the Southern Market replied, 'Ruler, don't follow form, don't follow convention and this will be your carriage.'

'The road is dark and long and there are no people along it. Who will accompany me? I have no rations, I have nothing to eat, so how can I follow the path to perfection?'

'Have simple needs, Sir, diminish your desires, Sir, then you can step out without any rations,' said the Master of the Southern Market. 'O ruler, you will be able to cross rivers and float upon the ocean, which, no matter how hard you stare, you will never see the end of, nor know where it goes. O Sir, those who bid you farewell will depart from the seashore while the ruler will journey out into the unknown!'

'The one who has responsibility for others always faces difficulties, and those who are recognized by others as their ruler also suffer. This is why Yao never had responsibility or allowed others to own him. Therefore, ruler, I suggest you get rid of difficulties, cast aside your worries and travel alone with the Tao which leads to the Country of Great Silence. If someone ties two boats together and then uses them to cross the lake, and he is hit by an empty boat, he won't be angry, no matter what sort of a temper he has. However, if there is a man in the other boat, he will shout at him to get out of the way! If nothing happens after his initial shout, he yells again and a third time, with a lot of abuse and swearing. To begin with he is not angry, now he is. To start with he had no one to be angry with, now there is someone. If a person can be emptied, and thus journey through this world, then who would harm him?'

Duke Ling of Wei wanted to cast new bells. So Pei Kung She, his collector of taxes, built a scaffold outside the city gate and in three months the bells were finished, top and bottom.

King Ching Chi saw this and asked, 'Master, what is this art of yours?'

Pei said, 'Centred on Oneness, how could I dare to try anything? I have heard it said, "After the carving and smoothing, revert to simplicity." Being slow, I have no comprehension; being still, I wander and drift; strangely, mysteriously, I let go what goes and greet what comes; what comes cannot be ignored and what goes cannot be held. I amble after the louts and thugs, wander after the humble and meek, seeing what becomes of them. In this way I collect taxes all day long and never have an argument. Just imagine how more significant this would be for someone who grasped the great path!'

Confucius was besieged in the area between Chen and Tsai and had no hot food for seven days. The Grand Duke Jen came out to express his concern and said, 'Master, do you think you will die?'

'Certainly,' said Confucius.

'Master, are you frightened by death?'

'Certainly.'

'I would like to tell you the Tao of never dying,' said Jen. 'There is a bird that dwells in the Eastern Ocean called Helpless. This bird is helpless for it flips and flops, flips and flops, as if it had no strength, flying only with the assistance of the other birds and jostling to return to the nest. None of them likes to be in front or behind, preferring to pick away at what others leave. Thus, when the bird flies, it is never alone, and no others outside the flock, such as humans, can do it any harm, so it avoids disasters.

'The straight tree is the first to be chopped down; the well of sweet water is the first to run dry. Sir, your intention is to display your knowledge in order to astonish the ignorant, and by developing your self, to cast a light upon the crudeness of others. You shine, you positively glow, as if you carried with you the sun and moon. All this is why you cannot avoid disasters.

'I have heard the great fulfilment man say, "The boastful have done nothing worthwhile, those who do something worthwhile will see it fade, fame soon disappears." There are few who can forget success and fame and just return to being ordinary citizens again! The Tao moves all, but the perfect man does not stand in its light, his Virtue moves all, but he does not seek fame. He is empty and plain, and seems crazy. Anonymous, abdicating power, he has no interest in work or fame. So he doesn't criticize others and they don't criticize him. The perfect man is never heard, so why, Sir, do you so want to be?'

Confucius said, 'Splendid!' then said farewell to his friends, left his followers and retired into a great marsh, put on animal skins and rough cloth and lived off acorns and chestnuts. He went out amongst the animals and they were not afraid, amongst the birds and they did not fly away. If the birds and animals were not alarmed, then neither should people be either!

Confucius asked Master Sang Hu, 'I have been exiled from Lu twice, a tree was toppled on top of me in Sung, all records of me have been wiped out in Wei, I was impoverished in Shang and besieged in Chen and Tsai. I have had to endure so many troubles. My friends and acquaintances have wandered off and my followers have begun deserting me. But why is this happening?'

Master Sang Hu said, 'Have you not heard of the man of Chia who ran away? Lin Hui threw aside his jade emblem[80] worth a thousand pieces of gold, tied his son to his back and hurried away. People asked, "Was it because the boy was worth more? Surely a child isn't that valuable. Was it because of all the effort required to carry the jade? But surely a child is even more trouble. So why throw away the jade emblem worth a thousand pieces of gold and rush off with the young child on your back?" Lin Hui told them, "It was greed that brought me and the jade emblem together, but it was Heaven that linked my son and me together."

'When the ties between people are based upon profit, then when troubles come, people part easily. When people are brought together

80. Symbol of authority as a minister.

by Heaven, then when troubles come, they hold together. To hold together or to separate, these are two very different things. The relationship with a nobleman can be as bland as water, that with a mean-spirited person sickly sweet as wine. However, the blandness of the nobleman can develop into affection, but the sweetness of the mean-spirited person develops into revulsion. That which unites for no apparent reason, will fall apart for no apparent reason.'

Confucius said, 'I have heard your advice with true respect!' And so, with an ambling gait and a leisurely air, he went home, gave up his studies and gave away his books. His followers no longer came to bow to him, but their regard for him grew greater.

One day Sang Hu also said to him, 'When Shun was close to death he commanded Yu, "Take care of what I say! Concerning the body, just let it go with the flow. Concerning feelings, let them follow their course. If you go with the flow, you avoid separation. If you follow the course of feelings, you avoid exhaustion. No separation, no exhaustion, so no need to adorn the exterior of the body. When you no longer need to do this, you are free of concern with material things."'

Chuang Tzu, dressed in a worn, patched gown made of coarse cloth and with shoes held together with string, went to visit the King of Wei. The King of Wei said, 'Why are you in such a state, Master?'

Chuang Tzu replied, 'This is poverty but not distress. If a scholar has the Tao and the Virtue but is unable to use them, that is distress. If his clothes are worn and shoes held together with string, that is poverty but not distress. This is known as not being around at the right time. Your Majesty, have you never seen monkeys climbing? When they are amongst plane trees, the oaks and camphor trees, they cling to branches and leaves with such ease that not even the archers Yi or Peng Meng could spot them. However, when they are amongst the prickly mulberry, thorny date trees and other spiky bushes, they move cautiously, looking from side to side, shaking with fear. This is not because their sinews and bones have gone stiff or unable to bend, but because the monkeys are not in their own environment and so cannot use their skills. Now that I find myself living with a benighted leader and with rebellious ministers above me, how can I avoid distress? Observe how Pi Kan's heart was cut out[81] – that illustrates my point!'

Confucius was confronted by troubles between Chen and Tsai and he had no hot food for seven days. He grasped a rotting tree in his left hand, while his right hand beat out a rhythm on a rotting branch and he sang the poem of the Lord of Piao. He had an instrument but no beat, he had sound but no blend of melody. The tree gave sound and the singer gave voice to a sadness that touched people's hearts.

Yen Hui, standing erect, arms folded, cast his eyes towards him. Confucius, anxious that Hui might overdo the respect and honour due to him, or that his love would make him vulnerable, said, 'Hui, it is easy not to care about what comes from Heaven. It is hard not to care about what comes from people. Nothing begins which will not end, Heaven and humanity are one. So who, now, is actually singing?'

'How can one avoid the inflections of Heaven with ease?' said Hui.

'Hunger, thirst, cold and heat and being unable to progress beyond barriers,' said Confucius, 'these are the effects of Heaven and Earth, aspects of ever-changing cycles. They are known as travelling together with others. The minister of a ruler dare not disobey. If he is true to his ruler, then how much more true should we be to respond to the decrees of Heaven!'

'What do you mean when you say it is difficult not to respond to the works of humanity?'

Confucius replied, 'Someone landing a new position goes out in all four directions at the same time. Honours and wealth become his without ceasing, but these do not come from who you are, they are just the external attributes of that particular job. The nobleman is no thief, an honest man is not a robber. Why should I be like that? It is said that there is no bird wiser than the swallow. If its eyes

81. Prince Pi Kan was murdered by the despot Chou, last ruler of Shang. This action was considered one of the reasons why the Shang Dynasty fell.

cannot find a good place, it will not give it another thought. If the food it is carrying falls from its mouth, it leaves it and goes on. It is cautious around humans, but it nests amongst them, finding protection by being close to the altars of the Earth and the Grain.'

'What do you mean, nothing begins that does not end?'

'The change and transformation of all forms of life goes on,' said Confucius, 'but we do not know who sustains this change. How, therefore, can we know beginnings? How can we know ends? There is nothing else to do but wait.'

'What do you mean when you say Heaven and humanity are one?'

'You have Heaven, therefore humanity is. You have Heaven, which is because it is Heaven. Humanity cannot create Heaven, because of humanity's own innate nature. The sage calmly passes on with his body, and that is the end.'

Chuang Tzu was wandering through the park at Tiao Ling, when he saw a strange jackdaw come flying from the south. Its wing-span measured seven feet and its eyes were large, about an inch across. It brushed against Chuang Tzu's forehead as it passed and then came to rest in a copse of chestnut trees. Chuang Tzu said, 'What sort of bird is this, with wings so vast but going nowhere, eyes so large but it can't see properly?' Hitching up his robe, he hurried after it with his crossbow in order to take a pot shot at it. On the way he saw a cicada which was basking in a beautiful shady spot, without a thought for its bodily safety. Suddenly, a praying mantis stretched forth its feelers and prepared to spring upon the cicada, so engrossed in the hunt that it forgot its own safety. The strange jackdaw swept down and seized them both, likewise forgetting its own safety in the excitement of the prize. Chuang Tzu sighed with compassion and said, 'Ah! So it is that one thing brings disaster upon another, and then upon itself!' He cast aside his crossbow and was on his way out, when the forester chased after him, shouting at him for being a poacher.

Chuang Tzu went home and was depressed for three months. Lin Chou, who was with him, asked him, 'Master, why are you so miserable?'

Chuang Tzu said, 'I was so concerned with my body that I

forgot my self. It was like looking into cloudy water, thinking it was really clear. Furthermore, I heard my Master say once, "When associating with the locals, act like a local." So I went out walking in the park at Tiao Ling and forgot my own self. A strange jackdaw touched my forehead, then settled in a copse of chestnut trees and there forgot its own true being. The forester thought I was to blame. This is why I'm miserable.'

Yang Tzu was travelling to Sung and stopped for the night at an inn. The innkeeper had two concubines, one beautiful, the other ugly. The ugly one was given all consideration, while the beautiful one was made to serve. Yang Tzu asked why this was, and a young boy from the inn said, 'The beautiful one knows her beauty, so we don't think of her as beautiful. The ugly one realizes her ugliness and therefore we don't think of her as ugly.'

Yang Tzu said, 'My followers, remember this! If you act rightly but unselfconsciously, you will be universally loved!'

賞善司

罰惡司

賞善

罰惡

CHAPTER 21

Tien Tzu Fang

Tien Tzu Fang was in attendance on the Marquis Wen of Wei,[82] and he frequently referred to Chi Kung. Marquis Wen said, 'This Chi Kung, is he your master?'

'No,' said Tzu Fang, 'but he comes from the same region as I do. In discussing the Tao with him I find he is often spot on, which is why I refer to him.'

'Is it the case, then, that you have no master?' said Marquis Wen. Tzu Fang said, 'I have.'

'Who then is your master?'

'Master Shun from the Eastern Wall,' said Tzu Fang.

'Then why have you never praised this great master?'

'He is indeed a man of Truth,' said Tzu Fang, 'having the appearance of a man but the expanse of Heaven. He is empty and his being is Truth; he is pure and holds all things. He greets those without the Tao with a proper manner, and they are enlightened, their conceits are dissolved. How could I present his thoughts?'

Tzu Fang left, and Marquis Wen sat profoundly shaken for the whole day and didn't say a word. He then summoned his ministers and said to them, 'How distant from us is the nobleman of complete Virtue! I used to believe that the words of the sages and the actions of benevolence and righteousness were the most perfect we could achieve. I have now heard of the teacher of Tzu Fang and my body is all at sixes and sevens, I don't want to move, my mouth is shut and I don't want to talk. That which I was studying has turned out

---

82. A remarkable politician who won freedom for the state of Wei, *c.* 400 BC.

to be a thing of straw. The whole state of Wei really is a weight on me!'

Wen Po Hsueh Tzu was travelling to Wei, when he stopped in the state of Lu. A citizen of Lu asked to see him, but Wen Po Hsueh Tzu said, 'Certainly not. I have heard that these noblemen of the Middle Kingdom are clear about the principles of ritual but foolish in their understanding of people's hearts. I do not wish to see him.'

He duly arrived in Wei but as he returned home he passed once more through Lu, and the citizen appeared again, asking to see him. Wen Po Hsueh Tzu said, 'He asked to see me before, now he's trying again. Obviously, he cares enough to say something to me.'

He went out to see the citizen and came back moaning softly. The next day he saw him again and again returned with a low moan. His servant asked, 'Why is it that, when you see this visitor, you come back moaning?'

He replied, 'I have said before, "These people of the Middle Kingdom are clear about the principles of ritual, but foolish in their understanding of people's hearts." Each time I see this visitor his coming forward and withdrawing is so precise it might have been calculated on a compass or set-square. His appearance is first like a dragon, then a tiger. He argues with me as if he was my son, and tries to give me advice like my father, which is why I am sighing.'

Confucius went to see him but did not say a word. Tzu Lu said, 'Sir, you have wished to visit Wen Po Hsueh Tzu for a while, yet when you saw him you didn't say a word. Why?'

'As soon as I saw him, I could see the Tao,' said Confucius. 'There was no need to say anything.'

Yen Yuan said to Confucius, 'Master, when you stroll, I stroll. When you stride, I stride. When you gallop, I gallop. But when you break into a headlong rush that leaves nothing but dust behind, I just stand and stare after you in astonishment.'

'Hui, what are you talking about?' said the Master.

'Master, when you stroll, I stroll; when you speak, I speak. When you stride, I stride; when you contrast, I also contrast. When you gallop, I gallop; when you speak of the Tao, I also speak of the Tao. But when I say you break into a headlong rush and leave the dust behind you and I just stand and stare, I mean you do not even need to speak to be believed, everyone salutes your universality and your lack of prejudice; even though you have no official status, people are inspired to follow you. I simply do not understand how this is.'

'Ah ha!' said Confucius. 'So we must enquire into this! There is no greater sadness than the death of the heart – beside which the death of the body is secondary. The sun rises in the east and sets in the west, and all forms of life are guided by this. All beings that have eyes and feet await the sun and then do what is necessary. When it rises, they come out; when it sets, they disappear. This is certain for all forms of life. They have to await their time of death; they have to await their time of birth.

'Having been given this prescribed shape, I hold to it unchangingly and in this way I wait for the end. I exist, acted upon by others both day and night without end, and I have no idea when I shall end. Obviously I am here in this particular shape and I understand my destiny, but not what has happened beforehand. This is how I am, day after day.

'I am sharing my ideas with you, and here we are side by side and you don't understand me. This is a shame! You can see the part of me that I have shown you, but that is no longer relevant – yet you still hunt for it as if it were. This is like looking for a horse after the sale is over. I am of the greatest service to you when I forget you, and you are of the greatest service to me when you forget me. Given this is so, why get so upset? It is my former self that you forget, and what I retain is what cannot be forgotten.'

Confucius went to see Lao Tzu and found him washing his hair. He had spread it out over his shoulders to dry. He stood there without moving, as if no one else existed in the world. Confucius stood quietly and then, after a while, quietly came into his vision and said, 'Were my eyes dazzled, is this really you? Just now, Sir, your body was as still as an old dead tree. You seemed to have no thought in your head, as if you were in another world and standing utterly alone.'

'I let my heart ponder upon the origin of beginnings,' said Lao Tzu.

'What do you mean?' asked Confucius.

'The heart may try to reason this out but doesn't understand it, and the mouth may hang open but can't find words to say. Still, I will attempt to describe this to you. Perfect yin is harsh and cold, perfect yang is awesome and fiery. Harshness and coldness emanate from Earth, awesomeness and fieriness emanate from Heaven. The two mingle and join, and from their conjunction comes to birth everything that lives. Maybe there is one who controls and ensures all this, but if so, then no one has seen any form or shape. Decay and growth, fullness and emptiness, at one time dark, at another bright, the changes of the sun and the transformation of the moon, these go by day after day, but no one has seen what causes this. Life has its origin from which it emerges and death has its place to which it returns. Beginning and end follow each other inexorably and no one knows of any end to this. If this is not so, then who is the origin and guide?'

'I want to ask what it means to wander like this,' said Confucius.

Lao Tzu said, 'To obtain this is perfect beauty and perfect happiness, and to obtain perfect beauty and wander in perfect happiness is to be a perfect man.'

'I would like to hear how this is done,' said Confucius.

Lao Tzu replied, 'Creatures that eat grass are not put out by a change of pasture. Creatures that are born in the water are not put out by a change of water. They can live with a minor change, but not with a change to that which is the most significant. Joy, anger, sadness and happiness do not enter into their breasts. All under Heaven, all forms of life, come together in the One. Obtain the One and merge with it and all your four limbs and hundred joints will become just dust and ashes. For death and birth, ending and beginning are nothing more than the sequence of day and night. Then you will never be disturbed in your contentment by such trifles as gain and loss, for example, good fortune or bad! Those who ignore the status of authority, casting it aside like so much mud, they know that their own self is of greater significance than any title. The value of your self lies within and is not affected by what happens externally. The constant transformation of all forms of life is like a beginning without end. What is there in this to disturb your heart? Those who comprehend the Tao are freed from all this.'

'Master,' said Confucius, 'your Virtue is like that of Heaven and Earth, but even you have to resort to these perfect words to guide you. Who amongst the great men of antiquity could have lived this out?'

Lao Tzu replied, 'I certainly do not. The flowing of the stream does nothing, but it follows its nature. The perfect man does the same with regard to Virtue. He does nothing to cultivate it, but all is affected by its presence. He is like the height of Heaven: natural; or the solidity of Earth, the brightness of sun and moon: all natural. There is no need to cultivate this!'

Confucius came out and commented upon all this to Yen Hui: 'When it comes to comprehending the Tao I am about as significant as a fly in vinegar! Had the Master not revealed things to me, I would never have understood the great unity of Heaven and Earth.'

Chuang Tzu went to see Duke Ai of Lu. Duke Ai said, 'There are many learned scholars in Lu but few of them study your works, Master.'

Chuang Tzu said, 'Lu has few learned ones.'

Duke Ai said, 'There are men wearing the dress of learned scholars throughout the state of Lu. How can you say there are few?'

Chuang Tzu said, 'I have heard that those learned ones who wear round caps on their heads, know the seasons of Heaven; those who wear square shoes know the shape of the Earth; those who tie semi-circular disks to their belts deal perfectly with all that comes before them. But a nobleman can follow the Tao without having to dress the part. Indeed, he might wear the dress but not understand the Tao at all! Should my Lord not be sure on this point, why not issue an order of state saying, "Any wearing the dress but not practising the Tao will be executed!"'

This is exactly what Duke Ai did, and five days later throughout the kingdom of Lu not a single learned one wore the dress! Only one old man wore the dress of the learned and stood at the Duke's gate. The Duke immediately called him in and discussed the affairs of the kingdom with him, and though they went through a thousand issues and tens of thousands of digressions, the old man was never at a loss.

Chuang Tzu said, 'So, in the whole kingdom of Lu there is just this one man who is among the learned ones. How can you claim there are many?'

Po Li Hsi[83] did not allow thoughts of fame and fortune to enter his heart. Instead, he looked after cattle, and his cattle prospered. Seeing this, the Duke Mu of Chin forgot Po Li Hsi's servile state and he turned over the running of the government to him. Shun of the Yu[84] family did not allow death nor birth to enter his heart, and this is how he could influence others.

Ruler Yuan of Sung wanted a map drawn up and so the artists flocked to him. They received their materials and instructions and formed up in line, licking their pencils and grinding their ink. There were so many that half had to remain outside. One artist arrived late, insolently and without any concern for speed. Having received his instructions and materials, he did not join the line, but went off to his own studio. The ruler sent someone to see what he was up to. He found him with his robe off, sitting cross-legged and almost naked. The ruler said, 'Splendid, this is indeed a true craftsman!'

King Wen[85] was touring the sights of Tsang and he saw an old man fishing. However, his fishing was not real fishing. He was not fishing as if he had to fish for any good reason, but just because he fished. King Wen wanted to summon him to take over governing the kingdom, but he was worried that such an action would upset his great ministers, uncles and cousins. He tried to erase the matter from his mind, but he could not bear the thought that all his people, all one hundred families, would be deprived of such a gift from Heaven. The next morning he summoned his great ministers and said, 'Last night I dreamed that I saw a man of quality, bearded and with a dark complexion, riding a dappled horse, half of whose hooves were red. This man ordered me, "Pass your government

83. A seventh-century BC minister who was taken prisoner when his state fell. He became a slave on a farm, but eventually rose to power again.
84. His family tried to kill him, but he would not seek revenge when in power.
85. Father of Wu who founded the Chou Dynasty. According to tradition, King Wen wrote the commentaries on the sixty-four hexagrams of the I Ching.

over to the old man of Tsang and the woes of your people will be healed!"'

The great ministers were certainly impressed and said, 'It was the late king, Your Majesty.'

King Wen said, 'Let us ask the diviner.'

The great ministers said, 'It is the command of the late King. Your Majesty should not doubt this, so there is no need for a diviner!'

So in due course the King handed over the government to the Old Man of Tsang. However, all the old order and regulations persisted unchanged and no new laws were sent out. Three years later King Wen toured his kingdom. He found that the officers in the districts had broken down the gates of the different groups and dispersed them, that the chiefs of the departments no longer bragged about their positions, and that no one brought illegal weights or measures into the country. The district officials had destroyed the fortified places and scattered those within, because they identified with those above them. The chiefs of departments sought no special honours, because they saw even the most mundane task as an honour. With no different weights and measures, the princes were no longer in two minds whether to use the official ones.

King Wen appreciated the true worth of having found a great teacher, and, facing north, he asked him, 'Could this government be extended to all the Earth?' The Old Man of Tsang looked confused and gave no answer. The next morning he gave orders with a distracted look, and by night he was gone and was never heard of again.

Yen Yuan asked Confucius about this. 'King Wen wasn't really up to it, was he? What was all that stuff about a dream?'

Confucius said, 'Silence, don't say a word! King Wen knew what he was about. Let there be no criticism of him! He only used the dream to extract himself from his difficulty.'

Lieh Yu Kou was displaying his skills at archery to Po Hun Wu Jen. He drew his bow fully back and placed a bowl of water upon his elbow. The arrow flew from his bow and no sooner had it gone than a second arrow was there and fired, followed by a third at the ready. And all this time he stood still as a statue.

Po Hun Wu Jen said, 'This is indeed the archery of an archer, not the non-archery of an archer. Let us go to the top of a high mountain, climbing up the rocks until we come to the edge of a drop eight hundred feet deep. Could you shoot then?'

So they set off, to the top of a high mountain, scrambling over the rocks, until they reached a drop of eight hundred feet. Here Wu Jen turned round and walked backwards towards the drop until his feet were half over the edge, whereupon he bowed to Yu Kou and asked him to join him. Yu Kou fell to the ground, sweat pouring from him, drenching him to his feet.

Po Hun Wu Jen said, 'The perfect man can stare at the azure Heavens above, or go down into the Yellow Springs below, or journey away to the eight ends of the cosmos, without affecting his spirit and original breath. Now here you are grovelling and your eyes agog. In such a state of mind, if you were to take aim, you would be in great danger!'

Chien Wu said to Sun Shu Ao, 'Sir, three times you were appointed Prime Minister without showing any enthusiasm and three times you were dismissed without showing any distress. To begin with I really didn't believe this. But now I see you, nose to nose, I see how calm and unruffled you are. Sir, have you some special influence over your heart?'

Sun Shu Ao said, 'Do I really exceed others? When I was offered the post, I did not feel I could refuse. When the post was withdrawn, I did not feel I could stop it. Neither having nor losing affect who I am, so there was no point in looking miserable. Do I really exceed others? I did not know where the glory lay, in the job or in me. If it is in the prime ministerial post, then why should it mean anything to me? If in me, then what did it have to do with being Prime Minister? With all these questions, I have decided just to wander in the four directions. What leisure do I have to speculate about whether my position is high or low?'

Confucius heard about this and said:

'He is a true man of the past:
the wise could not follow his words;
the charming ones cannot make him follow them,

nor the aggressive force him to do their will.
Neither Fu Hsi nor the Yellow Emperor could have made him
    be their friend.
Death and birth are momentous times but they do not affect
    him;
how much less do fame and fortune!
The spirit of one such as he can sail across the great mountain
    Tai
without the slightest difficulty,
enter into the deepest troughs of the ocean and not be wet,
or fill the lowest position without any anxiety.
He is filled with Heaven and Earth,
and the more he gives to others, the more he has.'

The King of Chu and the Lord of Fan were sitting together. Three of the King of Chu's servants came to report that the state of Fan had been destroyed. The Lord of Fan said, 'Fan's destruction does not deter me from preserving what is most significant. I say, "If the destruction of Fan is not sufficient to make me lose what I most value, then the preservation of Chu is not enough to ensure the preservation of what I should preserve. Viewed this way, Fan has not begun to be destroyed and Chu has not begun to be preserved.'

CHAPTER 22

The Shores of the Dark Waters

Knowledge strolled north to the shores of the Dark Waters, scaled the mount of Secret Heights and came upon Words-of-Actionless-Action. Knowledge said to Words-of-Actionless-Action, 'I want to ask you something. What sort of thought and reflection does it take to know the Tao? In what sort of place and in what sorts of ways should we undertake to rest in the Tao? What sort of path and what sort of plans do we need to obtain the Tao?' These three questions he asked of Words-of-Actionless-Action, but he did not answer. Not only did he not answer, he had no idea what to answer.

Knowledge did not obtain any answers, so he travelled to the White Waters of the south, climbed up on to the top of Doubt Curtailed and there caught sight of Wild-and-Surly. Knowledge put the same question to Wild-and-Surly. Wild-and-Surly said, 'Ah ha! I know, and I will tell you.' In the middle of saying this, he forgot what he was going to say!

Knowledge did not obtain any answers, so he went back to the Emperor's palace to see the Yellow Emperor and to ask him. The Yellow Emperor said, 'Practise having no thoughts and no reflections and you will come to know the Tao. Only when you have no place and can see no way forward will you find rest in the Tao. Have no path and no plans and you will obtain the Tao.'

Knowledge said to the Yellow Emperor, 'You and I know this, but the others did not know, so which of us is actually right?'

The Yellow Emperor said, 'Words-of-Actionless-Action was truly right. Wild-and-Surly seems right. In the end, you and I are not close to it.

'Those who understand, do not say.
Those who say, do not understand.
And so the sage follows the teachings without words.
The Tao cannot be made to occur,
Virtue cannot be sought after.
However, benevolence can be undertaken,
righteousness can be striven for,
rituals can be adhered to.
It is said, "When the Tao was lost, Virtue appeared;
when Virtue was lost, benevolence appeared;
when benevolence was lost, righteousness appeared;
when righteousness was lost, ritual appeared.
Rituals are just the frills on the hem of the Tao, and are signs of
    impending disorder."

'It is said, "One who follows the Tao daily does less and less. As
he does less and less, he eventually arrives at actionless action.
Having achieved actionless action, there is nothing which is not
done." Now that we have become active, if we wish to return to
our original state, we will find it very difficult! Who but the great
man could change this?

'Life follows death and death is the forerunner of life.
Who can know their ways?
Human life begins with the original breath;
When it comes together there is life,
When it is dispersed, there is death.

'As death and life are together in all this, which should be termed
bad? All the forms of life are one, yet we regard some as beautiful,
because they are spiritual and wonderful; others we count as ugly,
because they are diseased and rotting. But the diseased and rotting
can become the spiritual and wonderful, and the spiritual and
wonderful can become the diseased and rotting. It is said, "All that
is under Heaven is one breath." The sages always comprehend such
unity.'

Knowledge said to the Yellow Emperor, 'I asked Words-of-
Actionless-Action, and he didn't say anything to me. Indeed, not

only did he not say anything to me, but he didn't know what to say to me. I asked Wild-and-Surly and he was in the midst of explaining to me, though he did not say anything, then in the midst of it all he forgot what he wanted to say. Then I asked you and you know the answer, so why do you say you are not close to the answer?'

The Yellow Emperor said, 'Words-of-Actionless-Action was actually right, because he knew nothing. Wild-and-Surly was almost right, because he forgot everything. However, you and I are not close, because we know.'

When Wild-and-Surly heard about this, he concluded that the Yellow Emperor knew what he was talking about.

Heaven and Earth have great beauty but no words.
The four seasons follow their regular path but do not debate it.
All forms of life have their own distinct natures but do not
  discuss them.
The sage looks at the beauties of Heaven and Earth and
  comprehends the principle behind all life.
So the perfect man does without doing
and the great sage initiates nothing,
for, as we say, they have glimpsed Heaven and Earth.

Now even the Tao, spirit-like and with perfect clarity, in common with all other forms of life, undergoes the transformations of life. All life forms are already dead or living; they are square or round, and they do not comprehend their beginning.

Yet life goes on, just as it has done from time immemorial.
Even the vastness of distances between the six areas of the world
is encompassed by the Tao.
Indeed, even the smallest hair relies upon the Tao for its very
being.
Every living thing below Heaven,
those arising and those declining,
are guided by this. Yin and yang.
The four seasons are kept moving by it,
each within its own sphere.

Seeming lost in darkness, it still exists;
Glorious and free, it has no body: it is spirit.
All forms of life are guided by it,
though they do not know it.
This is what is called the root and origin.
It is this which we discern in Heaven.

Yeh Chueh asked Pi I about the Tao, and Pi I said, 'Attend to your body, concentrate upon the One, and the perfect harmony of Heaven will be yours.

'Rein in your understanding, unify your stance and the spirit will dwell within you.

'Virtue will be your beauty and the Tao will be your dwelling place.

'You will seem like a simple new-born calf and you won't try to understand the reason why!'

Before he could finish what he was saying, Yeh Chueh fell fast asleep. Pi I was very pleased indeed and wandered off singing this song:

'Body like a rotten tree stump,
Heart like cold dead ashes,
His understanding is true and real,
Not inclined to pursue questions.
Obscure, obscure, deeply dark,
Heartless, no advice forthcoming,
What sort of person is this!'

Shun asked Cheng, 'Is it possible to obtain the Tao and have it as mine?'

He said, 'As you aren't in control of your own body, how could you hope to obtain and hold the Tao?'

Shun said, 'If I don't control my own body, then who does?'

He said, 'Your shape is given you by Heaven and Earth. Life is not yours to have, it is the combining harmony of Heaven and Earth. Your innate nature and destiny are not yours to have, they are constructs given you by Heaven and Earth. Grandsons and sons are not yours to have: they are the sloughed-off skins bequeathed to you from Heaven and Earth. You should walk, therefore, as if you don't know where you are going; remain where you are without knowing why; eat without knowing what you're tasting. All this arises from the yang breath of Heaven and Earth. How can it then be possible for you to obtain and hold anything?'

Confucius said to Lao Tzu, 'Now, today, you seem relaxed, so I would like to ask about the perfect Tao.'

Lao Tzu said, 'You should cleanse and purify your heart through fasting and austerities, wash your spirit to make it clean and repress your knowledge. The Tao is profound and almost impossible to describe! I will attempt to offer some understanding of it:

'The brightly shining is born from the deeply dark;
that which is orderly is born from the formless;
the spiritual is born from the Tao;
the roots of the body are born from the seminal essence;
all forms of life give each other shape through birth.
Those with nine apertures are born from the womb,
while those with eight are born from eggs.
Of its coming there is no trace,
no sign of its departure,
neither entering the gate nor dwelling anywhere,
open to all the four directions.
Those who travel with the Tao will be strong in body,
sincere and profound in their thought,
clear of sight and hearing,
using their hearts without tiring,
responding to all without prejudice.
As a result of this, Heaven is high and Earth wide,
the sun and moon move and everything flourishes.
This is the Tao!

'Even the broadest knowledge does not comprehend it.
Reason does not mean wisdom, so the sage casts these aside.
There is something which is complete, no matter what you add;
is not diminished, no matter what you take away.
This is what the sage holds to.
It is as the ocean, deeply deep,

as the mountains, high and proud,
its end is its beginning,
it carries all forms of life and never fails.
The Tao of the nobleman is just external garb!
That which sustains all forms of life and never falters,
this is the true Tao!

'Here is a man of China, balanced between yin and yang,
dwelling between Heaven and Earth. For a while he is a man and
then he returns to the origin. Viewed from the perspective of the
origin, when life begins for him, he is just a collection of breath.
When he dies, whether he is young or very old, these different
destinies make little difference, his life-span is so short. What does it
mean then to ask which is good and bad between Yao and Shun?
The fruits of the trees and the trailing plants have their distinctive
patterns. Even human relationships, for all their troubles, have an
order and a structure. The sage does not oppose them when he
meets them: since he exceeds them by far, he has no need to hold on
to them. He responds to them harmoniously: this is his Virtue. He
greets them in friendship: this is his Tao. This is how Emperors and
kings have arisen.

'Human life between Heaven and Earth is like a white colt
    glimpsed through a crack in the wall, quickly past.
It pours forth, it overwhelms,
yet there is nothing that does not emerge.
It drifts, it swirls,
yet there is nothing that does not return.
Life is transformation, death is also transformation.
All living creatures are saddened, all humanity mourns.
However, it is simply the releasing of the Heavenly bowstring,
or the emptying of the Heavenly satchel,
a yielding and a changing which release the soul, as the body
    follows,
back at long last to the great Returning.
That without shape comes from shape,
that with shape returns to the shapeless.

'All people know this:
those with a perfect understanding do not discuss it,
while everyone argues how to set about achieving it.
Those who have achieved it do not discuss it.
Those who discuss have not achieved it.
Those who eagerly search with their keen eyes will not discern
    it. Be silent, do not debate.
The Tao cannot be heard, so it is better to close your ears than
    strive to hear.
This is called the great Achievement.'

Master Tung Kuo asked Chuang Tzu, 'That which is called the Tao, where is it?'
Chuang Tzu replied, 'There is nowhere where it is not.'
'But give me a specific example.'
'In this ant,' said Chuang Tzu.
'Is that its lowest point?'
'In this panic grass,' said Chuang Tzu.
'Can you give me a lower example?'
'In this common earthenware tile,' said Chuang Tzu.
'This must be its lowest point!'
'It's in shit and piss too,' said Chuang Tzu.
Master Tung Kuo had no answer to this. Chuang Tzu said, 'Sir, your questions miss the point. When Inspector Huo asked the superintendents of the market how best to test the value of a pig by treading down on it with his foot, they told him that the lower down the animal you pressed, the closer you were to finding the truth. So you should not look for the Tao in anything specific. There is nothing without it. The perfect Tao is like this – so it is called the Great. Complete, all embracing, universal: three different words but with the same reality, all referring back to the One.

'Imagine that we were wandering in the palace of No-Place.
Harmony and unity would be our themes, never ending, never
    failing!
Join with me in actionless action!
In simplicity and quietude!
In disinterest and purity!

In harmony and ease!
My intentions are now aimless.
I go nowhere and have no idea how I got there;
I go and I come and don't know why.
I have been, I have gone.
I have no idea when my journey is over.
I wander and rest in limitless vastness.
Great knowledge comes in and I have no idea where it will all
    end.

'If you can regard things as simply things, then you do not share
the limited nature of things. The limitless arises out of the limited,
and the boundless arises out of the restricted.

'We talk of fullness and emptiness; of withering and decaying.
The Tao makes them full or empty but is not defined by fullness or
emptiness. It creates withering and decay, but it is not defined by
withering or decay. It produces the roots and branches, but it is
neither root nor branch. It gathers together and it disperses, but it is
neither of these itself.'

Ah Ho Kan and Shen Nung were fellow students of Lao Lung
Chi. One midday Shen Nung was sitting on his seat with the door
shut and he was fast asleep, when Ah Ho Kan opened the door and
came in, saying,

'Lao Lung is dead.'

Shen Nung leaned forward, grasped his staff and rose to his feet.
Then he dropped his staff and burst out laughing, 'Our Heavenly
wise Master, he knew just how cramped and mean, arrogant and
wilful I am and this is why he has gone and cast me aside and died.
My Master has gone off! He has died without giving me words to
control my wildness!'

Yen Kang Tiao heard all this and said, 'The one who embodies
the Tao has noblemen from all over the world coming to him.
Now, regarding the Tao, you who haven't grasped even a tip of the
hair of it, not even a ten-thousandth part, nevertheless you still
know enough to curb your wild words and to die without uttering
them. How much more is this the case with someone who embodies
the Tao! You can look for it but it has no shape. You can listen for

it, but it has no voice. Those who discuss it call it deeply dark. To
talk of the Tao is not to know the Tao.'

Great Purity asked Endless, 'Sir, do you know the Tao?'

'I do not know it,' said Endless.

Then he asked Actionless Action, who replied, 'I know the Tao.'

'Sir,' asked Great Purity, 'about your knowledge of the Tao, do
you have some special hints?'

'I have.'

'What are they?'

Actionless Action said, 'I know that the Tao can elevate and
bring low, bind together and separate. These are the hints I would
give you to know the Tao.'

With these different answers Great Purity went to No Beginning
and said, 'Between Endless's statement that he doesn't know, and
Actionless Action's statement that he does know, I am left wondering which of these is right and which is wrong.'

No Beginning said, 'Not to know is profound and to know is
shallow. To be without knowledge is to be inward, to know is to
be outward.'

Then indeed did Great Purity cast his eyes upward and sigh, 'Not
to know is to know and to know is not to know! Who knows
about not knowing about knowing?'

No Beginning said:

'The Tao cannot be heard: what is heard is not the Tao.
The Tao cannot be seen: what can be seen is not the Tao.
The Tao cannot be spoken: what is spoken is not the Tao.
Do we know what form gives form to the formless?
The Tao has no name.'

No Beginning continued:

'To be questioned about the Tao and to give an answer means
that you don't know the Tao.

'One who asks about the Tao has never understood anything
about the Tao.

'Do not ask about the Tao, for the asking is not appropriate, nor
can the question be answered, because it is like asking those in dire
extremity. To answer what cannot be answered is to show no inner

understanding. When someone without inner understanding waits for an answer from those in dire extremity, they illustrate that they neither grasp where they stand outwardly nor understand the great Beginning within. So they cannot cross the Kun Lun mountains nor wander in the great Void.'

Starlight asked No Existence, 'Master, do you exist? Or do you not exist?'

Starlight could get no answer, but he looked upon the form of the other and saw a deep void. All day long he stared but could see nothing, listened but heard nothing, reached out his hand but held nothing.

Starlight said, 'Perfect! Who can reach such heights? I can imagine existence and non-existence but not non-existing non-existence; yet here we have non-existence of non-existence, how amazing!'

The swordsmith of the Grand Marshal was eighty years old, but he had not lost any of his skills. The Grand Marshal said, 'Master, you are so skilful! Do you have the Tao?'

He said, 'I do have the Tao. From the age of twenty onwards I have been devoted to making swords. I pay no heed to anything else, I look at nothing but swords. By being so constant I am now able to do it without thinking. Time brings one to such art, so imagine how much more significant this would be for one who used the same method but never ignored anything. Everything would depend on him and everything would be achieved!'

Jan Chiu asked Confucius, 'Is it possible to know anything about what there was, before Heaven and Earth?'

Confucius replied, 'It is. As it was in the past, so it is now.'

Jan Chiu got no further and left. The next day he saw Confucius again and said, 'Yesterday I asked if it's possible to know anything of what there was before Heaven and Earth and you said, Master, "It is. As it was in the past so it is now." Yesterday that seemed fine to me, but now it seems problematic. What does all this mean?'

Confucius said, 'Yesterday it was clear to you, because your spirit was ready for such an answer. Now it is problematic because you are no longer responding in the spirit, are you? There is no past, nor present, no beginning and no end. Is it possible to say that you had grandsons and sons before you had grandsons and sons?'

Jan Chiu did not answer. Confucius said, 'Enough, don't try to answer! Don't use life to give birth to death, don't use death to bring death to life. Do death and life depend upon each other? They are both held within the One. What was there before Heaven and Earth, was it a thing? That which creates things each in their own way is not a thing. Things that are produced cannot come before things that produce them because these already exist. Likewise, they were produced by things existing before them, and so on through time. The sage's love of humanity never ends and is based on this way of seeing.'

Yen Yuan asked Confucius, 'Master, I have heard you say that you should not welcome anything in, nor move out to greet anything. I would like to know how this is done.'

Confucius said, 'The people of old didn't change inwardly in the midst of external changes. Today people change inwardly but pay no attention to the externals. To note the changes around but not to change oneself is not to change. Where is change to be found? Where is there no change? How can one be affected by changes of the external? One needs to hold back from others.

'Hsi Wei had his park and the Yellow Emperor his garden. The Lord Shun had his palace and Tang and Wu had their manors. Then amongst the noblemen there were those such as the teachers of the Literati and the Mohists whose teachings caused people to begin considering what was right and what was wrong and arguing with each other, and the present day is even worse! Sages, in their dealings with others, do them no harm; those who do no harm cannot themselves be harmed. Only the person who does no harm can welcome others in or go out to meet them.

'The mountains and forest delight! The hills and valleys delight! However, this delight of mine ends and sadness comes. When sadness and joy come, I cannot prevent them. When they go, I cannot stop them. How distressing that the people of this world are but rest-houses for things. They know what they encounter but they do not know what they do not encounter. They know how to do the things they know, but not how to do those things they do not know. Not knowing, not doing, this is what traps humanity. Still some people attempt to escape from the inevitable. This is how it goes! Perfect speech is no speech; perfect action is no action. To know only what is known is a tragedy.'

CHAPTER 23

Keng Sang Chu

One of the followers of Lao Tzu was Keng Sang Chu, who had grasped something of Lao Tzu's teaching of the Tao. He went north and settled at the mountain of Wei Lei. He dismissed those servants of his who were brisk and efficient. He sent away any of his concubines who were kind and benevolent. Into his home he took the off-hand and rude, and employed the indolent and aggressive. Three years later Wei Lei had become a very prosperous place. The people of Wei Lei said to each other, 'When Master Keng Sang came here, we were frightened of him. Now, if we think about it day to day, there doesn't seem to be sufficient for everyone, but if we reckon him by the years, we can see there is more than enough to go round. It is possible that he really is a sage! Perhaps we should revere him as our priest before the dead and put all our altars of the grain and earth under his command.'

Master Keng Sang heard this, but he turned his face to the south and was certainly not pleased. His followers were perplexed by this. Master Keng Sang said, 'My followers, why do you think this is strange? When the life-giving breath of spring emerges, the plants begin to come to life, and then in autumn they produce their multitudes of fruits. Do spring and autumn do this of their own volition? They just follow Heaven's Tao. I have heard that the perfect man lives without effort within the confines of his house, leaving the different peoples to their own wild and unthinking ways. Now these busybodies of Wei Lei in their arrogant ways want to present their offerings to me and make me one of their leaders, as if I were really some kind of standard for others! This is why I am annoyed, because I remember the words of Lao Tzu.'

His followers said, 'Surely not. In ditches eight to sixteen feet wide the big fishes can't turn around, but the minnows and eels can. On a hill just six or seven feet high the big animals don't have space to hide themselves, but the cunning fox finds it perfect. Honour should be shown to the worthy and offices given to those who are capable, with preference shown to the good and thoughtful. In the past Yao and Shun behaved like this, so why shouldn't the people of Wei Lei! Master, let them do this!'

Master Keng Sang said, 'Come here my little ones! If a creature large enough to swallow a carriage whole leaves its mountain, it cannot avoid the dangers of being trapped in the net. If a fish great enough to swallow a boat whole is left stranded by the loss of water, it can fall prey even to the ants. This is why birds and creatures don't care how high they go to escape, nor do fish and turtles care how deep they go to escape. In the same way, those people who wish to preserve their bodies and lives are concerned only with how to hide away, and don't mind how remote their place of hiding is.

'Regarding the two masters you mentioned, what was so great about them as to be worthy of special mention? Their nit-picking philosophies make them like people who go around poking holes in walls and fences and sowing wild seeds in these places. They are like balding men contemplating combing their hair, or like a cook who counts each grain of rice before cooking! They take painstaking care, but to what end? They are useless to the world! If people of worth are elevated, there will be chaos as people fight to be promoted. If you choose people on the basis of their knowledge, then the people will try to steal this from each other. None of this makes the people any better. Indeed, what happens is that the people become more ambitious for gain. A son will kill his father for it and a minister will kill his ruler. People will steal in broad daylight and break down walls in the middle of the day. I say to you, the roots of all this great trouble will be found to have begun with Yao and Shun, and the consequences of this will remain for a thousand generations. A thousand generations later you will still have men who will eat each other!'

Nan Jung Chu sat upright on his mat looking perplexed and said,

'How can someone as old as I am study to achieve the state of which you speak?'

Master Keng Sang said, 'Keep your body in unity, hold on to life, don't become too anxious. Do this for three years and you can achieve the state of which I have spoken.'

Nan Jung Chu said, 'The eyes are a part of the body, I have never considered them to be anything other, but a blind person can't see through his eyes. Ears are a part of the body, I have never considered them to be anything other, but a deaf person can't hear through his ears. The heart is a part of the body, I have never considered it to be anything other, but the madman can't experience feelings with his. The body is also part of the body, but my soul seems separated from it, because I try to find my self, but why can't I find it? Now you say to me, "Keep your body in unity, hold on to life, do not become too anxious." Despite all my attempts to understand your Tao, this goes in one ear and out the other.'

Master Keng Sang said, 'That's all I can say. There is a saying, mud daubers are incapable of changing into caterpillars. The fowl of Yueh cannot hatch goose eggs, but those of Lu can. It is not that the virtue of one kind of hen is better than that of another. That one can and the other cannot is to do with their size, big and small. My talents are limited and cannot effect a change in you, Master. So, Sir, why don't you go south and see Lao Tzu?'

Nan Jung Chu gathered his provisions and set off, and after seven days and seven nights he arrived at the home of Lao Tzu.

'Have you come from Chu?' said Lao Tzu, and Nan Jung Chu replied, 'I have.'

'So, Sir, why have you brought this great crowd of other people with you?' Nan Jung Chu spun round and looked behind him in astonishment.

'Sir, don't you understand what I am saying?' said Lao Tzu.

Nan Jung Chu hung his head in shame and then looked up, sighed and said, 'Now I can't remember what to say in response and have therefore also forgotten what I was going to ask.'

'What are you saying?' said Lao Tzu.

'Do I have any understanding?' said Nan Jung Chu. 'People will call me a fool. Do I understand? This just upsets me. If I am not benevolent, then I distress others. If I am benevolent, then I distress myself. If I am not righteous, then I harm others. If I am righteous, then I upset myself. How can I get out of all this? These three issues perplex me, so following Chu's instructions I have come to ask you about them.'

Lao Tzu replied, 'Just now I looked deep into your eyes and I could see what sort of a person you are. What you have just said convinces me I am right. You are bewildered and confused, as if you had lost your father and mother and were looking for them using a pole to reach the bottom of the sea. You are lost and frightened. You want to rediscover your self and your innate nature but you haven't a clue how to set about this. What a sorry state you are in!'

Nan Jung Chu asked to be allowed to go into his room. He sought to develop the good and rid himself of the bad. After ten days of misery he came out and went to see Lao Tzu again.

'I can see that you have been washing and purifying yourself thoroughly,' said Lao Tzu, 'but you are still impure despite the outward cleanliness. Something is stirring inside you and there is still something rotten within. Outside influences will press upon you and you will find it impossible to control them. It is wiser to shut the gate of your inner self against them. Likewise, when interior influences disturb you and you find it impossible to control them, then shut the gate of your self so as to keep them in. To struggle against both the outside and inside influences is more than even one who follows the Tao and its Virtue can control, so how much more difficult it is for one who is just starting out along the Tao.'

Nan Jung Chu said, 'A villager fell ill and his neighbour asked how he was. He was able to describe his illness, even though he had never suffered from it before. When I ask you about the great Tao, it is like drinking medicine that makes me feel worse than before. I would like to know about the normal method for protecting one's life, that is all.'

'The basic way of protecting life – can you embrace the One?' said Lao Tzu. 'Can you hold it fast? Can you tell good from bad fortune without using the divination of the tortoise shell or the yarrow sticks? Do you know when to stop? Do you know when to desist? Can you forget others and concentrate upon your inner self? Can you escape lures? Can you be sincere? Can you be a little baby? The baby cries all day long but its throat never becomes hoarse: that indeed is perfect harmony. The baby clenches its fists all day long but never gets cramp, it holds fast to Virtue. The baby stares all day long but it is not affected by what is outside it. It moves without knowing where, it sits without knowing where it is sitting, it is quietly placid and rides the flow of events. This is how to protect life.'

'So this is what it takes to be a perfect man?' said Nan Jung Chu.

'Indeed no. This is what is known as the melting of the ice, the dissolving of the cold. Are you up to it? The perfect man is as one with others in seeking his food from the Earth and his joy from Heaven. However, he remains detached from consideration of profit and gain from others, does not get embroiled in plots and schemes nor in grandiose projects. Alert and unceasing he goes, simple and unpretentious he comes. This indeed is called the way to protect life.'

'So it is this which is his perfection?'

'Not quite,' replied Lao Tzu. 'Just now I asked you, "Can you become a little baby?" The baby acts without knowing why and moves without knowing where. Its body is like a rotting branch and its heart is like cold ashes. Being like this, neither bad fortune will affect it nor good fortune draw near. Having neither bad fortune nor good, it is not affected by the misfortune that comes to most others!'

One whose inner being is fixed upon such greatness emits a Heavenly glow. Even though he has this Heavenly glow, others will see him as just a man. Someone who has reached this point will begin to be consistent. Because he is consistent, people will unite with him and Heaven will be his guide. Those with whom people wish to unite are called the People of Heaven. Those whom Heaven guides are called Sons of Heaven.

Study is to study what cannot be studied. Undertaking means undertaking what cannot be undertaken. Philosophizing is to philosophize about what cannot be philosophized about. Knowing that knowing is unknowable is true perfection. Those who cannot grasp this will be destroyed by Heaven.

Draw on the generosity of life to sustain your body. Protect yourself from cares and you will give life to your heart. Revere what is central within and manifest it. Do this, and even if a multitude of evils befall you, they will be Heavenly in origin, not the works of fellow human beings. They will not overcome your serenity, they will not enter into your Spirit Tower.[86] Your Spirit Tower has its guardian but unless you know this guardian, it will not guard you.

If you cannot see this sincerity within you and you try to manifest it, it will fail. You will be invaded by external influences and will be unable to rid yourself of them. Then, whatever you do will inevitably fail. If you act badly in full public view, then people will seize you and punish you. If you act badly by night, then you will be seized by ghosts and punished. Understand this properly, know how you stand with regard to both people and ghosts and then reflect on this alone.

Someone who focuses on the internal is not interested in fame.
Someone who focuses on the external is intent on gaining whatever he can.
The one who does things which bring no glory, shines brightly in all he does.
One who looks to make gains at any cost is just a trader.
Others see he is just standing on tiptoe, but he thinks he is above all others.
Someone who struggles to succeed gets worn out,
while someone who doesn't really mind can't be possessed by such forces.
To exclude others is to show lack of concern and not to be concerned with others means that everyone is a stranger.
There is no weapon more lethal than the will – even Mo Yeh was inferior to it.
There are no greater adversaries than yin and yang, because

86. The heart and mind.

nothing in Heaven or on Earth escapes them.

But it is not yin and yang that do this, it is your heart that makes it so.

The Tao is in all things, in their divisions and their fullness. What I dislike about divisions is that they multiply, and what I dislike about multiplication is that it makes people want to hold fast to it. So people go out and forget to return, seeing little more than ghosts. They go forth and, to be sure, they say they have laid hold of something, but it is in fact what we call death. They are killed off and gone, just like a ghost. It is only when the formed learns from the unformed that there is understanding.

There is something which exists, though it emerges from no roots, it returns through no opening. It exists but has no place; it survives yet has no beginning nor end. Though it emerges through no opening, there is something which tells us it is real. It is real but it has no permanent place: this tells us it is a dimension of space. It survives, but has no beginning nor end: this tells us it has dimensions of time. It is born, it dies, it emerges, it returns, though in its emergence and return there is no form to be seen. This is what we call the Heavenly Gate. The Heavenly Gate is non-existence, and all forms of life emerge from non-existence. That which exists cannot cause things to exist. They all arise from non-existence. Non-existence is the oneness of non-existence. This is the hidden knowledge of the sages.

In former times people had a knowledge which was almost perfect. How nearly perfect? Some of them thought that in the beginning there was nothing and that the future brings nothing. There were others who believed that there was something in the beginning, and they saw life as decline and death as return, so they began to make divisions. Yet others said that at the beginning there was Non-Existence. Later there was life and with life there came immediately death. We believe non-existence to be the head, life the body and death the buttocks. Those who know that life and death are all One, we are all friends together. These three different perspectives, while diverging, belong to the same dynasty but are like the Chao and Ching families whose names show the line of succession and the Chu family whose name comes from its lands: they are not the same.

From the grime you have life, and when the grime is different in form, it is called different. You try to express this difference in words, though this is not a subject for words. But it is certain that this is not something you can understand. At the Winter Sacrifice you can indicate the intestines and the hooves of the sacrifice as being separate, yet they shouldn't be viewed as separate sacrifices. When someone visits a house they are thinking of buying, they inspect the whole house, from the ancestor shrines to the toilets, evaluating each part separately but also as a whole.

I will try to describe this discernment. It is rooted in life and has knowledge as its teacher, and from there proceeds to debate right and wrong. For example, we have fame and fortune, with people thinking they can determine what is really important. People think that they are the model of propriety and therefore try to make others see them like this, even to the point of dying for their views. These kinds of people believe that being an official means you are wise, and not being an official means you are a fool. They consider success as meaning they are famous and failure as being a disgrace. The people of this generation who follow this method are like the cicada and the little dove: they agree because they are the same.

If someone treads on another person's foot in the marketplace, he apologizes profusely for the accident. If an older brother treads on the foot of a younger brother, he comforts him. If a parent treads on a child's foot, there is no need to ask for forgiveness. There is a saying:

'Perfect behaviour does not discriminate amongst people;
perfect righteousness takes no account of things;
perfect knowledge makes no plans;
perfect benevolence exhibits no emotion;
perfect faith makes no oath of sincerity.'

Suppress the whims of the will and untie the mistakes of the heart.
Expunge the knots of Virtue,
unblock the flow of the Tao.

Honours and wealth,
distinctions and authority,
fame and gain,
these six are formed by the illusions of the will.

Looks and style,
beauty and reason,
thrill of life and memories,
these six are the faults of the heart.

Hatred and desire,
joy and anger,
sadness and happiness,
these six are the knots of Virtue.

Rejection and acceptance,
giving and taking,
knowledge and ability,
these six are the impediments to the free flow of the Tao.

When these four sets of six no longer trouble the breast,
then you will be centred.
Being centred, you will be calm.
Being calm, you will be enlightened.
Being enlightened, you will be empty.
Being empty, you will be in actionless action,
But with actionless action nothing remains undone.
The Tao is the centrepiece of the devotions of Virtue.
Life is the brightness of Virtue.
Innate nature is what motivates life.
Motivation which is untrue is lost.
Knowledge extends and knowledge plans.
But knowing what is not known is like looking at things like a
    child.
Action which arises because you cannot stop yourself is called
    Virtue.
When action arises from self, this is called governing.
These titles seem to contradict each other but in fact they agree.

Yi the Archer was a master at hitting the centre of the tiniest target, but he was foolish in that he could not stop wanting praise from others. The sage is skilful with regards to Heaven, but foolish in his dealings with people. Being skilful in both Heavenly concerns and human affairs is the mark of a complete man. Only an insect can be an insect, because what they are is given by Heaven. Does the complete man dislike Heaven? Does he hate what is of Heaven in people? If so, then imagine how much he hates the element of egocentricity in himself, which sets him and the rest of humanity above Heaven!

If a sparrow flew past Yi, he would have him, so good was he at his art. If everywhere in the world were to be caged, then the sparrows would be unable to escape. Indeed, this was why Tang caged Yi Yin by making him his cook and Duke Mu of Chin caged Po Li Hsi at the cost of five rams' skins. However, if you wish to cage people, you must use the things they like or you will never be successful.

A man whose feet have been chopped off casts aside fancy clothes, because his external appearance is incapable of being admired. A criminal condemned to death will scale the highest peaks, because he has no fear of life or death. If someone ignores the advances of friendship, he forgets about others and through forgetting others he is viewed as a man of Heaven. Such a person can be treated with respect, which will not please him, or be treated with contempt, which will not make him angry. This is because he is part of the Heavenly unity. Anyone who expresses anger but is not really angry will exhibit non-anger. Anyone who acts yet is not really acting, his actions will be non-action. If he wants to be still, he must be at peace. If he wants to be spiritual, he must calm his heart. When he wants to act, and to be successful, then he is moved by a force beyond him. That which one does because it is impossible to do other, that is the Tao of the sage.

CHAPTER 24

Hsu Wu Kuei

Through the kind offices of Nu Shang, Hsu Wu Kuei was able to see Marquis Wu of Wei. Marquis Wu greeted him fondly saying, 'Sir, you are unwell! The rigours of living in the wild mountain forests have been so great, and yet you have been kind enough to come and see me.'

To this Hsu Wu Kuei replied, 'I have come to comfort you, Sir, not for you to comfort me! Now, Sir, if you persist in sating your sensual appetites and desires and engaging in likes and dislikes, then you will adversely affect your true innate nature and your destiny. And if, Sir, you try to desist from sating your appetites and desires and make yourself change your likes and dislikes, then your ears and eyes will be afflicted. I have come to comfort you, and you, Sir, wish to comfort me!'

Marquis Wu looked very scornful and made no reply.

A little later Hsu Wu Kuei said, 'Let me tell you, Sir, how I judge dogs. The lowest kind of dog grabs his food, gorges himself and then stops, having the virtues of a fox. The ordinary sort of dog is always staring arrogantly at the sun. The most superior kind of dog appears to have forgotten himself. That is how I judge dogs, but that is nothing in comparison with how I judge horses. I judge horses by whether they run straight as a line, or curve round holding the centre, or turn as on a T-square, or circle like a compass. Such a horse I describe as being indeed a national horse, but not an international horse. A truly international horse is complete. He looks anxious, he appears to lose his way, to forget himself. However, a horse like this suddenly prances along or rushes past, kicking up the dust, and no one knows where he has gone.'

The Marquis was very pleased, and laughed.

Hsu Wu Kuei came out and Nu Shang said, 'Sir, what did you discuss with the ruler? When I discuss with him, I do so in a roundabout way using the *Book of Poetry* and the *Book of History*, and in this way I can discuss rituals and music. More directly, I use the Golden Tablets and the Six Bow Cases, and so guide him in decisions which have been very successful. Yet in all our meetings I have never seen him smile. So what is it that you discuss that makes him so pleased?'

'I simply explained how I judge dogs and horses,' said Hsu Wu Kuei.

'That was it?'

'Have you never heard of the exile from Yueh?' said Hsu Wu Kuei. 'A few days after leaving the country he was delighted if he met someone he had known in the country. A month after leaving the country he was delighted if he met someone he had seen in the country. A year after leaving the country he was delighted to meet someone who just looked as if he came from the country. The longer he was absent from his country, the more fond of it he became, is this not so? Those people who have retreated into the wild valleys where thick bushes block the path of even the weasels, and who have to struggle to move around, are delighted if they hear even the sound of a human footstep. How much more delighted are they if they hear the sounds of their own brothers and family talking and laughing beside them. Perhaps it has been rather a long time since a true man has sat and talked with your ruler!'

Hsu Wu Kuei went to see Marquis Wu, who said, 'Sir, you have been living in the forests of the mountains for a long time, surviving on acorns and chestnuts, filling yourself with onions and herbs and totally ignoring me! Now, is it old age? Do you want to eat meat and drink wine? Or have you come here to bless our altars of the Earth and the harvest?'

'Sir,' said Hsu Wu Kuei, 'I have lived in poverty and have never been able to eat or drink at Your Lordship's table, but I have come to bring comfort to you.'

'Really! Comfort me?' said the ruler.

'I wish to comfort both your body and your spirit.'

'What do you mean?'

'Heaven and Earth sustain all things,' said Hsu Wu Kuei. 'No matter how high you get, you should never consider that this shows you to be better. No matter how low you get, you should never consider that this shows you to be useless. You are ruler of the tens of thousands of chariots, the only ruler who taxes all the people of this country in order to satisfy the desires of your senses, even though your spirit does not wish to do this. The spirit prefers goodness and harmony and does not like wild living. Wild living is like an illness and this is what I have to comfort you over. What do you think of this, Sir?'

'Sir, I have wanted to see you for some time,' replied Marquis Wu. 'I wish to love the people and to act righteously and stop warfare. Would that do?'

'Certainly not. Loving the people is the beginning of harming the people. To act righteously and to cease warfare is the root of increased warfare. If you set about things thus, Sir, you will not succeed. All attempts to create beauty end in evil consequences. Your Grace may plan to act benevolently and righteously, but the result is the same as hypocrisy! You may give shape to things, but success leads to argument and argument leads to violence. Your Grace must not have hosts of troops massing in your forts nor lines of cavalry parading in front of the Palace of the Dark Shrine.

'Do not harbour thoughts that betray your best interests. Do not try to overcome others by cunning. Do not try to conquer others through plots. Do not try to defeat others by battle. If I kill the leaders and people of another ruler and seize the lands to satisfy my material wants, while my spirit is unsure of the validity of such actions, what is the point? Your Grace, the best thing is to do nothing, except develop true sincerity and thus be able to respond without difficulty to the true nature of Heaven and Earth. Thus the people will not die and it will not be necessary for you to have to enforce the end of warfare!'

The Yellow Emperor went to see Great Kuei at Chu Tzu Mountain. Fang Ming was the driver and Chang Yu travelled beside him. Chang Jo and Hsi Peng guided the horses and Kun Hun and Ku Chi rode behind the carriage. When they eventually arrived in the wild region of Hsiang Cheng, the seven sages were all confused and couldn't find anyone to ask the way.

They came upon a boy leading horses and asked him the way, saying, 'Do you know how to get to Chu Tzu Mountain?'

'Certainly,' he said.

'Do you know where Tai Kuei lives?'

'Certainly.'

'What a remarkable lad!' said the Yellow Emperor. 'Not only does he know how to reach Chu Tzu Mountain, he also knows where Tai Kuei lives. I would like to ask you how to govern everything below Heaven.'

'Governing everything below Heaven is surely the same as what I am doing at the moment, what's so hard about that?' said the lad. 'When I was younger, I liked to wander within the confines of the six directions but my eyesight began to fail. A wise elderly gentleman told me, "Climb up and ride in the carriage of the sun and explore the wild region of Hsiang Cheng." Now my eyesight is better and I am able to wander beyond the borders of the six directions. Ruling everything under Heaven is just like this. So what's the big problem?'

'Ruling everything under Heaven is, I agree, not your problem, my boy,' said the Yellow Emperor. 'However, I would like to hear how to do it.'

The lad did not answer. So the Yellow Emperor asked again. The boy said, 'Governing everything below Heaven is surely rather like leading horses! Get rid of anything that might harm the horses!'

The Yellow Emperor bowed twice to him, called him his Heavenly Master and departed.

If philosophers cannot see the effect of their ideas, they are not
   happy.
If debaters cannot argue cogently, they are not happy.
If interrogators cannot find candidates for criticism, they are not
   happy.
All of these are restrained by such attitudes.
Those scholars who are noticed by their generation rise to
   power.

Those who win the affections of the people consider high office
a reward.

Those with great strength enjoy a challenge.

Those who are brave and fearless revel in troubles.

Those skilled in sword and spear look for wars.

Those who are retiring rest on the laurels of their fame.

Those who are lawyers want more power to legislate.

Those who perform rituals and ceremonies enjoy their status.

Those who like benevolence and righteousness like to be able to
display them.

Farmers who cannot weed their fields are not contented.

The merchant who cannot trade at the market or by the well is
not satisfied.

The common folk like to have work to do from sunrise to
sunset, as they keep each other going.

The various craftsmen like to be using their skills.

If his wealth does not grow, the greedy man is unhappy.

If he is not getting more powerful, the ambitious man is
distressed.

Such people, driven by circumstance, are only happy when
things are changing, and when an opportunity arises, they inevitably
throw themselves into it. So they all proceed, like the changes of
the seasons, unchanging even though others change. They drive
their bodies and their innate nature and are overwhelmed by the
forms of life, never turning themselves back, which is sad!

Chuang Tzu said, 'An archer, not bothering to take aim, by sheer
luck hits the centre of the target. We could call him a good archer,
but in that case, everyone in the world could be called a Yi the
Archer, isn't that right?'

'OK,' said Hui Tzu.

Chuang Tzu said, 'People differ over what they consider to be
right, but everyone knows what they think is right. So everyone in
the world could be called a Yao, isn't that right?'

'OK,' said Hui Tzu.

Chuang Tzu said, 'So, there are four schools – the Literati,
Mohists, Yangists and Pingists – which along with your own, Sir,

make five. So which of these is right? Perhaps it is more like the case of Lu Chu? One of his followers said, "I have taken hold of your Tao, Master, and I can heat the pot in winter and make ice in summer." Lu Chu said, "But this is surely just using yang for yang and yin for yin. This is not what I would call the Tao. I will show you my Tao." So he tuned up two lutes and put one in the hall and the other in a private apartment. On striking the note Kung on one, the Kung note vibrated on the other. Likewise with the Chueh note, for the instruments were in harmony. Then he re-tuned one so that it was not in harmony with any of the five key notes. When this was played, all twenty-five of the strings on the other one vibrated, all faithful to their own note and all set off by the one note on the other lute. So, if you insist you are right, aren't you like this?'

Hui Tzi replied, 'The followers of Confucius, Mo, Yang and Ping,[87] like to tackle me in debate, each one trying to defeat the other, each violently trying to shout me down with their various arguments – but they haven't succeeded yet. So what about that?'

Chuang Tzu said, 'A citizen of Chi, not concerned by any mutilation,[88] sold his son to someone in Sung, where he became a gatekeeper. Yet this same man would go to great lengths to protect any of his bells or chimes. But he would not go looking for his son beyond the borders of his own country, such was his understanding of what is worthwhile! Or what if that well-known character, the citizen of Chu who was maimed and a gatekeeper, at midnight in another country, were to pick a fight with a boatman? Then he would never get across the river and would only have provoked the boatman's anger.'

Chuang Tzu was following a funeral when he passed by the grave of Hui Tzu. He looked round at those following him and said, 'The man of Ying had on the end of his nose a piece of mud as small as a fly's wing. He sent for the craftsman Shih to cut it off. Shih swirled his axe around and swept it down, creating such a

87. Ping is the title of the philosopher Kung Sang Lung.
88. A gatekeeper who could not run away was more valuable, so they were deliberately mutilated.

wind as it rushed past that it removed all trace of the mud from the man of Ying, who stood firm, not at all worried. The ruler Yuan of Sung heard of this and called craftsman Shih to visit him.

'"Would you be so kind as to do this for me?" he said.

'Craftsman Shih replied, "Your servant was indeed once able to work like that, but the type of material I worked upon is long since dead."

'Since the Master has died, I have not had any suitable material to work upon. I have no one I can talk with any longer.'

Kuan Chung was ill and Duke Huan, hearing of this, said, 'Father Chung, you are seriously ill. What if – which I had hoped I wouldn't have to say – your illness gets worse? Who should I hand over government of the country to?'

Kuan Chung replied, 'Your Grace, who do you wish to give it to?'

'Pao Shu Ya,' said the Duke.

'Not him! He is a good man, a scholar of integrity and he is honest, but he won't mix with those who are not the same as him. If he ever learns of someone's error, he won't forgive him, ever. If you put him in charge of the state, he will argue with you and upset everyone below him. Before too long you will view him as having done the unforgivable.'

'Then who can do this?' said the Duke.

The reply was, 'If I have to say anyone, then it should be Hsi Peng who should undertake this. He is the sort of man who forgets his high status and who will be supported by those below. He is ashamed that he is not like the Yellow Emperor, and is sorry for those who are not like him. The one who shares his Virtue with other people is known as a sage, he who shares his abilities with others is known as a worthy man. One who uses his worthiness to oppress others will never gain their support. One who uses his worthiness to lower himself can never fail to win the people's support. This man is hardly heard of in the country, nor does his own family have a great opinion of him. But as you ask me to speak, then I must say Hsi Peng.'

The King of Wu was sailing on the Yangtze River, and he moored in order to climb a mountain known for its monkeys.

When the monkeys saw him they fled in terror and hid in the bushes. However, there was one monkey who didn't seem bothered in the slightest, swinging around and showing off before the King. The King fired an arrow at him, which the monkey simply caught cleverly in his hand. The King then called up his followers to join the hunt and soon they had the monkey trapped and killed.

The King said to his friend Yen Pu I, 'This monkey showed off, relied on its skills and was rude to me, and this resulted in its death! Be warned by this! Ah, do not let yourself seem arrogant to others!' So Yen Pu I went home and began to study with Tung Wu, to eliminate this look of arrogance from his face, to give up happiness and to leave reasoning. Within three years he was praised by everyone.

Tzu Chi of the Southern Suburb was sitting, leaning on the arm of his chair, gazing into Heaven and singing. Yen Cheng Tzu came in and, seeing him, said, 'Master, you surpass all others. Is it true that your body can be made to look like a pile of dried bones and your heart be made like cold, dead ashes?'

Tzu Chi replied, 'I used to live in a cave in a mountain. At that time Tien Ho[89] came to see me for a visit, and the citizens of the kingdom of Chi congratulated him three times. I must have shown him who I am, since he obviously knew me. I must have been selling something and that is why he came to buy. If I had not displayed something, then how could he have known who or what I was? If I had not been selling something, then how could he have been able to buy anything? Oh dear! I do so pity those who lose themselves. I also pity those who pity others. However, I also pity those who pity those who pity others, but that was long ago.'

Confucius went to Chu, and the King of Chu offered a toast in wine. Sun Shu Ao stepped forward and raised the wine glass in his hand and I Liao from the Southern Market took some wine and poured it out as a libation, saying, 'You are like a man of old! They would make speeches.'

---

89. Chief Minister of Chi who actually controlled the state, but was admired for his respect for the hermit Tzu Chi.

Confucius said, 'I have heard of speech which is without words, but I have never spoken it. I shall do so now. I Liao from the Southern Market played with a set of balls and the problems between the two houses were solved. Sun Shu Ao slept quietly,[90] his fan waving gently, and the men of Ying prepared for war. How I wish I had a beak three feet long.'[91]

People like these follow the Tao that is not the Tao, and this discussion is the Argument Without Words. So it is that, when Virtue is fully integrated into the Tao and words stop where knowledge can know nothing more, there is perfection. The oneness of the Tao is beyond Virtue and what knowledge does not know is beyond what argument can cover. To label things as the Literati and the Mohists do is useless.

The sea does not reject the rivers that flow into it from the east; this is great perfection.

The sage holds both Heaven and Earth and his benign influence reaches out to all below Heaven, yet we know nothing of his background.

So it is that he has no official title while he is alive and no eulogies when he is dead. His reality is not known and labels do not stick to him: this is known as the great man.

A dog is not thought special just because it can bark, and no man is thought wise just because he can speak. Even less is he thought to be great. Anyone who thinks he is great is not to be counted as such, nor seen as virtuous. Nothing is greater than Heaven and Earth, but they do not seek greatness. One who knows what it is to be great does not go looking for it, does not lose it nor reject it and does not change his opinions in order to be great. He turns inward and finds what is without end. He follows the ancient ways and finds what never dies. This is the sincerity of the great man.

Tzu Chi had eight sons, and he called them before him, and summoned Chiu Fang Yin and said, 'Study the physiognomy of my sons and tell me which one is to be the greatest.'

90. Both men displayed coolness in times of trouble, and by their calm actions, not saying a word, stared down trouble.
91. The beak refers to the chattering of birds – noisy conversation.

'Kun is the most fortunate,' said Chiu Fang Yin.

Tzu Chi was stunned and yet also delighted. 'How is this?' he said.

'Kun will dine with the ruler of a kingdom and this will last all his life.'

Tears poured from Tzu Chi's eyes and he said unhappily, 'What has my son done to deserve this?'

'One who shares the table of a ruler of a kingdom brings blessings to all three sections of his family, and especially to his father and mother!' said Chiu Fang Yin. 'Now, Master, when I said this to you, you wept. This will disturb the fortune. The son is fortunate indeed, but his father is not so fortunate.'

Tzu Chi said, 'Yin, how do you know that this will be fortune for Kun? What you describe, the food and drink, only touches on the nose and the mouth, so how can you claim to know where such things come from? I have never been a shepherd, but a ewe gave birth to a lamb in the south-west corner of my fields. I have never been a hunter, but a flock of quail have arrived in the south-east corner of my fields.[92] If this isn't strange, then what is? When I go out wandering and travelling with my son, we journey through Heaven and Earth. We look for pleasure in Heaven and we look for nourishment from Earth. He and I don't get caught up in the affairs of the world, or in plots or in any strange practices. He and I ride upon the reality of Heaven and Earth and let nothing come between us. He and I are one in undisturbed unity and we not interested in doing what others think would be useful. Now you come and tell us that he has this crude and common "success"! In my experience, when something untoward happens, this is the result of something untoward having been done. This comes not from any action of mine nor of my son, but it must come from Heaven! Yes, this is what makes me weep.'

A little while after this he sent Kun to do some work in the kingdom of Yen. While on the road, bandits captured him. They decided that it would be difficult to sell him as he was, but if they

---

92. i.e., things come to me, although I have done nothing to deserve them.

cut off his foot, then they could sell him easily.[93] They did this, and
sold him in the kingdom of Chi, where, as fortune would have it,
he became a palace official in the palace of Duke Kang and so had
food to sustain him until the end of his days.

Nieh Chueh bumped into Hsu Yu and said, 'Master, where are
you heading?'

'I am escaping Yao.'

'What do you mean?'

Hsu Yu said, 'Yao has become obsessed with benevolence and I
am worried that he will be mocked throughout the world. Future
generations might even resort to eating each other because of this!
The people come together without difficulty. Give them love, and
they will care for you, assist them, and they will rally round you,
praise them, and they will be excited, upset them, and they will
desert you. Love and assistance arise from benevolence and righteousness, and while some people will deny benevolence and righteousness, the majority look to them for assistance. Benevolence and
righteousness conducted under these circumstances become insincere,
and possibly may be evil, like lending traps to others. Allowing one
man to determine what the world needs through his own powers is
like trying to comprehend everything in one moment. Yao knows
that the worthy man can assist the whole world, but he does not
know that such a person can ruin the whole world, for it is only
those outside this sphere of influence who can really understand.'

You have the gullible and the weak, you have the quick and vain
and you have the greedy and bent.

Those who are known as the gullible and the weak study under
just one master, they say yes to him and then feel privately smug,
believing that they have understood all that is necessary, when in
fact they have not grasped a single thing. These are known as the
gullible and the weak.

The quick and the vain are like lice on a pig. The lice find a place
where the bristles are long and well-spaced and they view this as a

93. Slaves were usually doormen, and one who could not run away was the most
valuable.

great palace or vast park. They might choose the groove between the hoof or the area of the nipples and the thigh and in such a safe place they consider this to be their quiet retreat. They do not know that one morning the butcher will make a sweep with his arm, lay out the grass, light the fire and that then they will be burnt up along with the pig. Their progress is limited and their retreat is limited. These are known as the quick and the vain.

The greedy and bent are similar to Shun. Mutton doesn't want ants, but ants want mutton, especially when it is off. Shun was also off: this was why the hundred tribes were so delighted with him and followed after him. Even though he changed his place of residence three times, each one was counted as a capital city. When he arrived at the wilderness of Teng, he had a hundred thousand families with him. Yao heard of Shun and gave him control over the new and untamed country and said he hoped Shun would bring benefits to all. When Shun was given this command, he was already quite elderly and his hearing and eyesight were poor, but he was unable to retire to his home. These are known as the greedy and the bent.

So it is that the spiritual man dislikes people crowding around him. If they insist on coming, he argues with them, and from this argument comes nothing of any benefit to anyone. Therefore, he ensures he has no attachment to anything, and nothing from which he is separated. Holding fast to Virtue and dwelling in harmony, he follows the world. This is what is known as the true man. He leaves knowledge for the ants, follows the style of fish and abandons the ideas of sheep.

See using the eyes, hear using the ears, have vision using the heart. If you do this the course is straight as if measured using a line, the changes are congenial. The true man of the past waited upon Heaven when dealing with people and did not wait upon people when dealing with Heaven. The true man of the past obtained it and was born, lost it and died, obtained it and died, and lost it and was born.

Medicines are like this. There is monkshood, ballflower, cockscomb and chinaroot. They each have their time when they are best suited, though to list all their uses would be impossible.

Kou Chien[94] retreated to Mount Kuai Chi with three thousand soldiers in armoured jackets and carrying shields, and Minister Chung alone understood how to save the disaster-ridden state, but he didn't know how to save himself from a tragic fate.

It is said that the eye of the owl is specially adapted and the leg of the crane has its right proportion. To try and cut out anything from these would be disaster to these creatures.

It is said that the wind blows over the river and the river is diminished. When the sun passes over the river, it loses something. If the sun and wind remain watching over the river, then the river will not be alarmed that they are doing anything to it, for it would continue to draw from the streams and go on its way. Water stays close to the earth and the shadow stays close to its source, for things stick together.

There is danger for the eye in seeing too clearly, danger for the ear in hearing too sharply and danger to the heart from caring too greatly. Indeed, it is dangerous to use any of our faculties. If these dangers are not dealt with, then disaster after disaster will ensue. To turn back from this to the original state takes much effort and time, but people consider these faculties as their greatest treasure, isn't that sad! As a result there is constant destruction of states and endless massacre of the people, while no one knows how to look into how this happened.

The foot only touches a small part of the earth, yet people can travel great distances into the unknown.

The knowledge of people is minor, and though minor it has to trust in that which they do not know, to know what is meant by Heaven. It is known as the great One, the great mystery, the great yin, the great eye, the great equal, the great skill, the great truth, the great judge. All this is perfection.

The great One knows,
the great mystery reveals,

94. King of Yueh who was overthrown by invaders and retreated to the mountain with his minister Chung. They won back the kingdom, but the King then feared Chung and made him commit suicide.

the great yin observes,
the great eye sees,
the great equal is the origin,
the great skill creates it,
the great trust touches it,
the great judge holds fast to it.

Heaven is in everything: follow the light, hide in the cloudiness and begin in what is. Do this and your understanding will be like not understanding and your wisdom will be like not being wise. By not being wise you will become wise later. When you ask questions, set no limits, even though they cannot be limitless. Although things seem to be sometimes going up and sometimes descending, sometimes slipping away, nevertheless there is a reality, the same today as in the past. It does not change, for nothing can affect it. Could we not say it is one great harmony? So why shouldn't we ask about it and why are you so confused? If we use that which does not confuse to understand that which does confuse, then we can come back to that which does not confuse. This will be the great unconfusing.

蒼松蔭：草閣滄
灣秋生丹楓夕
照閒軒浮詩翁
芳庭桂平中流
水眼千山

CHAPTER 25

Travelling to Chu

Peng Yang was once travelling to Chu and hoped that Yi Chieh would mention him to the King. But before the King would see him, Yi Chieh left to go home. So Peng Yang went instead to Wang Kuo and said, 'Sir, would you be kind enough to mention me to the King?'

Wang Kuo said, 'I'm not as useful a contact as Kung Yueh Hsiu.'

Peng Yang said, 'What sort of a person is this Kung Yueh Hsiu?'

'In winter he spears turtles beside the river, in summer he holidays in the mountains. Those passing ask him what he is doing and he answers, "This is where I live."'

'As Yi Chieh could not persuade the King to see you, what use will I be? I am not equal to Yi Chieh. He is the sort of man who has no virtue but who does have understanding, who is not lax with himself but devotes all his energy to furthering those around him. He's attracted to fame and fortune, so if he helps you, it is not because of any virtue but out of contrariness. It is like trying to pretend spring has come by putting on extra clothes, or wanting winter's cold winds to come and cool you in the summer. The King of Chu is also like this, overbearing and stern, and if he is upset by someone, he is as merciless as a tiger. No one except a toadying minister or one of true Virtue is able to discuss anything with him!

'The sage living humbly makes even his family forget their poverty; when he is powerful, he makes kings and dukes forget their status and properties and become humble. With life he just tags along and enjoys himself. With the people he delights in the successes of others and holds true to himself. Sometimes, without a word, he brings harmony to people. Simply by being with them, he transforms people until they feel towards him as do father and son who are on good terms with each other, in unity. All this happens without any effort, for he is guided by his heart. This is why I say wait for Kung Yueh Hsiu.'

The sage goes beyond confusion and diversity and makes everything into one body. Even though he does not know for certain how, he is true to his innate nature. He comes back to destiny and reacts appropriately, with Heaven as his guide, so that people follow him and accord him titles. If he was concerned with what he knew and what he did was inconsistent, then how could he be stopped?

If someone is born with a beautiful appearance, you can give them a mirror, but they will never know that they have a beautiful appearance if you never tell them so. Whether they know it or not, whether they are told or not, their fine appearance will never be changed. Other people admire their good fortune, for it comes from their innate nature. The sage loves the people and the people bestow titles on him, yet if they do not tell him, he won't know that he loves the people. Whether he knows it or he doesn't, whether he is told this or not, his love for the people is unchanged and their tranquillity in him is endless, for this is his innate nature.

Someone who sees his native kingdom or his old city is bound to be excited. Even if it has become nothing but mounds, trees and bushes, and when he enters it, he finds nine-tenths of those whom he knew gone, nevertheless he is most definitely glad to see the place. Imagine his joy when he sees what he used to see and hears what he used to hear, for it is like a mighty eighty-foot tower of which he has heard talk.

Lord Jin Hsiang grasped that core principle around which everything revolves and followed it to its end. He went with all other things, with no end and no beginning, no desire, no time. Every day he saw change, but he himself was one with what never changes, so there was never any need for him to stop! Anyone who seeks Heaven as his teacher will never obtain Heaven as his teacher. He will end up just following things, and no matter what he does, he cannot help it.

The sage has no thoughts of Heaven,
no thoughts of humanity,
no thoughts of beginning,
no thoughts of others.
He goes with his generation and does not stop.
He does everything and is never blocked.
Others want to unite with him, but then, what else could they
do?

Tang obtained the services of the rider Teng Heng and made him
his instructor. He followed this teacher but was not restricted by
him, so he was able to pursue his interests to their conclusion. This
resulted in various honours. These honours were superfluous and
revealed for all to see the twin aspects of what he had obtained.
Confucius commands, 'Work at what is at hand, that can be your
teacher.' Yung Cheng said, 'Remove the days and there are no
more years, no internal, no external.'

Ying of Wei made a treaty with the Marquis Tien Mou, but
Marquis Tien Mou broke it. Ying of Wei was furious and was
planning to send an assassin. The duke responsible for war heard of
this and said, 'Sire, you are the lord of ten thousand chariots and yet
you, as ruler, would use a common man to exact revenge! Let me
have two hundred thousand soldiers so that I can attack him,
capture his people and seize his cattle and horses, stoking up a fire
within him that will burn into his back. I shall then attack his
capital. When his commander Chi attempts to escape, I will strike
from behind and break his spine.'

Chi Tzu was ashamed when he heard this and said, 'We have
been building our walls up to eighty feet high and now, when they
are almost complete, we're about to make a breach in them. This
will be an immense waste of the convict labour we have used.
Now, we have not had to use our troops for seven years and this is
what Your Lordship's power rests upon. Yen is a trouble-maker
and you should take no notice of him.'

Hua Tzu heard this and did not agree. 'Those who say attack the
state of Chi are trouble-makers,' he said. 'Those who say don't
attack are also trouble-makers. The one who says those who urge

you to attack and those who don't are both trouble-makers, is himself a trouble-maker.'

'So, what should I do?' said the ruler.

'Just seek to discover the Tao!'

Hui Tzu heard this and brought Tai Chen Jen to see the ruler. Tai Chen Jen said, 'There is a creature known as the snail, do you know this, Sire?'

'For sure,' he said.

'It has on its left horn a kingdom called Provoke and on its right horn one called Foolish. These kingdoms are often arguing over territory and fighting. The dead are heaped up in multitudes with the defeated army fleeing – but within a few days they are back.'

The ruler said, 'Ha! What is this empty chatter about?'

'I just want to show Your Majesty what this is about. When you contemplate the four directions and up and down, Sire, is there any limit to them?'

The ruler said, 'No limit.'

'When the heart has wandered through unlimited realms, do you know how to return to this kingdom in such a way that its troubles seem to be insignificant?'

The ruler said, 'Certainly.'

'In the centre of these lands through which one wanders, is the state of Wei, and in the centre of this state of Wei is the capital, Liang, and at the centre of this capital Liang is the King. Is there really any difference between the King and the Foolish kingdom?'

The ruler said, 'No difference.'

After his visitor had departed, the ruler sat, dumbfounded, as if lost to the world.

Then Hui Tzu came to see him and the ruler said, 'That visitor, he is a great man, a sage cannot equal him.'

Hui Tzu said, 'If you blow a flute, you get a good sound, but if you blow on the pommel of your sword, you get a wheezing noise. Yao and Shun are often praised by people, but if you talk about them in front of Tai Chien Jen, then it sounds like one little wheeze.'

Confucius travelled to Chu and stayed at a tavern on Ant Hill. In the neighbouring house, the husband, wives and servants, male and female, climbed on to the roof to see him. Tzu Lu said, 'What are those people doing up there?'

Confucius said, 'They are followers of a sage. He is hidden among the people, hidden away in the fields. Fame no longer interests him, but his resolve is unlimited. His mouth speaks words, but his heart offers none. He is not at ease with this generation and his heart is not concerned with it. He is like someone who has drowned on dry land. I imagine he is Liao of the Southern Market?'

Tzu Lu wanted to bring him over.

Confucius said, 'Stop! He knows that I comprehend all this and he knows I am travelling to Chu. He assumes that I will seek promotion from the King of Chu and thus he views me as a time-server. Someone like him is embarrassed just hearing the words of a time-server, let alone being seen with him! And why do you believe he is still around?'

Tzu Lu went and looked and found the house empty.

The border guard at Chang Wu said to Tzu Lao, 'The ruler of a state must not be careless, nor should he be careless with the people. Previously when ploughing my fields, I was careless, and the result was a poor crop. When weeding, I was thoughtless, and the result was a diminished harvest. In recent years I changed my ways, I ploughed deep and was careful to bury the seed. My harvests are now plentiful and therefore I have all I need all year round.'

Chuang Tzu heard this and said, 'People today, when looking after themselves and caring for their hearts, are very much like this border guard's description. They ignore Heaven, wander from their innate nature, dissolve their real being, extinguish their spirit and follow the common herd. So it is that someone who is careless with their innate nature causes evil and hatred to arise, affecting their innate nature like rank weeds and bushes. These weeds and bushes, when they first appear, seem helpful and supportive, but slowly they affect the innate nature. They become like a mass of suppurating sores which break out in scabs and ulcers, oozing pus from this disease. This is how it is.'

Po Chu studied under Lao Tzu and said, 'I would like to be allowed to wander the world.'

Lao Tzu said, 'No! Everywhere under Heaven is the same.'

He asked again and Lao Tzu said, 'Where will you go first?'

'I will start with Chi.'

When he arrived in Chi he saw the corpse of a criminal. He lugged the body about to put it into the proper ritual position, took off his robes and covered the body, crying to Heaven and saying, 'My son, my son! Everyone under Heaven is in great trouble, and you, my son, have found this out earlier than the rest of us. It is said, "Don't steal, don't murder." However when praise and failure have been defined, suffering appears. When goods and fortunes have been amassed, argument appears. To establish things that bring suffering, to amass what brings argument, to cause distress and restlessness to others, one asks how is this possible?'

The scholar rulers of old saw their success in terms of the people and saw their failures in terms of themselves. They viewed the people as right and themselves as wrong. Thus, if even one person suffered, they would accept this as being their responsibility and retire. This is certainly not the case today. Today's rulers hide what should be done and then blame the people when they don't understand. They make the problems greater and punish those who cannot manage. They push people to the limit and execute those who can't make it. When people realize that they simply haven't the energy, they use pretence. When every day there is so much falsehood, how can the scholars and the people not become compromised! When strength is lacking, deceit is used; when knowledge is lacking, deception is used; when material goods are lacking, theft is used. But who really is to blame for these thefts and robbery?'

Chu Po Yu had lived for sixty years and he changed at sixty. He had never questioned that he was right, but he came to change his views and saw that from the beginning he had been wrong. Now it was not possible to know whether what he had been saying for fifty-nine years was right or wrong. All forms of life are born, yet it is not possible to see their source. They all go forth, but it is not easy to see by which gate. People all respect what they understand as knowledge, but they do not understand what their knowledge does not understand and so gain understanding. So isn't this simply great confusion? Well, well! There is no way out of that. This comes from saying definitely this, definitely that, doesn't it?

Confucius asked the Great Historians, Ta Tao, Po Chang Chien and Hsi Wei, 'Duke Ling of Wei enjoyed wine, women and song, and didn't look after the affairs of his kingdom, going off hunting with nets and bows, not attending to the sessions with the other lords. Why then is he called Duke Ling?'

Ta Tao said, 'Because this was so, he was titled so.'

Po Chang Chien said, 'This Duke Ling had three wives and he bathed with them in the same bathtub. However, when Shih Chiu appeared before him with imperial gifts, he himself would serve him. Duke Ling was corrupt in the first case and yet, when he saw a worthy man, he behaved quite correctly. This was the reason he was called Duke Ling.'

Hsi Wei said, 'Duke Ling died and divination was made to see whether he should be buried in the family tomb, but the oracle said no. When divination was made to see if he should be buried on Sand Hill, the oracle was good. When they dug down, they discovered a stone tomb. After cleaning it and looking carefully at it they found an inscription which said: 'Do not rely upon your descendants, Duke Ling will take this for himself.' It's obvious, therefore, that Duke Ling was called Ling long before he was born. However, you can't expect these two to know anything about all this!'

Little Knowledge asked Great Official Accord, saying, 'What do people mean when they say Talk of the Villages?'

Great Official Accord said, 'Talk of the Villages refers to the union of the ten surnames and hundred names into one code of living. What is different is united to form a commonality. What is in common is broken up to form the differences. If you point to different parts of a horse you do not have "a horse". However, if you have the whole animal in all its parts standing before you, you have a horse. In this way the hills and mountains arise, little layer upon little layer, and so become lofty, and the Yangtze and Yellow Rivers have become great through the conjoining of small streams.

'The great man shows his greatness by combining all the common aspects of humanity. So, when ideas come to him from outside, he can receive them but does not cling to them. Likewise, when he

brings forth some idea from within himself, they are like guides to
those around but they do not seek to dominate.

'The four seasons each have their own original life,
and Heaven does not discriminate,
so the cycle is fulfilled.
The five government offices have different roles,
but the ruler does not discriminate,
so the state is well run.
The great man does not discriminate
between war and peace,
so his Virtue is perfect.
All the forms of life are different,
but the Tao does not discriminate,
so it has no name.
Being nameless, it is also actionless action,
yet all life occurs.
The seasons end and begin;
the generations change and transform.
Inauspicious and auspicious fortune falls upon you,
sometimes unwelcomed,
other times welcomed.
Settle into your own views,
argue with others,
at times condemn those who are upright,
then those who are bent.
You should be like a great marsh land
with space for a hundred kinds of trees.
Or be like a great mountain
where the trees and grasses rest on the same ground.
This is what is meant by Talk of the Villages.'

Little Knowledge said, 'Surely, if we call this the Tao, that will
be enough?'

Great Official Accord said, 'Certainly not. For example, if we
add up all that is, it definitely exceeds the conventional description
of ten thousand things. However, we use the term "ten thousand
things" as a way of saying that the number of things is very large.

So also we use "Heaven and Earth" to describe great things, and "yin and yang" as original breaths of life which are vast, and the term "Tao" as being that term which covers them all. If we use this term to cover everything, there is no problem. However, if we try to go further and define this term by comparing it to what can be discerned, then we would be like those who call a dog and a horse by the same name, even though they are so different.'

Little Knowledge said, 'Within the limits of the four compass points and the six boundaries, where do the ten thousand things all have their origin?'

Great Official Accord said, 'Yin and yang reflect each other, oppose each other and control each other. The four seasons follow each other, give birth to each other and finish each other off. Good and evil, rejection and reception thus arose in definition against each other, giving rise to the distinction between male and female. People change from security to insecurity; auspicious and inauspicious fortune are born. Relaxation and tension are side by side. Collecting and scattering emerge and round it all off. These names and their developments can be examined and their actions recorded exactly. The notions of following in orderly sequence, of interaction, of returning when the limit has been reached, of starting again when they end, all this is inherent in things. Words can define them and knowledge can comprehend them, but that is all that can be said of things. The one who seeks the Tao does not try to go beyond this nor try to find the source. Quite simply, this brings all discussion to a close.'

Little Knowledge said, 'Chi Chen's point that there is no cause and Chieh Tzu's argument that there is a cause are two different perspectives. So which one is right and which one is mistaken?'

Great Official Accord said, 'Chickens cackle and dogs bark: this is what people know. However, even though they have this level of understanding, they can't explain how the chicken and dog have such different voices, nor can they conceive of what the future might be. We can examine and define to such a point that what is left is minute, or we can make it so great that we can't take it in. So whether you say there is a cause or there is not, you are still trapped in relative terms and so you're in error. If there is a cause, then that is true, if there is no cause, then there is nothing. If there is a name, there is reality and they really exist, if there is no name, there is no reality and no thing.

'It is possible to describe, to say, but these words take you away from its reality. Before things are born, they cannot stop being born, and once dead, they cannot resist going. Death and birth are not far apart, but what causes them is beyond our sight. Notions of a cause or no cause are irrelevant. I search for their historic roots but they disappear into the past. I look for the end of the future, but it never ceases to arrive. Infinite, unlimited, there are no words for this. To try to define it is to place it in the same category as "Is there a cause or is there not?" These are just words and they begin and end with things.

'The Tao does not have an existence, nor does it not have an existence. By using the title "Tao", we use a limited term. "Is there a cause or is there not?" are therefore words of very minor significance. Do they have anything to do with the great work? If what you say is of significance, then all day long you can discuss the Tao. If what you say is insignificant, you can talk all day long and all you will discuss is minor issues. The Tao takes us to the edge and neither words nor silence are able to describe this. No words, no silence, this is the highest form of debate.'

說法度生四十九
年.涅槃於穆王壬
申二月十五日住
世七十九年.
須菩提生時府庫
盡空故父卜云既善
且吉故曰空生亦
名善現又稱吉祥
尊者.十大弟子中
解空第一.
迦葉舊華言飲光.
以身有金光得名

金剛般若波羅蜜經

CHAPTER 26

Affected from Outside

It is not possible to determine what will affect us from outside us. For example, Lung Feng was executed, Pi Kan was sentenced to death, Prince Chi[95] pretended to be mad, E Lai[96] was murdered and Chieh and Chou both perished. All rulers want their ministers to be loyal, but such loyalty may not always be sincere. So Wu Yun was cast into the Yangtze and Chang Hung died in Shu, where the people preserved his blood for three years, by which time it had become green jade. All parents want their children to be filial, but filial sons are not necessarily so from love. This is why Hsiao Chi[97] was distressed and Tseng Shen[98] was sad.

If wood rubs against wood, it starts to burn.
When metal is heated, it melts.
When yin and yang go wrong,
Heaven and Earth are hugely disturbed.
Then comes the crash of thunder,
and fire from the midst of the rains
which destroys the great trees.
Gaining and losing,
the people are caught between them both
and there is no way out.
Trapped and entombed,

95. Pretended to be mad in order to escape the wrath of Chou, the last Shang Emperor.
96. A crony of Chou.
97. A model of filial piety, persecuted by his stepmother.
98. Another model of filial piety, hated by his father.

they can never complete anything.
Their hearts are strung out
as if suspended between Heaven and Earth,
sometimes comforted,
sometimes frightened,
plagued with problems.
Gain and loss rub against each other
and start fires beyond number
that burn up the balances of the heart in most people.
The moon cannot contain such fires.
All is destroyed,
the quest for the Tao ends.

Chuang Tzu's family were poor so he went to borrow some rice from the Marquis of Chien Ho. The Marquis of Chien Ho said, 'Of course. I am about to receive the tax from the people and will give you three hundred pieces of gold – is that enough?'

Chuang Tzu flushed with anger and said, 'On my way here yesterday I heard a voice calling me. I looked around and saw a large fish in the carriage rut. I said, "Fish! What are you doing there?" He said, "I am Minister of the Waves in the Eastern Ocean. Sire, do you have a measure of water you could give me?" Well, I told him, "I am going south to visit the Kings of Wu and Yueh and after that I would redirect the course of the Western River so it will flow up to you. Would that do?" The large fish flushed with anger and said, "I am out of my very element, I have nowhere to go. Give me just a little water and I can survive. But giving me such an answer as that means you will only ever find me again on a dried fish stall!"'

Prince Jen had a great fish-hook and a vast line. He baited the hook with fifty bulls, sat down on Mount Kuai Chi and cast his line into the Eastern Ocean.

Morning after morning he cast his line, but after a whole year he had still caught nothing. Finally, a great fish was hooked which dived into the depth, dragging the great fish-hook down with him. Then it turned and rushed to the surface and shot out, shaking its fins and churning up the sea so the waves rose like mountains and the waters turned white with its fury. The noise was like gods and demons fighting and terror spread over a thousand miles. Eventually, Prince Jen landed the fish and cut it and dried it. From Chih Ho in the east to Tsang Wu in the north, everyone had more than he could eat.

Ever since, those with little talent in later generations have told and retold this story, never ceasing to amaze people. If people take their rod and line and set off to fish in marshes and ditches, looking for minnows and sprats, then they will have some difficulty in catching a big fish. Those who make much of their little notions and strut around in front of officials are a long way off being companions of the greater comprehension. Indeed, if someone has never heard of Prince Jen, he is far from being competent to be one of this generation who rule the world.

A group of Literati students of the Odes of Ritual were robbing a grave. The main scholar in charge said, 'The sun is rising in the east, how's it going?'

The younger Literati said, 'We haven't got his clothes off him yet, but there's a pearl in his mouth.[99] As the Odes say,

'Green, green the grain
Dwelling on the slopes of the mound.
If during life you give nothing,
At death, does he deserve a jewel?'

So saying, they pulled back his beard and moustache and then one of them carefully prised open the mouth so as not to damage the pearl.

A follower of Lao Lai Tzu[100] was gathering firewood, when he chanced to meet Confucius. On his return he said, 'There is a man who has a long body and short legs, a slightly humped back and his ears far back. He seems like one who is preoccupied with all the troubles within the four oceans. I don't know who he is.'

Lao Lai Tzu said, 'This is Confucius. Call him over here.'

99. A jewel was placed in the mouth of a corpse to help pay its way through the Underworld.
100. A 'Taoist' teacher – not Lao Tzu.

Confucius came. Lao Lai Tzu said, 'Confucius! Rid yourself of your pride and that smug look on your face and you could then become a nobleman.'

Confucius bowed and retreated and then a look of astonishment came over his face and he asked, 'Do you think I could manage this?'

Lao Lai Tzu said, 'You can't bear the sufferings of this one generation, therefore you go and cause trouble for ten thousand generations to come. Do you set out to be this miserable, or don't you realize what you are doing? You insist that people should only be joyful in a way you prescribe. The infamy of this will follow you all your life. This is the action of a nondescript type of person, one who wants to rule through fame, who enjoys plotting with others, praising Yao and criticizing Chieh, when really you should just forget them and silence your tendency to glorify. What is wrong cannot but harm and what is active cannot fail to be wrong. The sage is cautious and hesitates before any action, and so always succeeds. But really, what can I say about your actions? For ultimately they are only bragging!'

The Lord Yuan of Song dreamt in the middle of the night that a man with dishevelled hair peered in at him through the side door and said, 'I have come from the depths of Tsai Lu and was on my way from the clear Yangtze as an ambassador to the Lord of the Yellow River, when a fisherman called Yu Chu caught me.'

Immediately Lord Yuan woke up and asked a diviner to find out what this meant.

'This is a sacred turtle,' said the diviner.

'Is there a fisherman called Yu Chu?' asked the Lord.

'There is,' he was told.

The Lord said, 'Command that Yu Chu comes here.'

Next day, Yu Chu arrived and the ruler asked him, 'What have you caught recently?'

He replied, 'I have caught a white turtle in my nets recently. It is about five feet in circumference.'

'Present your turtle,' said the ruler.

When the turtle came, the ruler couldn't decide whether to kill it or keep it. His heart was troubled, so he asked the diviner, who said, 'Kill the turtle and use it to make divinations and receive an oracle.' So the turtle had its shell removed and seventy-two holes drilled into its shell for divination.[101] Not one of them failed to offer a good oracle.

Confucius said, 'The sacred turtle could manifest itself in a dream to Lord Yuan but could not escape the nets of Yu Chu. It had sufficient wisdom to give seventy-two correct divinations, but it could not escape having its vital organs cut out. This is how it is, wisdom has its limits and even spirituality has something beyond its reach. Even perfect wisdom can be defeated by a multitude of scheming people.

'Fish seem not to fear nets, they only seem to fear pelicans. Rid yourself of petty knowledge and allow great wisdom to enlighten you. Rid yourself of goodness, and goodness will naturally arise. When a child is born, it needs no great teacher; nevertheless it learns to talk as it lives with those who talk.'

Hui Tzu argued with Chuang Tzu and said, 'What you say is useless!'

'You have to understand what is useless, then you can talk about what is useful,' said Chuang Tzu. 'Heaven and Earth are vast indeed and yet human beings only use the tiny part of the universe on which they tread. However, if you dug away beneath your feet until you came to the Yellow Springs, could anyone make use of this?'

'Useless,' said Hui Tzu.

'So indeed it is true that what is useless is clearly useful,' said Chuang Tzu.

Chuang Tzu continued, 'If someone has the itch to travel, what can stop him? But if someone does not wish to travel, then what can make him? The one who hides in conformity or the one who is distant and seeks oblivion, both fail to achieve perfect understanding and Virtue! They stumble and fall but do not recover. They crash

101. Heat was applied to the holes and the resulting cracks were read as prototype characters which furnished an answer to questions asked of the gods or ancestors.

ahead like fire and never look back. Even if they are a ruler with ministers, this too passes. These titles change with each generation and neither is better than the other. It is said that the perfect man leaves no trace of his actions.

'To respect the past and despise the present, this is what scholars do. Even the followers of Chi Hsi Wei, who view this generation in that way, are swept along without choice. Only the perfect man is able to be in the world and not become partisan, can follow others and not get lost. He does not absorb their teachings, he just listens and understands without any commitment.

'The eye that is penetrating can see clearly;
the ear that is acute hears well;
the nose that discriminates distinguishes smells;
the mouth with a keen sense of taste enjoys the flavours;
the heart that feels deeply has wisdom
and the wisdom that cuts to the quick is Virtue.

'Through all that is, the Tao will not be blocked, for if it is blocked, it gasps, and if it gasps, chaos breaks through. Chaos destroys the life in all. Everything that lives does so through breath. However, if breath will not come, this cannot be blamed on Heaven. Heaven seeks to course breath through the body day in and day out without ceasing: it is humanity which impedes this. The womb has its chambers and the heart has its Heavenly journey. However, if rooms are not large enough, then mother-in-law and wife will argue. If the heart does not wander in Heaven, then the six openings of sensation will compete with each other. The great forests, the hills and mountains surpass humanity in their spirit because they cannot be overcome.

'Virtue overflows into fame and desire for fame overflows into excess. Plans arise from a crisis and knowledge comes through argument. Obstinacy fuels resolution and official actions arise from the desires of all. When spring comes, the rains come along with the sunshine, the plants surge into life and harvesting tools are made ready again. Half of all that has fallen begins to sprout, and no one knows why for sure.

'Quietude and silence are healing for those who are ill;
massage is beneficial to the old;
peaceful contemplation can calm the distressed.
To be sure, it is only the disturbed person who needs these.
Someone who is at ease and is untroubled by such things has no
    need of this.
The sage reforms everything below Heaven, but the spiritual
    man does not enquire how.
The worthy person improves his generation, but the sage does
    not enquire how.
The ruler governs the country, but the worthy person does not
    enquire how.
The petty man makes do in these times, but the ruler does not
    enquire how.

'The gatekeeper of Yen Gate had a father who died and the
gatekeeper was praised for the extremities of self-deprivation he
inflicted on himself, and was honoured by the title of Model
Officer. Some others in the area also underwent such extremities,
and half of them died. Yao offered the country to Hsu Yu and Hsu
Yu fled from him. Tang offered the kingdom to Wu Kuang and
Wu Kuang became angry. Chi To heard this and retreated with his
followers to the waters of the Kuan, where the local nobles came
and commiserated with him for three years. For the same reason,
Shen Tu Ti threw himself into the Yellow River. A fish trap is used
to catch fish, but once the fish have been taken, the trap is
forgotten. The rabbit trap is used to snare rabbits, but once the
rabbit is captured, the trap is ignored. Words are used to express
concepts, but once you have grasped the concepts, the words are
forgotten. I would like to find someone who has forgotten the
words so I could debate with such a person!'

城隍

土地

第二章 玉歷之圖像

CHAPTER 27

Supposed Words

Supposed words constitute nine-tenths of discourse, quotes make up seven tenths and flowing words are brought forth every day, refined by the influence of Heaven.

Supposed words which constitute nine-tenths are similar to people who are brought in from outside. For example, no father is used as a reference for his son, for the father cannot be as objective as someone not of the family. It is not my fault but the fault of other people (who otherwise wouldn't listen to me), for otherwise people would only pay attention to what they already know and dismiss anything else. Thus they say that whatever agrees with them is right, but whatever they dislike they call wrong.

Quotes make up seven-tenths and are there to stop arguments, which they do because they are respected as the words of sagacious elders. However, those who are old but have not grasped the warp and weft, the root and branch of things cannot be quoted as sagacious elders. A person like this hasn't understood the Tao. Nor has he understood the Tao of humanity. He is just a sad remnant of another time.

Flowing words are spoken every day and they harmonize through the influence of Heaven, continuing for ever and so extending my years. If nothing is said about them, they remain in agreement, and agreement is not affected by words: words are in agreement but agreement is not words. So it is said, 'say nothing'. Words say nothing, so you can talk all your life and say nothing. In contrast you can live your life without speaking and have said things of worth.

There is that which makes things acceptable and that which makes things unacceptable.
There is that which makes things certain and that which makes things uncertain.
How is this?
Because it is.
How is this not so?
It is not so, because it is not so.
How does this occur?
Because it occurs.
How does this not occur?
It does not occur, because it does not occur.

Everything is defined by what is right and everything is defined by what is possible. If there is nothing, then it cannot be. If there is nothing, then it cannot occur. If there are no flowing words every day, influenced by Heaven, then how could all this persist? All forms of life arise from the same base and in their diverse forms they succeed each other. They begin and end like an unbroken circle, and none can say why. This is the influence of Heaven. This influence of Heaven is the harmony of Heaven.

Chuang Tzu asked Hui Tzu, 'In reaching the age of sixty, Confucius has changed his views sixty times, so what he once held to be right he now holds to be wrong. So who knows now whether what he once called right he hasn't fifty-nine times called wrong?'

Hui Tzu said, 'Confucius sincerely tries to pursue understanding and tries to act in accord with this.'

'Confucius has abandoned that,' said Chuang Tzu, 'but he doesn't talk about it. Confucius said, "We all received our abilities from the Great Origin, and we should try to show them in our lives." Our singing should accord with the chords and our speech should be an example. But you parade profit and righteousness before us, and your likes and dislikes, and what you approve and disapprove, and you produce nothing more than servile agreement. To ensure people's hearts submit, so that they dare not resist, that would make everyone under Heaven rest secure. Dear oh dear! I have no chance of managing all this!'

Tseng Tzu twice held power but twice he changed his heart, saying, 'At first, when I was caring for my parents, my salary was three fu of rice, but I was happy. The second time I received three thousand chung of rice, but my parents were gone and I was sad.'

One of the followers of Confucius said, 'Surely Tseng Tzu can be described as being free from the folly of entanglement?'

'But he was already entangled,' replied Confucius. 'If he had been free, why should he have been so sad? He would have viewed both his three fu and his three thousand chung as just so many sparrows or mosquitoes flying in front of him.'

Yen Cheng Tzu Yu said to Tzu Chi of the Eastern Suburb. 'When I listened to your words, Master, the first year I was just a country bumpkin. The second year I was happy to be led. The third year I began to journey with you. The fourth year I was just a thing. The fifth year I began to progress. The sixth year the ghosts came into me. The seventh year Heaven's perfection came. The eighth year I could not understand death nor life. The ninth year I achieved the great mystery.

'When life completes its purpose, death results. What is, follows, and each of us has to contemplate death, for it's the path we tread. That which lives in yang is without a path. Is this certain? How does all this happen? Why is it not so here? Heaven has its time and space and Earth has its calculating peoples. Yet how can I discern all this? We have no idea when and how life will end. But how can we try and decide that they are not destined? Given that we have no idea how and when they began, how can we try and decide that they are destined? Given that there is something there, how is it possible to claim that there are no ghosts? If there is nothing there, how can we possibly claim that there are ghosts?'

The Outline asked the Shadow, 'A few minutes ago you were looking down, now you are looking up; a few minutes ago your hair was piled up, now it is hanging down; a few minutes ago you were sitting down, now you are standing up; a few minutes ago you were walking, now you are standing still. Why?'

Shadow said, 'Petty! Petty! Why do you ask me about all this? This is all true to me but I haven't a clue why I do it. I am like the shell of a cicada or the shed skin of a snake: something which seems real but is not. In the sunlight I appear, in darkness I disappear. However, do you think I arise from these? For they are themselves dependent upon others. When it comes, I come also. When it goes, I go with it. If they arise from the mighty yang, so do I. However, there is no point in asking about the mighty yang!'

Yang Tzu Chu travelled south to Pei, Lao Tzu went west to Chin but Yang asked him to go to the border at Liang where they met. Lao Tzu stood in the middle of the road, gazed up to Heaven and said with a sigh, 'At first I thought you could be taught, but now I know it is not possible.'

Yang Tzu Chu said nothing. Later they arrived at the inn and he went to fetch water in order to wash his teacher, and a towel and a comb. Removing his shoes outside the door, he crawled across the floor and said, 'Earlier, Master, your follower wanted to ask you about what you said, but you were busy and I did not dare to. Now, it seems an appropriate time, so I would like to ask what I've done wrong.'

Lao Tzu said, 'Such pride and arrogance, such elevation and certainty; who could bear being with you? The greatest purity is soiled, overflowing virtue is not enough.'

Yang Tzu Chu, when he first arrived at the inn, was greeted by the people there. The innkeeper brought out a mat, his wife brought towels and a comb. Others in the inn respectfully moved aside from their mats. However, when he came back, everyone tried to shove him off his very own mat!

撫孤松而盤桓

癸亥清龢余蓄做宋人筆

CHAPTER 28

Abdication

Yao wanted to abdicate the country to Hsu Yu, but Hsu Yu would not accept. He then offered it to Tzu Chou Chih Fu. Tzu Chou Chih Fu said, 'You wish me to be the Son of Heaven, which is fine. But unfortunately I suffer from a deep-rooted and painful disease which I am currently trying to overcome. As I need to use all my energy to deal with this, I am unable to rule the country.'

The country is of course of tremendous significance, yet he would not put his life at risk, so why do so for even less important things? Someone who doesn't wish to rule the country is exactly the person to ask to do so.

Shun wanted to abdicate the country to Tzu Chou Chih Po, but Tzu Chou Chih Po said, 'At this time I have an unpleasant and disturbing illness and I am using all my energy to deal with it, which means I have no time to rule the country.'

It is said that the country is the greatest of ventures, but he would not risk his life for it, which shows how those who have the Tao are very different from the ordinary person.

Shun tried to abdicate in favour of Shan Chuan, but Shan Chuan said, 'Here I am in the midst of space and time. During the winter I wear skins and furs, in summer I wear vine leaves and linen. In the spring I plough and plant and my body is exercised by this. In the autumn I harvest and pile up and then I rest and eat. When the sun rises I wake up and work, while at sunset I rest. I journey where I will between Heaven and Earth to my heart's desire. So why would I want to rule the country? Alas, Sire, you do not understand!' So he said no and went away, deep into the mountains, and no one knew where he went.

Shun wanted to abdicate the country to his friend the farmer of Shih Hu. The farmer of Shih Hu said, 'But you have such strength and endurance, my Lord!' Realizing that Shun's Virtue would not be enough, he collected his wife, took hold of his son's hand and went off into the islands of the coast. He never ever came back.[102]

The great king Tan Fu[103] lived in Pin, and the Ti peoples invaded. He tried to pay them off with skins and silks but this did not satisfy them. He tried to appease them with dogs and horses, but they didn't like that. He offered them pearls and jade but they didn't like that, for the Ti peoples were only interested in his lands.

Great King Tan Fu said, 'To live here with the older brothers, to despatch the younger brothers to death, to live amongst the fathers and despatch the sons to death – I cannot do it! My children, stay here! Does it really matter whether I rule you or the Ti people do? I have heard people say that you should not use that by which you care for the people, to harm the people.' Then he picked up his staff and riding crop, and left. However, the people came after him, all following one another, and soon they founded a new country under Chi Mountain.[104]

The great King Tan Fu knew how to care for life. Those who honour life, even if they are rich and powerful, misuse what should nourish, and so cause injury to themselves. Likewise, even if they are poor and lowly, they will endanger themselves for the sake of profit. The people of this generation, if they achieve greatness and title, are then preoccupied with holding on to them. Looking only for profit, they forget the risks involved. Surely this is madness!

The people of Yueh assassinated their rulers three times in one generation. Upset by all this, Prince Sou fled to the caves of Tan,

102. All the preceding instances of virtuous rulers wishing to abdicate in favour of sages, wise advisers or ministers, are drawn from history or mythology, and many have been explained more fully earlier.

103. Founder of the Chou state. He is mentioned in the *Book of Songs* in similar terms as a model of wise kingship.

104. The Sacred Mountain of Chou, site of the original oracles which form the *I Ching*.

which meant that the kingdom of Yueh was without a ruler. The people of Yueh tried to find Prince Sou but couldn't, until they discovered the caves of Tan. Prince Sou refused to come out, but the people of Yueh smoked him out with noxious fumes. Then they put him in the royal carriage. Prince Sou grasped the strap and hauled himself up into the carriage, looked to Heaven and said, 'O ruler, O ruler! Couldn't I have been spared all this?' Prince Sou was not frightened of being the ruler, it was all the troubles that go with it that he was afraid of. It can be said of Prince Sou that he was not willing to allow the concerns of the kingdom to damage his life and it was exactly because of this that the people of Yueh wished to have him as their ruler.

The countries of Han and Wei were at war over a territorial dispute. Master Hua Tzu went to see Marquis Chao Hsi of Han, who looked worried. Master Hua Tzu said, 'Now imagine that the people of the world were to present you with a document which read, "If you lay hold of this with your left hand, you will lose your right hand; lay hold with your right hand, and you will lose your left hand; however, if you lay hold of this, you will also rule the world." So, Lord, would you do so?'

The Marquis Chao Hsi said, 'I wouldn't touch it.'

Master Hua Tzu said, 'Excellent! From that point of view, I can certainly see that two hands are more important than the whole world. Furthermore, your body itself is more important than just your two hands. The whole of Han is much less important than the whole of the world and this scrap of land you are fighting over is of less significance than Han. However, surely, my Lord, if you so value your body and your life, you should not be following a path of misery and distress trying to seize this territory!'

Marquis Chao Hsi said, 'Splendid! I have been offered all sorts of advice from different people, but I have never before been offered words of such wisdom.'

Master Hua Tzu, it can be said, knew the difference between what was significant and what was minor.

The ruler of Lu had heard that Yen Ho had gained the Tao and so he sent a messenger bearing gifts of silk to start up discussions with him. Yen Ho was sitting in the doorway of his simple house, dressed in coarse hemp cloth and feeding a cow. The ruler of Lu's messenger arrived and Yen Ho met him.

The messenger asked, 'Is this Yen Ho's house?'

Yen Ho replied, 'This is Ho's house.'

The messenger proceeded to offer the gifts to him, but Yen Ho said, 'I think that unfortunately you have got your instructions confused. If you present these to the wrong person, you will get into trouble. I suggest you return and check that you are doing the right thing.'

So the messenger went back, ensured his instructions were accurate and then came back to look for him, but he could not find him. It is true that those like Yen Ho really do hate honours and wealth.

It is said, the true purpose of the Tao is in caring for yourself, its edges are concerned with running the country and the family, while it is only its dregs which are concerned with ruling the world. So, from this we can understand that what Emperors and kings do is surplus to what the sage does, for it does not relate to care of the self or of life.

The leaders of this generation, that is to say most of them, throw away their lives in pursuit of material gain. Isn't it pathetic! When the sage starts something, he will certainly have considered what he is doing and why he is doing it. Now this is like a man who takes the pearl of the Marquis of Sui and shoots a bird in the sky with it, high up in the air. People would obviously laugh at him. Why is this so? Because he has used something of great value to obtain something of little value. Now surely life is even more valuable than the pearl of the Marquis of Sui!

Master Lieh Tzu was in great poverty and had a hungry look about him. A visitor spoke about this to Tzu Yang, Prime Minister of Cheng, saying, 'Lieh Tzu Kou looks like a scholar who has the Tao, yet here he lives in your state and you let him exist in poverty?' Prime Minister Tzu Yang sent an officer to see him with a gift of rice. Master Lieh Tzu greeted him and bowed, but twice refused the gift.

After the messenger had gone, Master Lieh Tzu went inside, and his wife looked scornfully at him and beat her breast saying, 'I have been told that the wife and children of one who has the Tao have comfort and happiness, but right now we are starving. The ruler understood his mistake, and sends you some food to eat, Master. But the Master refuses it. Is this then our destiny?'

Master Lieh Tzu laughed and said, 'The ruler does not know me. He sent the rice because someone told him to. Likewise, one day someone could speak against me and he could treat me like a criminal. That is why I will not accept.' As it so happened, the people rose against Tzu Yang in civil war and put him to death.

When King Chao of Chu[105] was forced into exile from his country, sheep-butcher Yueh fled also and followed King Chao into exile. King Chao eventually returned in triumph to his kingdom and rewarded those who had followed him. When he met sheep-butcher Yueh, Yueh said, 'Oh great King, you lost your kingdom, and Yueh lost his butcher's shop. The great King has regained his kingdom and Yueh has regained his butcher's shop. I have received back what I needed, so why should you speak of rewarding me?'

The King said, 'Make him!'

Sheep-butcher Yueh said, 'The great King lost his kingdom but not because of anything I did, so I could not be punished for that. The great King has regained his kingdom, again not because of anything I did, therefore I wouldn't expect to rewarded for that.'

'I want to meet him,' said the King.

Sheep-butcher Yueh said, 'The laws of the kingdom of Chu say that someone must have achieved great deeds and been the recipient of acclaim before he can be called to meet the King. Now, my knowledge did not save the kingdom, nor was I courageous enough to die in battle with the invaders. When the armies of Wu entered Ying, I was terrified of the danger and fled from the invaders. I did not purposely follow the King. Yet the King intends breaking with convention and wants to see me. This is not the sort of thing I want the rest of the world to hear about me.'

The King said to Tzu Chi, the War Minister, 'Sheep-butcher Yueh occupies a lowly place, yet what he says about righteousness is

105. The country was invaded by Wu, but he regained his kingdom within a year, in 506 BC.

very profound. I want you to promote him to one of the three most senior positions in the government.'

Sheep-butcher Yueh said, 'I appreciate that being one of the three most senior ministers is more noble than being a sheep-butcher, and that ten thousand chung is a better salary than what I currently earn. However, I cannot, through my desire for profit, allow the ruler to become known for being so profligate with his favours! I dare not accept, but wish simply to return to my stall as a sheep-butcher.' He never did accept.

Yuan Hsien[106] lived in Lu, where his house was only a few steps wide and looked as if its thatch was shorn grass. Its broken door was made from brushwood and the door-posts were of mulberry wood. Earthenware pots minus their bottoms and stuffed with rags served as the two windows, while the house leaked above and was damp below, but he sat contentedly playing music.

Tzu Kung,[107] wearing an inner robe of purple and an outer one of white and travelling in a carriage drawn by large horses, the top of which could not fit through the gate, came to see Yuan Hsien. Yuan Hsien emerged at his gate to greet him, wearing a hat made of bark and slippers worn down to the heel, holding a staff made of hellebore.

Tzu Kung said, 'Good grief, Sir! You must be in terrible distress.'

Yuan Hsien replied, 'I have heard say that to have no money is to be poor, and to have studied but to have no way to use one's studies is to be in distress. Now, I may be poor, but I am not in distress.'

Tzu Kung stepped back in astonishment and embarrassment.

Yuan Hsien laughed and said, 'To act only in order to be praised; to pretend to be even-handed and yet to be biased; to study just so as to show off; to teach just in order to boast; to hide your real intentions behind a pretence of righteousness and benevolence; to show off through extravagant use of horses and chariots, I can't bear all this!'

Tseng Tzu lived in Wei, wearing a worn hemp quilt coat and no

106. One of Confucius' followers, famous for not being bothered by his poverty.
107. One of Confucius' followers, renowned for his wealth.

outer garment, with a haggard and emaciated visage and his hands and feet callused and hardened. He could go three days without lighting a fire, ten years without having a new set of clothes. If he put his hat on straight, the straps broke; if he pulled his coat together, his elbows came through the cloth; and if he pulled on his shoes, his heels broke through at the back. Nevertheless, as he shuffled along, he sang the Odes of Sacrifice of Shang[108] with a voice that penetrated Heaven and Earth as if it came from a struck bell or a chiming stone. The Son of Heaven could not get him to be a minister nor could the princes make him their friend. Thus it is with those who feed their souls while forgetting their body. Those who feed their bodies forget about ideas of profit, and those who follow the Tao forget about the concerns of the heart.

Confucius said to Yen Hui, 'Hui, come here! Your family is poor and you are lowly, so why not seek high office?'

Yen Hui replied, 'I don't want to be an official. I have fifty acres of farm land outside the city, which supplies me with basic foods. I have ten acres of land within the outer wall and this supplies me with luxuries. I take delight in playing my lute and I am more than happy just to study the Tao of my Master. I don't want any positions.'

Confucius looked upset. Then his demeanour changed and he said, 'What a splendid mind you have, Hui! I have heard it said,

'"One who knows he is contented will not get mixed up in the pursuit of gain;
one who truly understands what is good will not be worried by any loss;
one who knows himself inwardly will not be worried by lack of external positions."

'I have been preaching this for a long time, but now I see it embodied in you, Hui, and I have certainly benefited from that today.'

Prince Mou of Wei from Chung Shan said to Chan Tzu, 'My

---

108. Ancient ritual hymns.

body is here beside the rivers and oceans, but my heart is back in the courts of Wei. What advice can you give me?'

Chan Tzu said, 'Value life. If you value life then you will put profit into perspective.'

'I understand all that,' said Prince Mou of Wei from Chung Shan, 'but I find I can't overcome my feelings.'

Chan Tzu said, 'If you can't handle your feelings, how can you avoid harming your spirit? If you can't control your emotions, but nevertheless try to to stop yourself following them, you will harm yourself twice over. Those who do this double injury to themselves are not counted amongst those with long life.'

Wei Mou had command of ten thousand chariots, so for him to retire and live alone in the caves and cliffs was much more difficult than for a scholar. He may not have had the Tao, but we can say he had the intention.

Confucius was trapped in between Chen and Tsai and for seven days he did not eat cooked food, simply a vegetable soup without any rice.

His face was drawn and haggard yet he sat contentedly playing his lute and singing inside the house. Yen Hui was outside choosing the vegetables, and Tzu Lu and Tzu Kung were talking to each other.

They said to Yen Hui, 'Our Master has twice been chased out of Lu, he has fled from Wei, had his tree chopped down in Sung, been in distress in Shang and Chou and is now trapped between Chen and Tsai. If anyone kills the Master, they will be free of any guilt; if anyone imprisons him, they will be without blame. Yet here he sits, endlessly playing and singing. Can a noble gentleman be so lacking in shame as this?'

Yen Hui had nothing to say in reply, so he went in to report this conversation to Confucius. Confucius laid aside his lute and said, 'Those two are just petty people. Tell them to come here and I will explain to them.'

Tzu Lu and Tzu Kung came in. Tzu Lu said, 'The current situation is one of considerable distress!'

'What sort of talk is this?' said Confucius. 'When the nobleman flows with the Tao, that is called flowing. When he cannot flow with the Tao, he doesn't flow. Now, I hold to the Tao of righteousness and benevolence and am thus able to confront this chaotic generation, so what prevents me from flowing? Looking within, I am unconcerned by any difficulties of the Tao and I confront any problems which arise without losing my Virtue. When we see the winter coming and the frost and snow arrive, that is when we appreciate the endurance of the pine and cypress. The difficulties between Chen and Tsai are in fact a blessing!'

Confucius picked up his lute and started to play and sing again. Tzu Lu siezed hold of a shield and began to prance about while Tzu Kung said, 'I had no idea that Heaven is so high and Earth so far below.'

The people of the past who had the Tao were happy if they were trapped and happy if they could flow. Their happiness was unconnected to either of these. If they had the Tao and its Virtue, then being trapped or flowing were simply to them like the regular succession of cold and hot or wind and rain. So Hsu Yu was content on the warm slopes of the Ying River and Kung Po enjoyed himself on the top of Kung Hill.[109]

Shun wanted to hand over the world to his friend from the north, Wu Tse, but Wu Tse said, 'You are a strange person, my Lord, for at first you lived in the fields and ditches and then you went into the gate of Yao. As if that were not enough, he now wants to drag me into his awful mess and taint me with his crimes. I am ashamed to be seen with you.' And having said this, he threw himself into the deep waters of the Ching Ling.

Tang[110] was planning to attack Chieh and so he visited Pien Sui, who said, 'It is nothing to do with me.'

'Then who can help?' said Tang.

'I don't know.'

Tang looked for advice from Wu Kuang, and Wu Kuang said, 'It is nothing to do with me.'

---

109. Kung Po ruled for fourteen years, then in 828 BC retired to Kung Hill as a hermit.

110. He overthrew the tyrant ruler Chieh, last king of the Hsia Dynasty, and founded the Shang Dynasty.

'Then who can help?'

'I don't know.'

'Could Yi Yin?' said Tang.

'He is a violent man who acts disgracefully. I don't know more than that.'

So Tang went to Yi Yin and they planned the attack together. When Chieh had been conquered, Tang offered to abdicate to Pien Sui. Pien Sui said, 'When you were planning to attack Chieh, you asked my advice, so you must consider me a villain. Now you have conquered Chieh, you offer the throne to me, so you must also think I am ambitious. I was born into this disorderly generation, yet a man who has nothing of the Tao comes to me twice, trying to stain me with his actions. I cannot stand to hear these words repeated time and time again.' So saying, he threw himself into the waters of the Chou River and died.

Tang wanted to offer the throne to Wu Kuang and said, 'The man of wisdom has planned this, the fighting man has carried it out and now the benevolent one should take over, for this is the Tao of the past. So why should you not do so, Sir?'

Wu Kuang refused: 'To overthrow the ruler is not righteous; to massacre the people is not benevolent; to cause distress to others and to take your own pleasure is not honourable. I have heard it said that, if someone does not act righteously, don't accept their commission. If a generation is without the Tao, don't set foot on their land. So there is no question of me accepting! I cannot stand looking at you any longer.' And so saying, he fastened a stone to his back and drowned himself in the River Lu.

Earlier, in the time of the Chou Dynasty's triumph,[111] there were two scholars who lived in Ku Chu called Po Yi and Shu Chi. The two said to each other, 'I have heard that in the west there is a man who has the Tao, so let's go and visit him.' When they reached the sunlit side of Mount Chi, King Wu heard about them and sent Shu Tan to see them. He suggested they make an agreement, saying, 'Your wealth will be second in rank and your titles of the first rank

111. c. eleventh century BC.

if you agree to this proposal, and seal it with blood and bury it.'[112]

The two friends looked at each other and burst out laughing. 'Huh, how odd!' they said. 'This is not what we would call the Tao. In the ancient past Shen Nung had the whole world, and he carried out the ritual sacrifices at the appointed times and with great respect, but he never dreamt of praying for blessings. When sorting out the people, he was true and honest and did what was right, but never expected anything from them. He liked to rule fairly, and when necessary would be stern and strict. He didn't exploit the failures of others in order to further his own powers. He didn't use other people's weaknesses to increase his own strength. He didn't exploit favourable openings in order to make profit. But now the Chou Dynasty, seeing that the Yin have fallen into disarray, suddenly seize the government from them, asking advice from the leaders and bribing the ordinary people. They have brought out their weapons and offered sacrifices and made pacts with people to try and show how serious they are. They shout their own praises in order to impress the people and they attack just for the sake of gain, which is just to overthrow disorder and replace it with tyranny.

'We have heard that, even if by good luck the scholars of old lived in peaceful times, they did not shirk public office. However, if they lived in a time of chaos, they tried not to remain in office if they could help it. Now the world is in darkness and the Virtue of the Chou has rotted. Rather than stay here and be associated with it, it is better if we flee and thus maintain our purity.' The two scholars went north to Mount Shou Yang, where they died of starvation. Now, if men like them have managed to avoid getting any fame or fortune, they did so by being high-minded and conscientious in behaviour, taking pleasure in their own ideas without having to lower themselves to serve the world. This is what these two scholars achieved.

112. This describes traditional ways of concluding a contract by smearing it, and the parties to it, with blood from a sacrifice.

娑囉娑囉

四十三

此是五濁
惡世也

CHAPTER 29

Robber Chih

Confucius was friendly with Liu Hsia Chi, whose brother was called Robber Chih. Robber Chih had nine thousand followers who pillaged wherever they wished in the land, attacking and robbing the princes, breaking into houses, stealing the people's cattle and horses, seizing their wives and daughters. Having stolen so much wealth, they forgot their families, ignored their fathers and mothers and did not sacrifice to their ancestors. Whenever they rampaged through the countryside, if it was a big kingdom, the people guarded their walls, and if it was a small kingdom, the people fled into their forts. All the multitude of peoples dreaded them.

Confucius said to Liu Hsia Chi, 'Those who are fathers should be able to set out the law for their sons, and those who are elder brothers should be able to instruct their younger brothers. If a father is unable to set out the law for his son, and an elder brother is not able to instruct his younger brother, then the filial relationship between father and son and between elder and younger brother is pointless. Now, Sir, you are one of the best scholars of this generation, and your younger brother is Robber Chih, who threatens the whole world, yet you have not instructed him well. I am ashamed of you. I suggest I go on your behalf, Sir, to try and advise him better.'

Liu Hsia Chi said, 'Sir, you have said that a father should set out the law for his son and that elder brothers should instruct their younger brothers. However, if the son will not listen to the father, or if the younger brother pays no attention to his elder brother, then even if someone comes with skill such as yours, what can he do? Furthermore, Chih is a man whose heart is like a gushing fountain, and whose will is like a hurricane, strong enough to see off any enemy and clever enough to gloss over his evil. If you agree with him, he is pleased, but if you disagree with him, he becomes angry and he will curse you with the most foul language. Do not go and see him, Sir.'

Confucius did not listen. Accompanied by Yen Hui as his driver, and with Tzu Kung by his side, he went off to see Robber Chih. Robber Chih was camped with his followers on the sunlit side of Mount Tai, savouring a meal of human livers. Confucius stepped down from the carriage and went to see the officer in charge of visitors.

'I am Confucius of Lu,' he said, 'and I have heard that your commander is a man of lofty righteousness.' And he bowed twice to the officer.

The officer went in and passed on the message. On hearing this, Robber Chih flew into a great rage. His eyes blazed like bright stars and his hair stood on end under his hat.

'This must be that crafty one from Lu kingdom, the man Confucius, is it not? Tell him this from me: "You talk away, inventing phrases and eulogizing the kings Wen and Wu. Your hat is so decorated it is like the boughs of a tree and your belt is skin from the ribs of a cow. The more you say, the more ridiculous it is. You eat yet you do not plough, dress without ever weaving. You wag your lips and use your tongue like a drumstick. You just decide what you think is right and wrong and lead the rulers astray, preventing scholars from studying the roots of the whole world. You establish notions of filial piety and fraternal duty just as you fancy, yet you also want to wriggle your way into favour with the princes, the wealthy and the nobility. Your wickedness is vast and your sins weighty. Get off home now, for if you don't then I will take your liver and add it to this meal."'

Confucius sent another message in: 'I have the friendship of your brother Chi and so I hope for the favour of being able to view your feet from below the tent.'

When the officer passed this on, Robber Chih said, 'Tell him to come here!'

Confucius hurried forward, and declining the mat offered, he stepped back and then bowed twice to Robber Chih. Robber Chih was still in a terrible temper. He stretched out his legs, placed his hand upon his sword and glared with his eyes, speaking with a roar like a tigress defending her young: 'Confucius, come here! If what you say pleases me, you will live. If it angers me, you will die.'

Confucius said, 'I have heard that there are three kinds of Virtue in this world. The highest Virtue is to grow tall and strong with wonderful looks so that all, young and old, noble and commoner, are delighted to see you. The middle Virtue is to understand Heaven and Earth and to be able converse eloquently on all subjects. The lowest Virtue is to be brave and fearless, resolute and dashing, gathering all to oneself and leading them.

'Anyone who has just one of these Virtues is suitable to stand facing south and be called the Lone One, the Ruler. Now, here you are with all three. You soar up to eight feet two inches; light pours forth from your face and eyes; your lips look as though coloured with vermilion; your teeth are like rows of precious shells; your voice is in tune with the musical notes, yet you are simply called Robber Chih. Surely this is something to be ashamed of, and I disapprove of you.

'However, should you so wish, you could listen to my ideas and send me as your ambassador to Wu and Yueh in the south, to Chi and Lu in the north, east to Sung and Wei and west to Chin and Chu, arguing with them that they should form a great walled city several hundred li wide. From there they could rule over towns containing several hundred inhabitants, and I would argue that you should be established there as lord. Then you could begin your career again with this city. You can stop fighting, send your followers home, bring your family together there and offer sacrifices to your ancestors. This is what a sage would do, or a true scholar, and it is what the whole world desires.'

Robber Chih was in a towering rage. 'Confucius, come here!' he roared. 'The sort of person who can be won over by promises of profit or reformed through speeches are simply fools, idiots and the most common sort. That I am tall and strong, and so handsome that everyone delights to see me, is a virtue descended from my parents. Even if you hadn't told me, don't you think I'd know this?

'What's more, I have heard that those who praise people to their face will also speak against them behind their backs. Now, Confucius, you tell me about a great walled city filled with people, and you hope to make me change by such promises of profit, attempting to make me follow your words like some common person. But how long would such a place survive? There is no walled city as big as the whole world which was ruled by Yao and Shun, yet their descendants own so little land that they can hardly stick the point of an awl into it! Tang and Wu announced themselves as Sons of Heaven, but within a few generations their dynasties were dead and gone. Surely this was because what they had was considered such a valuable prize?

'What is more, I have heard that in the past[113] the birds and animals were many and the people few. As a result, the people lived in nests to escape the animals. During daylight they gathered acorns and chestnuts and during darkness they hid in their tree nests. This is why they were known as the Nest-Building People. In the ancient past the people didn't know how to make clothes. During the summer they gathered firewood and in the winter they kept warm by burning it. This is why they were called the People who Know how to Keep Alive. In the time of Shen Nung the people lay down in peace and contentment and rose in serene security. The people knew their mothers but not their fathers, and they lived side by side with the elks and deer. They ploughed and ate, they wove and made clothes, never dreaming of harming others, for this was the era of the perfect Virtue.

'However, the Yellow Emperor was unable to sustain this era of Virtue. He battled with Chih Yu in the area of Cho Lu until the blood flowed over a hundred miles. Yao and Shun ascended the throne, establishing hordes of ministers. Tang exiled his ruler Chieh and King Wu murdered his ruler Chou, and from then on the strong oppressed the weak and the many abused the few. From

113. The following paragraphs describe traditional myths of the founding of civilization by, amongst others, the Three August Ones.

Tang and Wu until now they have all been instruments of disorder and confusion. Now, Sir, you come here promoting the ways of Kings Wen and Wu, using your skills in debate to teach them to the whole world and to all generations. Dressed in your distinctive garb and wearing a narrow belt, armed with false speeches and hypocritical behaviour, you fool the many lords and princes of diverse countries and prowl around looking for riches and fame. There is no greater robber than you, Sir. Why doesn't the whole world, which calls me Robber Chih, call you Robber Confucius?

'Using your sweet words, you persuaded Tzu Lu[114] to follow you. You caused him to put aside his high cap, to lay down his long sword and attend to your teachings, with the result that the whole world says, "Confucius is able to suppress violence and stop evil." But in the end Tzu Lu attempted to murder the ruler of Wei, messed that up and his body was pickled and hung over the east gate of the city, so, yes, Sir, your teachings were no good to him.

'Do you call yourself a scholar, of some skill, a sage? You have been driven out of Lu twice, fled from Wei, got into trouble in Chi and been besieged in Chen and Tsai. There is nowhere in the world that will have you. You advised Tzu Lu and this resulted in his being pickled. On one hand you can't care for yourself, and on the other, you can't help others. Is this Tao of yours worth anything?

'There is no one thought more of by all generations than the Yellow Emperor, yet the Yellow Emperor could not maintain the harmony of Virtue, for he fought on the battlefield of Cho Lu and the blood flowed for a hundred miles. Yao was not compassionate, Shun was not filial, Yu was paralysed down one side,[115] Tang exiled his ruler, King Wu attacked Chou and King Wen was imprisoned at Yu Li. These seven men are thought of as lofty by the whole world. However, if we study them carefully, we can see that the pursuit of profit made them all act against what was true and violate their innate selves. Their actions cause deep embarrassment.

114. A follower of Confucius, previously renowned for his fighting abilities.
115. Yao murdered his son; Shun exiled his mother's youngest brother; Yu worked without ceasing for twelve years to harness the floods of the Yellow River and damaged his health as a result.

'When the world discusses worthy scholars, Po Yi and Shu Chi are mentioned. However Po Yi and Shu Chi both refused the role of ruler for the state of Ku Chu and preferred to go and die of starvation in the mountains of Shou Yang, where no one buried them. Pao Chiao showed off and condemned the world. He embraced a tree and stayed there till he died. Shen Tu Ti spoke out in protest but was ignored, so he fastened a stone to his back and drowned himself in the river, where the fish and turtles ate him. Chieh Tzu Tui was a perfect follower, and cut out a piece of his own flesh for his lord, Duke Wen, to eat. However, later on the Duke ignored him and Chieh Tzu Tui was angry and stormed off into the woods where he burnt himself to death hugging a tree. Wei Sheng had an assignation with a young woman under a bridge, but the woman did not turn up. The water began to rise, but rather than leave, he wrapped his arms around the pillar of the bridge and died. These six men are hardly to be distinguished from a dog torn to shreds, a pig that is drowned or a beggar with his begging bowl in hand. They all succumbed to their desire for fame and honour and so they despised death. They did not nourish the roots of their life nor live out the time allocated by destiny.

'The world discusses loyal ministers and says that none were better than Prince Pi Kan and Wu Tzu Hsu. However, Wu Tzu Hsu's body sank in the river and Pi Kan's heart was cut out. These two are called models of loyal ministers by the whole world, but they both ended up being laughed at by everyone. Taking the cases above down to Wu Tzu Hsu and Pi Kan, none of them deserves respect.

'Regarding the speech you have given me, Confucius, were you to tell me about ghosts, then there would be no way I could tell whether you are right or not. However, if you talk to me about this world and its affairs, which is all you have dwelt upon so far, then I have heard it all before!

'Now I will tell you about the innate nature of things. Eyes wish to look upon beauty, ears to hear music, the mouth to taste flavours, the breath of life to persist. A man of considerable age will live to be a hundred, one of middle age will be about eighty and one of lesser years will be sixty. If you remove the time lost on recovering from illness, mourning the dead, worrying and being anxious, then this leaves you with only four or five days in every month when you can open your mouth and laugh. Heaven and Earth are without end, but humans die when their time is up. Take the longest period of possible finite time and compare it with what is without limit: it is gone as swiftly as when a horse dashes past a crack in a wall. Anyone incapable of fulfilling their will and innate nature and achieving their full years cannot be described as having gained the Tao. I reject everything you have said, Confucius. Get a move on and go. I don't want to hear anything more from you. Your Tao is foolish, deceitful, artful, vain and hypocritical, incapable of sustaining the inner harmony of truth and so it's not worth talking about!'

Confucius bowed twice and hurried off. Leaving by the gate, he mounted his carriage, dropping his reins three times. His eyes were glazed and he could not see; his face was the colour of dead ashes. Supporting himself on the crossbar of his carriage, his head hung down, he seemed to be losing his life's breath. He journeyed back to Lu and when he arrived at the eastern gate, he chanced upon Liu Hsia Chi.

'So here you are at the city gate,' said Liu Hsia Chi. 'I haven't seen you for days. Your carriage and horses have got dusty. Have you been by any chance to see Chih?'

Confucius looked to Heaven and groaned. 'I most certainly did,' he said.

'Chih was infuriated by what you said, I suspect?'

'He certainly was,' said Confucius. 'I am rather like someone who has given himself moxibustion treatment, even though he was not ill. I dashed off and stroked the tiger's head and played with his whiskers and I only just escaped from his mouth!'

Tzu Chang asked Man Kou Te, 'Why do you not try and do better? If you don't, your words will not be believed. If your words are not believed, you will not be employed. No proper employment means no gain. So whether you view this from the perspective of fame, or consider it in terms of profit, then righteousness is the true thing to do. If you can cast aside fame and fortune, and revert to the true calling of your heart, then you can see that a real scholar should not let a single day go by without pursuing a true course!'

'The one without shame grows rich,' said Man Kou Te, 'and the one in whom many place their trust becomes famous. So it would appear that the grandest reputations and profit come to those who are both trusted and without shame. So if you're concerned with reputation or gain, then trust is crucial. If, however, you cast aside thought of fame and fortune, and revert to the true calling of your heart, then you will see that the scholar follows the path of his Heavenly nature!'

'In the past,' said Tzu Chang, 'Chieh and Chou both enjoyed the honour of being the Sons of Heaven; all the wealth of the world was theirs. Now if you say to a mere sweeper, "Your behaviour is like Chieh or Chou," he will look embarrassed and his heart will be disturbed by such words, for even the lowliest person despises them. Confucius and Mo Ti, however, were poor and common people. Now, however, if you say to a prime minister that his conduct is like that of Confucius and Mo Ti, he will be abashed and look disconcerted and proclaim that he is not worthy, for these two are revered by all scholars. So, to be as powerful as the Son of Heaven does not mean you are respected. And to be poor and common does not mean you will automatically be despised. The difference between being honoured and despised is to be found in the worth or worthlessness of your behaviour.'

Man Kou Te said, 'Minor criminals are locked up while great criminals are made into lords and rulers. Yet in the gates of such lords, righteous scholars are to be found. In the past, Hsiao Po, Duke Huan murdered his elder brother and made his sister-in-law his wife. However, Kuan Chung still became his minister. Chang Tien Cheng murdered his ruler and usurped his country, but Confucius still accepted gifts from him. In their debates they condemn such people, but in their actions they acquiesce before them. Surely their words and their deeds must have been in conflict with each other in their breasts! This is why the Book says, "What is evil and what is beautiful? The successful is considered the head and the unsuccessful is the tail."'

'Sir,' said Tzu Chang, 'if you don't pay attention to the normal ways of behaviour, and make no distinction between near and distant family, between noble and commoner, between elder and younger, how can you maintain the order of the five arrangements and the six kinships?'

Man Kou Te replied, 'Yao killed his eldest son and Shun exiled his uncle. Do either of these have proper regard for the rules about near and distant kinship? Tang exiled his ruler Chieh and King Wu overthrew his lord Chou. Do either of these have proper regard for the distinctions between noble and commoner? King Chi usurped his brother and the Duke of Chou killed his elder brother. Do either of these have proper regard for the distinction between elder and younger? The Literati speak hypocritically and the Mohists say everyone should be loved equally. Do either of these have proper regard for the distinction between the five arrangements and the six kinships?

'Add to this that you, Sir, are concerned with reputation, while I care about profit. In reality neither fame nor fortune are in accord with principle and they cannot stand examination in the light of the Tao. The other day we referred this to the one who is unbound by opinion. He said,

'"The mean person desires wealth,
The nobleman desires fame.
In the ways in which they affect their true form,
and change their innate natures,
they are different.
But as they both cast aside what they have
in pursuit of something they don't have,
they are identical."
So it is said,
Do not be a mean person,
Turn again and desire the heavenly within.
Do not be a nobleman,
Pursue the path of Heaven within.
Whether bent or true,
See all in the light of Heaven.
Learn to face all four directions,

and flow with the tides of the seasons.
Whether right or wrong,
Hold firm to that centring point within.
Alone fulfil your will.
Travel only in the company of the Tao.
Do not stray from your path,
Do not try to be perfect in righteousness,
For then you will fail at what you do.
Make no haste to become wealthy,
Take no risks for fame,
Or you will lose the Heavenly within.

'Pi Kan's heart was cut out, Tzu Hsu's eyes were put out: this is what faithfulness gave them. Kung the True spoke against his father,[116] Wei Sheng died by drowning, so misfortune was the result of their loyalty. Pao Chiao stood till he dried out and Shen Tzu would not defend himself,[117] so harm was the result of their integrity. Confucius never saw his mother and Kuang Tzu never saw his father: these are the mistakes of the righteous. These are the models passed down from generation to generation. They clearly indicate that the scholar who is determined to be faithful in his words and firm in his actions pays the price and brings upon himself such disasters.'

Not Enough asked Knowing Harmony, 'There is no one who doesn't seek fame and fortune. When someone is rich, everyone wants to know him. They are willing to abase themselves, hoping to impress. To have others fall down before you is one way of ensuring long life and comfort for the bodily needs as well as peace for the mind. Do you alone have no idea of this, Sir? Do you have no understanding or simply lack the will power? Or have you decided what is right and resolved never to deviate from this?'

Knowing Harmony said, 'Now there is this man who lives around here and who was born at the same time as us: we who see ourselves as scholars, who have cast aside the common lot of this

116. Because his father stole a sheep.
117. Because to do so he would have had to indict his father.

generation and risen above it. He has given up trying to define the principle of right. He studies the ancient past and this present time, the different views on what is right and what is wrong. He follows this degenerate generation in changing as the world changes, ignoring what has been deemed important, casting aside what is worthy, just doing whatever he wants. Yet is he not wrong in thinking this will prolong life, give the body all it needs for pleasure and joy to his will? He swings from grief and distress to happiness and joy, yet doesn't understand how these affect the body. He suffers fear and fright and excitement and delight, yet this does nothing to help him understand why. He knows what is to be done, but not why it should be done. Indeed, you might have all the status of being a Son of Heaven and all the wealth of the whole world, yet still not escape disaster and distress.'

Not Enough said, 'There is nothing that riches cannot give you. They bring the best in beauty and the summits of power, which neither the perfect man nor the sage can ever achieve. They buy strength and bravery from others which then make the owner feared and powerful. They can buy up the wisdom and the skills of others which then make the owner seem wise and knowledgeable. They can entice the virtues of others so that the owner can seem a man of consequence and principle. Even though he has no kingdom of his own, the wealthy man is as much respected as a ruler or even a father. Furthermore, music, beauty, good food and power can be enjoyed even by those who have never studied them before. The body can enjoy these without ever having had to learn from others.

'Desire, dislikes, what to pursue and what to avoid: no one needs to be taught about these, for they are part of our innate nature. Nor am I the only person under Heaven to think like this. Who could ever give them up?'

Knowing Harmony said, 'The wise man does things because of his concern for the well-being of everyone, and he does not do anything against convention. So if he has enough, he doesn't seek for more, for as there is no need, he needn't seek for anything. However, if there is too little, then he will seek for more. To do this he goes in all directions but would never see himself as being self-indulgent. If there is too much, he gives it away. He can give away all under Heaven and still not see himself as open-minded.

'Open-minded or greedy are not caused by any external influence, they arise from the inborn state of being of each of us. Someone might be as powerful as the Son of Heaven, but never use this to dominate others. He could own the whole world, but never use his wealth to degrade others. He sizes up the situation and bears in mind the harm that could be inflicted upon his innate nature. This might lead him to withdraw from something he is offered – but not in order to win false praise and honour. Yao and Shun were Emperors and there was harmony, but not because they strove to be benevolent, for they would not permit what was good to harm them. Shan Chuan and Hsu Yu could have become Emperors, but they refused, not because they sought to impress by this but because they did not wish to inflict harm upon themselves through this. All of these followed what was to their advantage and refused what was harmful, and so the whole world celebrates them. Though they gained praise, they did not act as they did in order to have such praise.'

Not Enough replied, 'But in order to do this they distressed their bodies and renounced what was pleasurable, restricting themselves to a meagre existence in order to survive. They were like those who exist for years in sickness and distress, waiting to die.'

'Peaceful contentment is happiness,' said Knowing Harmony, 'while excess is dangerous. This is true for all things, but most especially in the case of wealth. Rich men hear the sounds of the bell and drum, flute and pipe, and their mouths are stuffed full of the most tasty meats and fine wines, until they are satiated and have forgotten what they are supposed to be doing. This is a disorderly state. Sinking into the depths of their desires, they are like someone carrying a heavy burden up a hill. This is bitter suffering. They desire riches and hope to find some comfort there. They desire power and try to hold on to it all. In the quiet of their private moments they sink into indulgence. Even if their bodies are fit and tanned, they become inflated with pride. This is a state of sickness. Desiring wealth, lusting after profit, they fill their rooms to over-flowing and cannot desist. They are unable to escape this lust, they want even more and they ignore all those who advise against this. This is a state of disgrace. They heap up their wealth beyond anything they could ever use, but cling to it frantically. Even when they know the distress it causes, they want yet more and more. This state is called pathetic. Behind doors, they fear robbers and thieves. Out of doors, they are afraid of being mugged. They fortify themselves at home with towers and moats, and when travelling they dare not walk alone. This is the state of terror. These six states are the worst possible. But they forget them all and seem to have lost the faculty of reason. Once disaster comes, even if they wish to draw on all their innate nature or use up all their wealth, they can't regain a single day of peacefulness. So it is that those who look for fame will not find it and those who look for fortune will not be able to find it. To wear out their minds and destroy their bodies in searching for these – surely this is simply terrible delusion!'

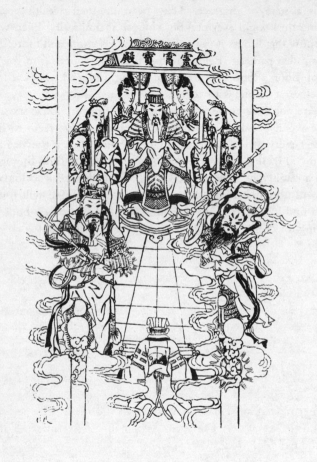

CHAPTER 30

The Lover of Swords

In the past King Wen of Chao loved swords. Specialists came to his gate, over three thousand of them, all experts in swordsmanship. They were his guests. Day and night they fought before him until the dead or wounded each year were more than a hundred. But the King never ceased to be delighted at watching them. This went on for three years, then the country began to fall apart and the other princes began to plot its overthrow.

Crown Prince Kuei was distressed by this, and he presented the situation to his followers:

'If there is anyone here who can persuade the King to put away these swordsmen, I will give him a thousand pieces of gold,' he said. His followers replied,

'Chuang Tzu can do this.'

The Crown Prince sent an ambassador with a thousand pieces of gold to Chuang Tzu. Chuang Tzu refused the gold but returned with the ambassador. He came in to see the Crown Prince and said, 'Oh Prince, what is it you wish to tell me that you send me a thousand pieces of gold?'

'I have heard, Sir, that you are an illustrious sage,' said the Crown Prince. 'The gift of a thousand pieces of gold was a gift for your attendants. However, you have refused to accept this, so what more dare I say?'

Chuang Tzu said, 'I have heard that the Crown Prince wants to use me to help the King give up his abiding passion. If in trying to do so I upset the King and fail to achieve what you hope for, then I might be executed. So what use would the gold be to me then? Or, if I could get the King to give up, and fulfil your hopes, what is there in this whole kingdom of Chao that I could not ask for and be given?'

'You're right,' said the Crown Prince. 'However the King will only see swordsmen.'

'That's all right. I'm quite good with a sword,' replied Chuang Tzu.

'Fair enough,' said the Crown Prince, 'but the swordsmen the King sees are all tousle-headed with spiky beards, wearing loose caps held on with simple, rough straps and robes that are cut short behind. They look about them fiercely and talk only of their sport. The King loves all this. Now, if you go in wearing your scholar's garb you will start off on completely the wrong foot.'

'With your permission I will get a full swordsman's outfit,' said Chuang Tzu.

Within three days he had got this and returned to see the Crown Prince. The Crown Prince took him to see the King, who drew his sword and sat waiting for him. Chuang Tzu walked slowly into the hall through the main door. When he saw the King, he did not bow.

'What instruction have you for me, that you have persuaded the Crown Prince about beforehand?' demanded the King.

'I have heard that the King likes swords and so I have brought my sword for the King to see.'

'What use is your sword in combat?'

'My sword can kill one person every ten paces, and after a thousand miles it is not faltering.'

The King was pleased and said, 'There can be no one else like you under Heaven!'

'A fine swordsman opens with a feint then gives ground, following up with a cut, stalling his opponent before he can react,' replied Chuang Tzu. 'I would like to show you my skills.'

'Rest awhile in your rooms, Master, and await my commands,' said the King. 'I shall make arrangements for the contest and I will call you.'

The King spent the next seven days testing his swordsmen. More than sixty died or were severely wounded, leaving five or six who were selected and commanded to present themselves in the hall.

Then he called in Chuang Tzu and said, 'Now, this very day I shall pit you against these men to show your skills.'

'I have longed for such an opportunity,' said Chuang Tzu.

'Sir, what sort of sword will you choose, long or short?' asked the King.

'Any kind will do,' said Chuang Tzu, 'but I have three swords, any of which I could use if the King agrees. But first I would like to say something about them and then use them.'

'I would like to hear about these three swords,' said the King.

'I have the sword of the Son of Heaven, the sword of the noble Prince and the sword of the commoner,' said Chuang Tzu.

'What is this sword of the Son of Heaven?'

'The Son of Heaven's sword has as its point the Valley of Yen, and the Great Wall and Chi and Tai mountains as its blade edge. Chin and Wey are its ridge, Chou and Sung are its hilt and Han and Wei its sheath. On all four sides it is surrounded by barbarians and it is wrapped in the four seasons. The Sea of Po encompasses it and the eternal mountains of Chang are its belt. The five elements control it and it enacts what punishment and compassion dictate. It comes out in obedience to yin and yang, stands alert in spring and summer and goes into action in autumn and winter. Thrust forward, there is nothing in front of it; lift it high, and there is nothing above it; swing it low, and there is nothing below it; spin it around, there is nothing encompassing it. Raised high, it cleaves the firmaments; swung low, it severs the very veins of the Earth. Use this sword but once and all the rulers revert to obedience; all below Heaven submit. This is the sword of the Son of Heaven.'

King Wen was astonished and seemed to have forgotten everything else.

'What of the sword of the noble Prince?' he asked.

Chuang Tzu said, 'The sword of the noble Prince, its point is sagacious and courageous people; its blade is those of integrity and sincerity; its ridge is those of worth and goodness; its hilt is those who are trustworthy and wise; its sheath is of the brave and outstanding. When this sword is thrust forward, it encounters nothing; when wielded high, it has nothing above it; when swung low, it has nothing below it; when swirled about, it finds nothing near it. Above, its guidance comes from Heaven and it proceeds with the three great lights.[118] Below, it is inspired by the square, stable nature of the earth, proceeding with the flow of the four seasons. In the middle lands it restores harmony to the people and is in balance with the four directions. Use this sword but once and it is like hearing the crash of thunder. Within the four borders everyone obeys the laws and everyone attends to the orders of the ruler. This is the sword of the noble Prince.'

'What of the sword of the commoner?'

'The sword of the commoner is used by those who are tousle-haired with spiky beards, wearing loose caps held on by ordinary coarse cords, with their robes cut short behind. They stare about them fiercely and will only talk about their swordsmanship while fighting before the King. Raised high, it cuts through the neck; swung low, it slices into the liver and lungs. The people who use the sword of the commoner are no better than fighting cocks who at any time can have their lives curtailed. They are useless to the state. Now you, O King, have the position of the Son of Heaven but you make yourself unworthy by associating with the sword of the commoner. This is what I dare to say.'

The King brought him up into his hall where the butler presented a tray of food, while the King strode three times round the room.

'Sire, sit down and calm yourself,' said Chuang Tzu. 'Whatever there was to say about swords has been said.'

Following this, King Wen did not go out for three months and all his swordsmen killed themselves in their own rooms.

118. Sun, moon and stars.

CHAPTER 31

The Old Fisherman

Confucius wandered through the Black Curtain Forest and sat down beside the Apricot Tree Altar. His followers started reading their books while Confucius played his lute and sang. He was not even halfway through the song when a fisherman stepped out of his boat and came towards him. His beard and eyebrows were white and his hair was wild, while his sleeves hung down beside him. He walked up the slopes until he reached the drier ground and then stopped, resting his left hand on his knee and his chin in his right hand, and listened until the song was over. Then he called over Tzu Kung and Tzu Lu and the two of them went to him.

'Who is that?' he said, pointing at Confucius.

'He is a nobleman from Lu,' replied Tzu Lu.

The fisherman then enquired as to Confucius' family. Tzu Lu replied, 'The family of Kung.'

'What does this man of Kung do for a living?'

Tzu Lu was working out what to say when Tzu Kung replied, saying, 'This man of the Kung family in his innate nature holds fast to loyalty and faithfulness; in his behaviour he shows benevolence and righteousness; he makes the rituals and music beautiful, and balances human relationships. He pays respect above him to the ruler of his generation and in his dealings with those below him he tries to transform the ordinary people, as he wants to bless the whole world. This is what this man of the Kung family does.'

The fisherman enquired further, 'Does he have any land over which he rules?'

'No,' said Tzu Kung.

'Is he an adviser to a king?'

'No.'

The stranger laughed and backed away, saying, 'So benevolence is benevolence, yet he won't escape without harm to himself. Exhausting the heart and wearing out the body puts his true nature in jeopardy. Sadly, I believe he is far removed from the Tao.'

Tzu Kung went up and told Confucius about this. Confucius laid aside his flute and stood up, saying, 'Maybe he is a sage!' and he went down the slope to find him. He reached the water's edge as the fisherman was about to pole away. Seeing Confucius, he poled back again and confronted him. Confucius stepped back somewhat hastily, bowed twice and went forward.

'What do you want, Sir?' said the stranger.

'Just now, Master, you said a few words but didn't finish,' said Confucius. 'Being unworthy, I do not understand them. So I would like to be with you and to hear even just the sounds of your words in the hope that they might enlighten me!'

'Oh-ho, you have a good love of study, Sir!'

Confucius bowed twice and stood up. 'Ever since I was little I have pursued study, and now here I am sixty-nine years old, yet I have never heard the perfect teaching, so what can I do but keep my heart open?'

The stranger said, 'Like seeks like and each note responds to its own. This is the boundary established by Heaven. I will not discuss that which concerns me, but will concentrate on what you need to know about. You, Sir, are wrapped up in the affairs of the people. The Son of Heaven, the noble princes, the great ministers and the common folk, when these four groups do what is right, there is the beauty of unity. If these four groups break apart, then there is terrible great disorder. If ministers do what they should and the ordinary people are concerned with what they do, then no one infringes upon another.

'Fields in ruin, leaking roofs, lack of food and clothing, unjust taxes, disputes between wives and concubines, disorder between the young and the old, these are what trouble the common folk.

'Inability to do the job, being bored by their work, bad behaviour, carelessness and laziness in those below, failure to succeed, insecurity in employment, these are what trouble the great ministers.

'Lack of loyal ministers, civil war in the kingdom, workmen with no skills, tributes that are worthless, poor positioning at the spring and autumn gatherings, the disquiet of the ruler, these are what trouble the noble princes.

'Yin and yang out of harmony, fluctuations in heat and cold which damage all, oppression and rebellion by nobles, all leading to uprisings, ravage and abuse of the people, the rituals badly performed, the treasury empty, social relationships in turmoil and the people debauched, these are what trouble the Son of Heaven and his people.

'Now, Sir, at the higher end of the scale, you are not a ruler, nor a noble nor even a minister in a court, while at the other end you are not in the office of a great minister with all his portfolios. Nevertheless, you have decided to bring beauty to the rituals and the music and to balance human relationships and thus to reform the ordinary people. Isn't this rather overdoing it?

'Furthermore, there are eight defects that people are liable to, as well as four evils that affect their affairs, which must not be ignored:

'To be involved with affairs that are not yours is to be overbearing.

'To draw attention to yourself when no one wants you is to be intrusive.

'To suck up to someone with speeches designed to please is to be sycophantic.

'Not to distinguish between good and evil in what others say is to be a flatterer.

'To gossip about other's failings is to be slanderous.

'To separate friends and families is to be malevolent.

'To give false praise in order to hurt others is to be wicked.

'Having no concern for right or wrong, but to be two-faced in order to find out what others know, is to be treacherous.

'These eight defects cause disorder to others and harm to the perpetrator. A nobleman will not befriend one who has them, nor will an enlightened ruler appoint such a person to be a minister.

'With regard to the four evils of which I spoke, they are:

'Ambition – To be fond of taking on vast enterprises, altering and changing the old traditions, thus hoping that you can increase your fame and standing.

'Greediness – To be a know-all and to try and get everything done your way, seizing what others do and claiming it as your own.

'Obstinacy – To see your errors without doing anything to change them and to persist in doing things the wrong way.

'Bigotry – To smile upon someone who agrees with you but when that person disagrees, to disown and despise them.

'These are the four evils. If you can cast aside the eight defects and avoid the four evils, then you are at a point where it is possible to be taught.'

Confucius looked sad and sighed, bowed twice, stood up and said, 'Lu has exiled me twice, I have fled from Wei, they have felled a tree on me in Sung and laid siege to me between Chen and Tsai. I have no idea what I did to be so misunderstood. Why was I subject to these four forms of trouble?'

The stranger looked distressed, then his expression changed and he said, 'It is very difficult, Sir, to make you understand! There was once a man who was frightened by his own shadow and scared of his own footprints, so he tried to escape them by running away. But every time he lifted his foot and brought it down, he made more footprints, and no matter how fast he ran, his shadow never left him. Thinking he was running too slowly, he ran faster, never ceasing until finally he exhausted himself and collapsed and died. He had no idea that by simply sitting in the shade he would have lost his shadow, nor that by resting quietly he would cease making footprints. He really was a great fool!

'You, Sir, try to distinguish the spheres of benevolence and righteousness, to explore the boundaries between agreement and disagreement, to study changes between rest and movement, to pontificate on giving and receiving, to order what is to be approved of and what disapproved of, to unify the limits of joy and anger, and yet you have barely escaped calamity. If you were to be serious in your cultivation of your own self, careful to guard the truth and willing to allow others to be as they are, then you could have avoided such problems. However, here you are, unable to cultivate yourself yet determined to improve others. Are you not obsessed with external things?'

Confucius, really cast down, said, 'Can I ask you about truth?'

'True truth is simple purity at its most perfect,' replied the stranger. 'To be without purity, to be without sincerity means you cannot move other people. So if you fake mourning and weeping, then no matter how thoroughly you do this, it's not real grief. If you make yourself act angry, even if you sound very fierce, this won't inspire awe. If you force yourself to be affectionate, no matter how much you smile, you cannot create harmony. True grief may make no sound but is really sorrowful; true anger, even if there is no manifestation of it, creates awe; true affection doesn't even need to smile but creates harmony. When someone has truth within, it affects his external spirit, which is why truth is so important. In terms of human relationship it works thus:

'in service of parents, it is affection and filial piety;
in service of rulers, it is loyalty and integrity;
in celebrations, it is enjoyable pleasures;
in conducting the mourning rituals, it is sadness and grief.

'For in loyalty and integrity, service is all-important; in celebration, enjoyment is all-important; in mourning, grief is all-important; in service of parents, making them content is all-important.

'The splendour of service doesn't mean just doing the same thing every time. When making your parents content, you don't worry about what to do. In getting jolly at a festival, you don't get worked up about the crockery. In mourning at times of death, you don't get het up over the precision of the rituals. Rituals have emerged from the common needs of the ordinary people. Truth itself comes to us from Heaven: this is how it is and it never changes. So the sage models himself upon Heaven, values truth but does not kowtow to convention. The fool does the opposite. He cannot take his model from Heaven and so is swayed by the mundane. He simply doesn't know the value of truth, but is under the domination of the ordinary people and so is affected by this common crowd and is never at peace. Sadly for you, Sir, you started early in such nonsense and have only recently heard of the great Tao!'

Confucius yet again bowed twice, stood up and said, 'Now that I have had the opportunity to meet you, I feel as if I have been blessed by Heaven. Master, if you wouldn't be embarrassed by this, will you allow me to join those who serve you and to be taught by you, and therefore tell me where I might find your house? I want to go there to hear your teachings from you and to complete my study of the great Tao.'

The stranger replied, 'I have heard it said that if you find someone with whom you can walk, then go with him to the deepest mysteries of the Tao. However, if it is someone you cannot walk with, and he doesn't know the Tao, do not link yourself with him, and then you cannot be blamed. Do what you must, Sir! I will now depart from you, Sir, I will depart from you!' With this he pushed off with his pole and went away through the reeds.

Yen Yuan returned with the carriage and Tzu Lu held out the strap for Confucius to pull himself up and in, but Confucius did not look their way. He waited till the last ripples had died away and he could no longer hear the sound of the pole and then he returned and climbed into his seat.

'I have been your servant for many years, Master,' said Tzu Lu, running alongside the carriage, 'but I have never before seen you behave with such awe towards another. The rulers of ten thousand chariots, of a thousand chariots, when they see you, Sir, they never put you in another room or treat you with anything less than the respect due to an equal, while you yourself always conduct yourself with an air of rigid politeness. Now this old fisherman stood tall before you with his pole, while you bent double like a musical chime bar, and you always bowed twice before speaking to him. Wasn't this going a bit too far? We are all wondering about this. Why did this fisherman command such respect from you?'

Confucius leaned upon the crossbar of his carriage, sighed and said, 'Oh, Yu, it's very hard to change you! You have studied ritual and order for so long, yet your base and mean heart has not yet been changed. Come here and I will explain! If you meet someone who is older than you and are not respectful, then this is a failure of etiquette. If you meet a worthy person and fail to offer respect, this is a lack of benevolence. If the fisherman was not a perfect man, he would not have the power to make others humble before him. If people do not humble themselves before him, they are lacking in sincerity and thus are unable to obtain the truth, so they harm themselves. Sadly, there is nothing worse that can befall us than the lack of such benevolence, but you alone, O Yu, risk such a calamity!

'Furthermore, the Tao is that by which all the forms of life have life. All that lose it die. All that obtain it live. To struggle against it in practice is to face ruin. To flow with it is to succeed. So it is that where the Tao is, the sage will honour it. Now the old fisherman most certainly has the Tao, so how could I risk not showing respect to him?'

紅柿園林秋色好綠荷池
館曉涼生　先夫子唐夫先生本
對晚大言　王念慈

CHAPTER 32

Lieh Yu Kou

Lieh Yu Kou[119] was on his way to Chi but he returned before he got halfway down the road. He encountered Po Hun Wu Jen, who said, 'Why have you come back?'

'I was frightened.'

'What scared you?'

'I went into ten soup shops en route,' said Lieh Yu Kou, 'and in five of them I was served before anyone else.'

'Really? But what exactly alarmed you?' said Po Hun Wu Jen.

'Even if you try to hide the inner true nature of someone, the body gives it away like a traitor and shines out. Once this is external, it overpowers the hearts of people and makes them treat you, for petty reasons, like someone who is a noble or venerable. From such actions all sorts of problems arise. Now, soup sellers don't make much in the way of profit and have only their soup to sell. If such people, with so little to offer and so little power, treat me thus, imagine what would happen were I to meet the lord of ten thousand chariots! With his body worn out by the concerns of state, and his wisdom stretched by its governance, he would offer all this to me and ask me to solve his problems! That is what alarmed me.'

'How very perceptive of you!' said Po Hun Wu Jen. 'However, given who you are, people will still come to you!'

Shortly after this, Po Hun Wu Jen went to see Lieh Tzu's home and found the doorway full of the shoes of his many visitors. Po Hun Wu Jen stood facing north, with his staff upright in his hand and his chin resting upon it, until his chin became creased. He stood there some time, then he went away without a word.

119. The full name of Lieh Tzu – see p. xiv.

The porter at the gate went in to Lieh Tzu and told him about this. Lieh Tzu grabbed his shoes and ran barefooted after Po Hun Wu Jen, catching up with him at the outer gate, where he said, 'Sire, having come here, are you now going to go away without giving me some medicine?'

'It is pointless,' he replied. 'I said to you that people would crowd round you, and so they have. It is not your fault that they come, but you cannot keep them away, so what use was my warning? It is the way your extraordinary attributes shine forth which attracts people to you and makes them happy. But if you so move others, this in turn disturbs you to the very roots of your being. But there is nothing more to be said about this. The sort of people who gather round you will never tell you this. The silly words they speak actually poison a person. There is no comprehension and no conception of this among them, so who can make this clear to you? The clever person labours on and the wise person is distressed. However, someone without skills looks for nothing. He eats what he wants and wanders around, drifting like an empty boat, aimlessly, vacuously.'

A man of Cheng called Huan studied texts at a place called Chiu Shih. After three years Huan had become one of the Literàti and just as the Yellow River spreads its blessing over nine miles on either side, so did he bestow blessings upon the three levels of his family relations. He helped his younger brother study the teachings of Mo, and he and his brother debated, though his father always took the brother's side. Ten years later Huan committed suicide. He appeared to his father in a dream saying, 'It was I who had your son trained as a Mohist. Why don't you acknowledge this by taking a look at my grave where I have become the berries on the cypress?'

When Creation blesses someone, it blesses not that which is human in the person, but that which is from Heaven. In the same way was Huan's brother guided to be a Mohist. When Huan thought he was the one who made his brother a Mohist, he despised his own family and was like the people of Chi who try to prevent others from also drinking from the well. It is said that nowadays, in this generation, we have only people like Huan. They act as if only they are right.

However, note that people who have Virtue do not even know

this, and imagine how much more this is true of those who have the Tao! In the past people like Huan were known as those who have escaped Heaven's retribution.

The sage rests where there is true rest and does not rest when there is no real rest. The bulk of humanity rests when there is no real rest and does not know how to truly rest.

Chuang Tzu said, 'To know the Tao is easy, not to speak about it is hard. Knowing and not saying, this is to aspire to the Heavenly. Knowing and saying, this is to be subject to the human element. In the past people paid attention to the Heavenly, not to the human.'

Chu Ping Man studied how to slay the dragons[120] under Cripple Yi and it cost a thousand pieces of gold, which was all his family had. Three years later he had mastered the art but he could never use it.

The sage sees what is thought to be necessary as unnecessary, so there is no call for warfare. The ordinary person sees what is not necessary as necessary, with the result that there is frequent warfare. The one who looks to warfare always resorts to it in any situation. But relying upon warfare leads to destruction.

The comprehension of the petty person does not go beyond the external wrappings and the ephemera of gifts, business cards and letterheads. He exhausts his spirit on that which is insignificant and vacuous, but wants to be seen as leading others to the Tao and as bringing all things into the great Oneness. Someone like this will most certainly get lost in time and space. His body is trapped and can never know the great beginning. The perfect man, in contrast, concentrates his spirit upon that which was before the beginning and rests in the strangeness of being in the fields of nothingness. Like water he flows without form, or pours out into the great purity. How pathetic you are! Those of you whose understanding is no greater than the tip of a hair, and who do not understand the great peacefulness!

A man from Sung, called Tsao Shang, was sent by the King of Sung as an ambassador to the state of Chin. When he left Sung he

120. Study the Tao.

was given only a few carriages. However, the King of Chin was so delighted with him that he gave him a hundred more. On returning to Sung he met Chuang Tzu and said, 'Living in poor streets of an impoverished village, making sandals and starving, with a shrivelled neck and a sickly face, this I cannot stand! But being in the confidence of a ruler of ten thousand chariots and being given a hundred of them, this I enjoy and am good at.'

Chuang Tzu said, 'Well now. When the King of Chin falls ill, he summons his doctor who lances the ulcer or squeezes the boil and as a reward receives one carriage. The doctor who applies a suppository gets five carriages. The lower down the service, the more carriages given. So, Sir, I assume you must at least have been licking his piles to have been given so many carriages? Be gone, Sir!'

The Duke Ai of Lu asked Yen Ho, 'If I were to take Confucius as the main prop of my government, would the problems of the country be resolved?'

'To take on Confucius would be dangerous!' replied Yen Ho. 'He likes to decorate feathers and to use flowery language in his work and cannot differentiate the trunk of issues from the mere branches. He is willing to distort true nature in order to convince the people, and yet he has no understanding of what he is doing. He draws inspiration from his own heart and judges according to his own lights, so how could you put such a person in charge? Do you approve of him? Could you entrust things to him? If you do so, it is a mistake. Surely a person who makes the people turn away from reality and learn what is hypocritical is no fit model for the people. If you care about the future, you should forget this idea.'

It is hard to govern people and not to forget yourself, for this is not Heaven's model. Merchants and traders won't want to be associated with someone like this. Their lowly position might make you think they are the same, but such a charge rankles with them.

Punishments on the outside are inflicted with metal and wood instruments. Punishments to the inner person are inflicted by agitation and excess. When minor people encounter external punishments, the instruments of metal and wood deal with them. When they encounter internal punishments, it is the yin and the yang that consume them. Only the true man can avoid both external and internal punishments.

Confucius said, 'The human heart is more dangerous than mountains or rivers, more difficult to know than Heaven. Heaven has its seasons of spring, summer, autumn and winter, and its times for sunrise and sunset. But humanity has a thickly cloaked exterior and its true nature is hidden deep within. So it is that someone can have an honest face but be miserly; can be truly gifted but be without skills; seem featherbrained but actually have a very clear plan; appear firm but be bent; look slow but be fast. Thus, those who gather around righteousness as if it were there to slake their thirst will later flee from righteousness as if it were a fire.

'So it is that the nobleman observes those working for him at a distance and considers their loyalty, and observes them close at hand to consider their respect. He tests their skills by confronting them with difficult issues and tests their knowledge by suddenly asking a question. He tests their faithfulness by getting their commitment and he tests their benevolence by giving them wealth, while he tests their fortitude and resolve by informing them of coming dangers. By getting them drunk he tests their ability to take care of themselves and by mixing them with all manner of people, he tests their chastity. By these nine tests, it is possible to uncover the unworthy ones.'

When Cheng Kao Fu[121] received the first grade of office, he bowed his head. When he received the second grade, he bent his back. On receiving the third grade, he doubled over and ran along the wall, hugging it. Who would not have him as a model! But a common fellow, on receiving his first grade, puts on airs. On receiving his second grade, dances on top of his carriage. On his third grade, dares to address his uncles by their personal names! How far removed this is from Hsu in the time of Tang!

There is nothing more dangerous than for Virtue to have a heart, but for that heart to have eyelashes that obscure vision. For if they have such eyelashes, then they can only look within and this leads to

---

121. An ancestor of Confucius, eighth century BC.

ruin. There are five evil Virtues, of which the central one is worst. What am I talking about when I say the central Virtue? The central Virtue is that which makes people think well of what they say but despise what others say.

There are eight extreme conditions which limit people, three that assist and six repositories in the body. The eight things that bring trouble if someone has all eight in excess are: beauty, a good beard, height, size, strength, class, bravery and courage.

The three that will bring advancement are: following and copying others; bowing and scraping; and ambition to be better than others.

The six repositories are: knowledge that goes out to all things; bravery, determination and the many troubles they create; benevolence, righteousness and the many requests that arise; comprehending life in its essence – a massive task; understanding knowledge is a lesser thing; comprehending the great destiny you follow after – comprehending the lesser destiny, you are just swept along.

A man went to see the King of Sung and was given ten carriages, and with the ten carriages he went and showed off with them to Chuang Tzu.

Chuang Tzu said, 'Up on the Yellow River there lives a family which earns enough to eat by weaving things out of rushes. Their son was diving in the very deepest pools when he found a pearl worth a thousand pieces of gold. His father said to him, "Bring me a stone and I will smash it to pieces. A pearl worth a thousand pieces of gold must have come from a pool nine levels deep, from under the chin of the Black Dragon. My son, to have got this pearl, the dragon must have been asleep, for had he been awake, you would have been cut to pieces, my son!" Now the kingdom of Sung, is it not really deeper than the nine levels pool; and the King of Sung, is he not really more ferocious than the Black Dragon? My boy, if you were able to get these carriages, he must have been asleep. For if the King of Sung had been awake, you would be in pieces by now, my lad!'

Someone offered Chuang Tzu a court post. Chuang Tzu answered the messenger, 'Sir, have you ever seen a sacrificial ox? It is decked in fine garments and fed on fresh grass and beans. However, when it is led into the Great Temple, even though it most earnestly might wish to be a simple calf again, it's now impossible!'

Chuang Tzu was dying and his followers wanted to provide a glorious funeral. Chuang Tzu said, 'I will have Heaven and Earth as my shroud and coffin; the sun and moon as my symbols of jade; the stars for my pearls and jewels; all the forms of life as my mourners. I have everything for my funeral, what is there missing? What more could I need?'

His followers said, 'We are worried, Master, that the crows and kites will eat you.'

'Above ground I shall be eaten by crows and kites,' said Chuang Tzu, 'and below ground by worms and ants. Aren't you just being rather partisan in wanting to feed only one of these groups, so depriving the others?

'Trying to use what isn't equal to produce equality is to be equally unequal. Trying to prove something by something uncertain is only certain to make things uncertain. The person whose eyesight is clear and thinks he understands is victim to these sights, whereas the one who is guided by the spirit perceives the reality. That there is a difference between what we see with our eyes and what we know through our spirit is a wisdom from long ago. But the fool relies upon his eyes and loses himself in what is merely human, and everything he does is just a façade – how sad!'

此是觀世音菩薩解鼻齅諸香開五輪指

CHAPTER 33

Governing the World

There are many ways of running the world, and each of those who use a particular one considers theirs to be so good as to be incapable of improvement. In the past, this was known as the way of the Tao, but where is that now? I say, 'There is nowhere where it is not.' You say, 'Where does the spirit come from? Where does enlightenment emerge from?' 'The sage brings them to be and the king completes them, and the origin is the One.'

The one who is not cut off from his primal origin is known as the Heavenly man.

The one not cut off from the true nature is known as the spiritual man.

The one who is not cut off from the truth, is known as the perfect man.

The one who views Heaven as the primal source, Virtue as the root and the Tao as a gate, and sees change and transformation as natural, such a one we call a sage.

The one who makes benevolence the model for kindness, righteousness the model for reason, ritual the model for behaviour, music the model for harmony, who is content in benevolence and pity, we call such a one a nobleman.

This is how the people should be governed: laws should be seen as defining difference, and their titles as indications of status. Comparison should be used to provide evidence and enquiry to establish decisions, so that they can be numbered one, two, three, four and so on, and thus give the hundred ranks their ranking. One should be observant in business, and should ensure adequate food and clothing, and that the cattle are fed and cared for and the grain stored. One should be concerned for the old, the infirm, the orphans and the widow.

The people of the past were so thorough! They were equals in spirituality and enlightenment, they were as all-seeing as Heaven and Earth. They tended all the forms of life and unified the whole world. Their care reached all people, they clearly perceived the roots of all things and they were attentive to even the smallest details. Their influence extended to the six directions and the four quarters, so that small and great, coarse or fine, there was no place that they were not. Their insights, as discernible in their laws and practices, were passed down from age to age in their codes and in the *Histories*. In Tsou and Lu[122] there are scholars, gentlemen of the girdled class who can understand what is to be found in the *Book of Poetry* and the *Book of History*, in the *Rites* and the *Music*.

The *Book of Poetry* has the Tao of the will, the *Book of History* has the Tao of events, the *Rites* has the Tao of conduct, the *Music* has the Tao of harmony. The *Book of Changes* has the Tao illustrating the yin and yang and the *Spring and Autumn Annals* has the Tao of titles and procedures. These teachings are found across the face of the whole world, and in China they are mentioned by many of the hundred schools of philosophy of the Tao.

Everywhere under Heaven is in great disarray, the worthy ones and the sages have no light to shed, the Tao and Virtue are no longer united, and the whole world tends to see one aspect and think that they have grasped the whole of it. They can be compared to the ear, the eye, the nose and the mouth. Each has its own light to shed but you cannot interchange their functions. Likewise, the hundred schools of philosophy have their points and each has its time of usefulness. Though this is true, nevertheless not one of them covers the whole truth, just like the scholar who lived in one corner. He tried to judge whether Heaven and Earth are beautiful, to grasp the principle of all forms of life, to calculate the worth of the ancient wise men. Yet it is rare indeed for one such as he to be

122. Home states of Mencius and Confucius.

able to encompass all the beauty of Heaven and Earth, or to describe that which is spiritual and clear.

As a result, the Tao which is within the sage and which manifests itself externally in the king fell into obscurity and was dulled, was constrained and became lost. The people of the whole world just followed their own desires and were their own judges. Sadly, the hundred schools persist, fated to never be able to unite again, or agree. The scholars of these later generations did not see the purity of Heaven and Earth united, and the great wisdom of the ancient ones of the Tao was scattered and torn by the world.

To show no model of extravagance to later generations, to leave all forms of life unaffected, to avoid embroidering ritual, to rule oneself by strict regulation in one's behaviour so as to be ready to deal with crises, thus helping other generations: this was what the ancients took to be the Tao.

Mo Ti and Chin Hua Li heard of their opinions and were pleased. But they pursued them to great excess and and were too particular in applying the opinions to themselves. Mo Tzu wrote a treatise called 'Against Music', and united this with 'Moderation in Economics'. He did not believe in singing during life, nor in mourning at death. He taught universal love and universal consideration. He forbade warfare and would allow no space in his Tao for anger. He thought study good and did not disagree with others. But he did not agree with the primal kings but rather attacked the rituals and music of the ancient times.

The Yellow Emperor had Hsien Chih music, Yao had Ta Chung, Shun had Ta Shao, Yu had Ta Hsia, Tang had Ta Huo, King Wen had the music of the Pi Yung Hall and King Wu and Duke Chou created Wu music.

In ancient times the rituals for mourning outlined exactly what was due to the noble and the ordinary, the highest and the lowest. The coffin of the Son of Heaven had seven layers, those of the nobles five layers, those of the prime ministers had three layers, those of officers two layers. Now Mo Tzu only said there should be no singing during life, and at death no mourning. For everyone he would just have a plain wooden coffin, three inches thick and with no outer case. If he teaches people this, he can have no real affection for people. If he did this for his own funeral, then he does not have much affection for himself.

Yet this has not led to the ignoring of Mo Tzu's Tao. Far from it, even though people continue to sing when he says no singing, people continue to feel like crying when he says no crying, people still want to be happy after he has said no happiness. Is what he advocates really human? A life that is laborious and a death which is insignificant: this Tao is one of great thoughtlessness. Making people sad and depressed by practices which are hard to follow cannot be seen as the Tao of the sage. It is universally against human nature, and the whole world rejects it. Even if Mo Tzu himself could stand it, how can the rest of the world be expected to live this way? With the whole world so opposed, this Tao has wandered far from the ways of the real king.

Mo Tzu thought a great deal of his Tao, saying, 'In the past, when Yu held back the waters and controlled the Yangtze and Yellow Rivers, he sent them to flow through the lands of the four barbarian tribes and the nine provinces. They were united with the three hundred rivers, the three thousand streams and the smaller streams too many to number. Yu himself carried the sandbags and dug with the spade, until he had united all the rivers of the whole world, and there was no hair left on his legs from his knee to his ankle. He washed his hair in the pouring rain and combed it with the harsh winds, while creating the ten thousand states. Yu was a great sage, but he wore out his body for the sake of the whole world.' The result is that in later years Mohists wear skins and coarse cloth, wooden shoes or hemp sandals, never stop night or day, and view such fervent activity as their highest achievement. They say, 'Anyone who cannot do this is not acting in the spirit of Yu and is not worthy of being called a Mohist.'

The followers of Hsiang Li Chin and the disciples of Wu Hou and the Mohists of the south such as Ku Huo, Chi Chih, Teng Ling Tzu and so forth, all recite the texts of Mo, but they argue and do not agree on these texts, calling each other heretical Mohists. In their debates they argue about hard and white, about sameness and difference, and they dispute the use of terms such as odd and even. They consider the main teacher of their group as a sage, each hoping that their particular one will be seen as the teacher by later generations. These same arguments continue up to the present time.

Mo Ti and Chin Ku Li had perfectly good ideas but were wrong in what they proceeded to do. They have made later generations of Mohists feel that they have to labour on until there is not a hair left on their calves, their driving ambition being to outdo each other. This is the height of their folly and the low point of their unity. Indeed, it is true that Mo Tzu was one of the good of this world and you will not find his equal. He was weary and worn, but do not despise him for he was a scholar of ability.

This should be the purpose of the heart:
not to be trapped by convention,
nor to be concerned with adornments;
not to be thoughtless in treating others,
nor to be in opposition to the crowd;
to want the whole world to live in peace and balance
for the sake of the people's unity,
to look to the needs of others as well as yourself.

This should be the purpose of the heart and this is what the ancient ones considered to be the Tao's way. Sung Chien and Yin Wen heard of these ideas and were pleased. They made their hats in the shape of Hua Mountain as their distinguishing feature. In their intercourse with all forms of life, they accepted difference as given. They discoursed upon the nature of the heart and they sought a unity proceeding from the heart. By such concerns they sought to unite everyone in joyfulness and to harmonize all within the boundaries of the oceans. Their greatest desire was to see this achieved everywhere, by their efforts. They could face insults and not be disturbed; they struggled to save the people from warfare; they aimed to prevent aggression and to silence arms and thus to deliver future generations from violence. In pursuit of such ideals, they walked across the whole world, advising the high and teaching the low, and even though the world would not listen, they just continued even more strongly and would not give up. So it is said that high and low were tired of seeing them, but they never gave up putting themselves forward.

Indeed, this is so, but they did too much for others and too little for themselves, saying, 'All that we ask and need is five pints of rice and this will suffice.' It is inconceivable that the Master had enough by this means. Even though the followers were hungry, they never forgot the whole of the world, persevering day and night without ceasing, saying, 'We have to take care to preserve lives!' What wonderful aims these masters have for their generation! They say, 'The nobleman does not scrutinize others too harshly, nor does he take from others to adorn himself.' If an idea does not benefit the world, then they see that it's not worth struggling with. They see banning aggression and ridding the world of violence as their major area of concern, and see diminishing their own desires and feelings as an internal goal. They sought this both on a grand scale and a small scale, both in subtle things and in the more common way, and when they had perfected this, they stood tall.

This was the way of the ancient one who followed the Tao:
public-spirited and completely non-partisan,
flexible and not fixed upon one idea,
open-minded and without a guide,
following others without a second thought,
not casting anxious glances,
not using knowledge to make plots,
not choosing one thing rather than another,
instead going with all:
this was the way of the ancient one who followed the Tao.

Peng Meng, Tien Pien and Shen Tao[123] heard of these ideas and were delighted. They believed that all the various forms of life are held in the Tao. They said, 'Heaven can overarch but not support; Earth can support but not overarch; the great Tao embraces all but cannot distinguish between them. We conclude that all forms of life have that which they can do and that which they cannot do. It is said, if you select, you abandon comprehensibility; if you contrast, then you lose perfection. But the Tao leaves out nothing whatsoever.'

123. Shen Tao is known as an originator of certain Legalist concepts.

So it was that Shen Tao put aside knowledge and any concern for himself, went where he could not avoid going, seeking always to be without interest and pure in all that he did, seeing this as being true to the Tao, and saying that understanding is not understanding, thus viewing knowledge as dangerous and struggling to be rid of it. He was without ambition and so he was carefree, taking no responsibility and scorning those in the world who praised the worthy. Drifting and unconcerned, he did nothing and laughed at those whom the world saw as sages. Cutting corners, smoothing the rough, he flowed and twisted with all things. He ignored right and wrong and simply worked at avoiding trouble. Having nothing to gain from knowledge or reflection, and with no understanding of what was going on, he went through life with a lofty ease and disregard. He walked only when he was pushed, and only started when he was forced to. He was like a whirlwind, like a feather spinning round and round, like the turning of a grindstone. He had integrity, he was without any wrong, without failure or excess, whether in action or in stillness. How was this possible? Those who are without knowledge are free from the tribulations of self-promotion, from the entrapment that arises from working with knowledge. Whether moving or resting, he never left the proper path, and throughout his life was never praised. I would like to be one without knowledge, not trapped in the teachings of a sage. Such people, like the very earth itself, never lose the Tao. People in positions of authority laughed at him together, saying, 'Shen Tao's Tao is not for the living but is the way for those who are already dead, which is why they are so odd.'

Tien Pien was the same, for he studied under Peng Meng and understood that one should not make distinctions. Peng Meng's master said, 'The Tao of the scholars of old taught that nothing is right and nothing is wrong. Their essence was like the wind; how can it be expressed in words?' But he was always opposed to the views of others, never seeing things as they saw them, and he was prone to cut corners. What they named the Tao he said was not the Tao, and what was called right he always had to argue might be wrong. Peng Meng, Tien Pien and Shen Tao did not properly understand the Tao. Nevertheless, they had all had the chance to hear about it.

To consider the origin as pure and that which emerges as coarse; to view accumulation as inadequate; to live by oneself in peace and with spiritual clarity, this is what in ancient times was known as the way of the Tao. Kuan Yin[124] and Lao Tzu heard these ideas and were pleased. They founded their system upon the belief that nothing exists ultimately, and they were guided in this by the notion of the great one. Gentleness and weakness combined with humility and self-emptying were its distinguishing features and its core was the prevention of harm to all forms of life.

Kuan Yin said, 'One who does not exist in self sees others as they really are. His movement is like water, his calmness like a mirror, his response is like that of an echo. When he is empty, he seems to have forgotten; unmoving, he is as still as water; peaceful, he is as one with all; he views success as failure, and he never tries to take the lead but always to follow.'

Lao Tzu said, 'Know the masculine but hold to the feminine, become the valley of the whole world. Know your purity but hold to the impure, be a channel for the whole world.' Most people choose to be first, he chooses to be last and says that he will accept the dregs of the whole world. Most people choose fulfilment; he chooses to be empty. He has never hoarded, so has more than enough; he prefers to be alone, yet has many around him. Living by actionless action, he mocks at ability. While others look for good fortune, he feels free to bend and twist. He says that he only wishes to avoid blame. He considers what is most profound to be the core and takes what is most severe as his guide, and he says that which is strong will break and that which is sharp becomes blunted. He is always open-handed and tolerant with all and seeks no harm to any. This can be called perfection.

Kuan Yin and Lao Tzu! Truly great men of the past!

The blank and the motionless have no form;
change and transformation are never at rest;
what is death?

---

124. The traditional name of the Gatekeeper to the West, who asked Lao Tzu to write the *Tao Te Ching* before he left China for good.

what is life?
what is the companionship of Heaven and Earth?
where does the spirit of clarity go?
when forgotten, what becomes of it?

All forms of life are gathered around us, yet none of them is our destination. In the past people thought this was the way of the Tao. Chuang Tzu heard of these ideas and was pleased. He taught them using strange and mysterious expressions, wild and extraordinary phrases, and terms which had no precise meaning. He taught what he believed, yet was never partisan, nor did he view things from just one perspective. He saw the whole world as lost in foolishness and thus incapable of understanding anything sensible.

Therefore he used supposed words to offer a constant insight, quotes to have a ring of truth and flowing words to give greater depth. He came and went with the spirit of Heaven and Earth but he never viewed all the forms of life as being beneath him. He did not dispute right and wrong, but dwelt alongside his generation and its ways. Some might consider his writings insignificant, for they are inoffensive and fluent. But though his words are varied, in amongst the twists and turns there is more than might be expected, for there is much which is true and eternal. He travels with the Creative above and he makes friends with those below who view life and death as meaningless and who see neither beginning nor end. His vision of the origin is vast and penetrating, ever expanding and open-minded, unshackled by anything or anybody. It can be said that he is in accord with the Author of the Tao, and soars to the highest heights. Indeed this is so, but he still continues to explore with us the changes and transformations that arise within all, and come from him. His teachings have never been fully appreciated, as they are difficult and subtle.

Hui Shih made many efforts and all his books would fill five carriages, but his Tao was false and confused and what he said never hit the centre. Jumping from idea to idea, he would say things like:

'The greatest thing has nothing outside it and we call this the great One. The smallest thing has nothing inside it and we call this the smallest One.'

Or:

'No substance, incapable of being hoarded, yet greater than a thousand miles.'

Or:

'Heaven is on the same level as Earth and the mountains are equal to the marshes.'

Or:

'When the sun is in the centre, it is in the decline. That which is born is dying.'

Or:

'That which is very similar is different from that which is only a little similar and this is called being a little different. All forms of life are similar and all differ. This we call the great similarities and differences.'

Or:

'The south is limitless but has borders.'

Or:

'Today I left for Yueh and arrived yesterday.'

Or:

'That which is joined is separated.'

Or:

'I know where the centre is of the whole world, north of Yen and south of Yueh.'[125]

Or:

'Love embraces all forms of life and Heaven and Earth are of One.'

Hui Shih made these great statements to help the whole world to be more creative in debate and other speakers throughout the world were delighted to follow his lead, saying,

'An egg has feathers,
a chicken has three feet,
Ying has the whole world,
a dog could be called a sheep,
horses have eggs,

125. Extreme north and extreme south.

a toad has a tail,
fire is not hot,
mountains emerge from the mouth,
chariot wheels never touch the ground,
eyes cannot see,
pointing is not the same as being there,
being there is not the culmination,
the tortoise is longer than the snake,
a T-square does not work,
a compass doesn't make circles,
chisels do not fit into handles,
a bird's shadow never moves,
swift though the arrowhead is, at times it is neither moving nor
    still,
a dog is not a dog,
a bay horse and a black ox make three,
a white dog is black,
a motherless colt never had a mother,
if you have a pole one foot long and every day you cut off half,
ten thousand generations will not exhaust it.'

These are the sorts of sayings speakers came up with in response to Hui Shih, rattling on in this fashion eternally to the end of their lives.

Huan Tuan and Kung Sun Lung are to be numbered amongst these. They were more vocal than others, overwhelming the hearts of the people and changing their ideas. But they could not subdue people's hearts, they just encompassed them with argument. Hui Shih drew upon his knowledge every day to argue with these speakers, these talkers from around the world, as can be seen from the examples above.

Indeed, Hui Shih's style of speaking illustrates that he thought himself the very best, saying that Heaven and Earth are also equal! Shih certainly maintained his vigour, but unfortunately he had no real skill.

In the south there was a man with very odd views called Huang Liao, and he enquired why Heaven and Earth didn't fall or collapse, where the wind and rain come from, likewise the thunder and lightning. Hui Shih didn't try to avoid these questions and, without pausing to think, he charged right in and gave answers to everything affecting all the forms of life, without ceasing, with no end of words. Nevertheless, he feared he hadn't said enough, so he began embroidering his answers with fantastic theories. If he spoke contrary to what others thought, he saw this as confirmation of the veracity of what he said and was delighted at the fame he gained. In this he was indeed like all other such speakers. He was weak in terms of true Virtue and forceful in his engagement with what is external. He trod a dark and confused path.

From the perspective of the Tao of Heaven and Earth, we can see that Hui Shih's ability was simply like the buzzing of a mosquito or gnat. What was the real use of it? Certainly, he can be credited with founding one school of thought, though to be honest I have to say he needed to follow the Tao more! Hui Shih found no sense of achievement in doing this. Instead he persisted in trying endlessly to diagnose all the forms of life, until finally all he is remembered for is his fame as a debater! Poor old Hui Shih! With all that talent he never obtained any significant achievement. Racing after the multitude of things in this world and never returning, he was indeed like someone who tries to have the last word with an echo, or who tries to show that you can outrun your shadow.

What a shame!

Index

Chang Tien Cheng, 268

Chang Wu, 229

Chang Wu Tzu, 18

Chang Yi, 159

Chang Yu, 212

change, 56–8, 151, 174, 180, 197, 201, 214, 226, 230

Change (Emperor of the South Sea), 64

Chao, King of Chou, 253–4

Chao family, 205–6

Chao Hsi, Marquis of Han, 251

Chao Wen (lute player), 14

Chao (state), 77n.

Chaos (Emperor of the Centre), 64

chapped-hand cream, 5–6

Chen (state), 62

Cheng Kao Fu, 292 and n.

Cheng of the North Gate, 118–19

Cheng, 190–1

Cheng (state), 289

Cheng Tzu Chan, 39–40 and n.

Cheng Tzu Yu, 246

Chi, 2

Chi, Master, 8–9

Chi, Prince, 236 and n.

Chi (state), 30, 33, 76–7, 152, 160, 215, 217, 220; attack on, 227–8

chi (breath of Heaven), 87

Chi Che, 98

Chi Chen, 233

Chi Chih, 299

Chi Chu, 27

Chi Hsien (shaman of spirits), 62–3

Chi Hsing Tzu, 161

Chi Kung, 177

Chi Mountain, 250, 258

Chi To, 242

Chi Tzu, 227

Chiang Lu Mien, 98

Chieh (evil ruler), 27 and n., 50, 82, 84–5, 144, 236, 268–9

Chieh (state), 258

Chieh Tzu Tui, 266

Chieh Yu, 4 and n., 60–61

Chieh Yu (madman of Chu), 35

Chien Ho, Marquis of, 237

Chien Wu, 4, 51, 60–61, 184

Chih, Robber, xxii, 69–70, 77, 78, 82, 84–5, 104, 261–77

Chih, ruler, 141

Chih Chang Man Chi, 102–4

Chih Chi, 141

Chih Ho, 238

Chih Yu, 264

Chin (musician), 120

Chin (state), 19, 99, 291

Chin Chang (master), 54

Chin Hua Li, 298

Chin Ku Li, 300

Chin Shih, 24

Ching (woodcarver), 162–3

Ching family, 205–6

Ching Ling, 257

Ching-shou (form of music), 22

Ching Tzu, 164

Chiu Fang Yin, 219

Chiu Shih, 289

Chiu Yu insects, 154

Cho Lu (battlefield), 265

Chou, Duke of, 122

Chou Dynasty, 67 and n., 258–9

Chou (Shang Emperor), 27 and n., 144, 236, 268–9

Chu, King of, 146, 185, 217, 225

Chu family, 206

Chu (state), 2, 35, 38, 42, 77 and n., 99, 112, 141n., 151, 158, 215, 217, 253; King of, 225; travelling to, 225–34

Chu Chiao, 18

Chu Hsien, 159

Chu Jung, 79 and n.

Chu Liang, 57

Chu Ping Man, 290

Chu Po Yu, 32, 230

Chu To, 154

Chu Tzu Mountain, 212–13

Chu Yuan, 33

Chuan Hsu, 51

Chuang, Duke, 163

Chuang Tzu; on benevolence, 118; on carelessness, 229; and Confucius, xx–xxi, xxviii; on desiccated skull, 151–